Legal Issues in Social Work, Counseling, and Mental Health

SAGE SOURCEBOOKS FOR THE HUMAN SERVICES SERIES

Series Editors: ARMAND LAUFFER and CHARLES GARVIN

Legal Issues in Social Work, Counseling, and Mental Health

Guidelines for Clinical Practice in Psychotherapy

Sage Sourcebooks for

the Human Services
37

Robert G. Madden

SAGE Publications
International Educational and Professional Publisher
Thousand Oaks   London   New Delhi

For information:

SAGE Publications, Inc.
2455 Teller Road
Thousand Oaks, California 91320
E-mail: order@sagepub.com

SAGE Publications Ltd.
6 Bonhill Street
London EC2A 4PU
United Kingdom

SAGE Publications India Pvt. Ltd.
M-32 Market
Greater Kailash I
New Delhi 110 048 India

Printed in the United States of America

Library of Congress Cataloging-in-Publication Data

Madden, Robert G.
    Legal issues in social work, counseling, and mental health: Guidelines for clinical practice in psychotherapy / by Robert G. Madden.
       p. cm. — (Sage sourcebooks for the human services; vol. 37)
    Includes bibliographical references and index.
    ISBN 0-7619-1233-9 (pbk.: acid-free paper). — ISBN 0-7619-1232-0 (cloth: acid-free paper)
       1. Mental health personnel—Legal status, laws, etc.—United States. 2. Psychotherapists—Legal status, laws, etc.—United States. 3. Social workers—Legal status, laws, etc.—United States.
    I. Title. II. Series: Sage sourcebooks for the human services series; v. 37.
    KF2910.P75M33   1998
    344.73′044—dc21   97-45285

This book is printed on acid-free paper.

    99 00 01 02 03 10 9 8 7 6 5 4 3

Acquiring Editor:	Jim Nageotte
Editorial Assistant:	Fiona Lynn
Production Editor:	Sherrise Purdum
Production Assistant:	Karen Wiley
Designer/Typesetter:	Janelle LeMaster
Print Buyer:	Anna Chin

To Doreen, my life partner,
for your love, emotional support, encouragement,
unfailing belief in me, and for your gentle editing:
You make it all possible and meaningful.

CONTENTS

PREFACE

The influence of the legal system on American society has never been more prominent than during the decade of the 1990s. Whether because of relaxed rules for filing lawsuits, the social phenomena of turning to the courts to solve all disputes, or the media coverage of trials and other legal procedures, mental health workers have seen their practice increasingly affected by the law. The specialized language and procedures of the legal profession make it difficult for most nonlawyers to participate in this part of the democratic process. As a clinical social worker and an attorney, I have found myself in the role of educator with both professions. Clinicians need to know how to respond to legal issues related to practice and lawyers need to know the roles and perspectives of mental health practitioners.

This book grew out of my experiences training and consulting with lawyers, social workers, counselors, and other mental health professionals. When faced with an impending legal issue, most clinicians become intimidated. Their focus is directed at avoiding or at least minimizing the scope of their involvement. They seldom understand the expectations of lawyers or the opportunities to influence the legal process. I believe that the demystification of the law is necessary to enable clinicians to feel empowered by their interactions with the legal system and thus make the law more therapeutic for clients and more supportive to mental health professionals. This book is intended to help readers feel more confident and competent when faced with legal issues in practice.

The increased attention to the legal issues has been focused primarily on malpractice risk reduction. This perspective is limiting and reactive. If mental health professionals understand and embrace opportunities to influence legal decisions, they can develop a more sophisticated approach to handling legal issues as they arise in practice. Further, they can structure practice policies so as to reduce the potential of causing harm to clients and, from this strategy, reduce the risks of being sued.

Many times when I complete a legal presentation to mental health clinicians, I see a look of dread and fear on people's faces. A common response is that these issues are never thought about until there is a problem. Practice policies may be lax or nonexistent, and clients' legal rights may be routinely ignored. It is time to stop avoiding the law and denying the obvious legal implications of mental health practice. I hope that the readers of this book will use the information to be prepared for the inevitable interactions with the legal system.

This book begins with an examination of the role of the law in society, especially the ways in which the law influences practice. Succeeding chapters analyze various aspects of clinical practice including record keeping and confidentiality, the standard of care for particular treatment situations, and the business and management issues faced by agencies and private practitioners. The final chapter illustrates some of the legal issues often faced by clients. I hope students and clinicians read the book to improve their knowledge of the law, but because the legal issues are complex, this book also can be used as a reference source, as legal issues arise in practice.

The use of case descriptions throughout the book is intended to illustrate the workings of the courts, to provide insight into the manner of legal decision making, and to expose the reader to the orientation of legal professionals. Some of the case material is presented in narrative style, while other cases are quoted directly from the legal opinions issued by the courts. Cases have been chosen carefully to address specific legal issues. As a result, only those sections of the opinion that relate to the mental health issue have been reproduced. In most cases, the text has been edited for readability and the internal citations have been omitted from the court opinions. Readers are directed to the official case report for the complete text and for the exact language of the cases.

The legal information in this book is intended to educate the reader about general legal principles. None of the information in this book should be considered legal advice. Practitioners are urged to consult with a local lawyer because each jurisdiction has its own statutes and case law and may not follow the majority view on a particular issue. Local chapters of professional organizations often maintain lists of attorneys who have knowledge or experience in mental health law.

The legal issues in mental health practice are too numerous and complicated to be treated in any single volume. Given that the law is constantly evolving, it is my hope that more practitioners and scholars will participate in study and communication about the variety of ways the law influences practice and, just as important, the many ways clinicians can influence the law.

ACKNOWLEDGMENTS

To my sons, Bryant and Kyle: Thanks for understanding those times when I had to work. I would rather have played. To my parents for inspiring me and supporting my development as a person.

I would like to acknowledge the help of my friends and colleagues who read the manuscript. Your wise counsel and honest criticisms are sincerely appreciated: Pat Doherty, Raymie Wayne, Melissa Parody, and Chris Garrahan.

To my colleagues at St. Joseph College for supporting my scholarship. To the faculty at the University of Connecticut School of Law for your generous hospitality while I was a visiting scholar working on this project.

And to series editor Charles Garvin, Jim Nageotte, and the staff at Sage: your guidance, support, and experience enriched this book.

Chapter 1

SOCIETY, THE LAW, AND
MENTAL HEALTH PRACTICE

In American society, the law's presence is inescapable. The stub from the parking garage has a disclaimer denying liability if something happens to cars parked in the facility. A manufacturer includes a warning right on its stepladder not to use the top two steps or it cannot be held responsible for a subsequent fall or injury. A sign is posted at a highway construction project warning that the road is legally closed, imploring drivers to pass at their own risk. Meanwhile, no alternative routes are available and tolls are still being collected on that stretch of highway. Celebrity trials and sensationalized crime stories have captivated the United States during the 1990s. The machinations of courts and lawyers have come to be regarded as a form of entertainment, analyzed and criticized each night on television. Many individuals whose lives are touched by the legal state emerge disillusioned. As the law increasingly permeates our daily interactions, it is tempting to sink comfortably into the rhetoric that the legal system has become ridiculous at best, controlling and perverse at worst.

In the fields of social work, counseling, and psychotherapy, practitioners have come to fear the very idea that clients or their families might resort to legal action if unhappy with the results of therapy. Substantial time and energy are expended responding to subpoenas in divorce or custody cases. The legal complexities of managed care contracts and partnership/corporation agreements are spelled out in indecipherable language. However, the increasing intrusion of the legal

1

system into the practice of psychotherapy should not be seen as a wholly unwelcome development. Rather, in some ways, it reflects the growing legitimacy and prestige of psychotherapy and a potentially useful means for improving practice. Unfortunately, the increased legal presence also reflects a paucity of clear practice standards, embryonic outcome research, and a limited history of developing sound practice procedures and business policies.

The legal system is most threatening to clinicians when it directly implicates their practice. A psychologist was accused of breaching her confidentiality duty by releasing a client's records pursuant to a subpoena without first seeking the client's consent. A youth counselor worried for months that she would be sued after a 14-year-old girl reported in a session that she was going to the dormitory rooms of some college boys for "parties." The counselor did not report this to anyone and the girl subsequently was raped and beaten after consuming alcohol at one of the parties. A social worker in private practice was threatened with a lawsuit by a woman who was accosted by one of the social worker's clients in the waiting room; the client had begun to decompensate during a session, became paranoid, and refused to leave the building. A psychiatrist and his hospital were both sued for negligent prescription of drugs and failure to hospitalize a patient who was in outpatient therapy for two months. The patient committed suicide despite twice-weekly therapy, drug intervention, and attempts by the psychiatrist to get the patient to admit himself (he did not meet the criteria for involuntary admission).

None of these recent cases reached a trial but all of them resulted in substantial anxiety for the professionals. The cases illustrate the unpredictable nature of the legal risks faced in practice. Practitioners' lack of knowledge and discomfort with the legal system can cause intense stress that negatively affects practice. Often, preventive actions could have been taken if therapists had known the legal standards. Other times, practitioners would have benefited from an understanding of the purposes of legal proceedings and their role in a case so they could have responded appropriately. Unless the legal system is demystified, clinicians will continue to be intimidated and fail to take advantage of the opportunities to improve conditions for clients, practitioners, and the very process of delivering mental health services.

This book is geared to mental health professionals from a variety of disciplines including social work, psychology, counseling, and mental health nursing. Although these disciplines differ in approach and philosophy, they share many commonalities. Each discipline has a unique role in providing mental health services but the legal issues for practice are remarkably similar across the disciplines. The clinical process of working with people who are experiencing emotional or mental health problems triggers a common set of legal expectations regulating the behavior of clinicians and protecting the rights of consumers. Throughout the book, the terms *clinician, counselor,* and *psychotherapist* are used interchangeably and case examples have been selected to illustrate the legal issues across the spectrum of professional training. Specific standards of practice and codes of ethics exist for each profession, but an overall knowledge of the legal system and the ways in which it influences practice is essential to all who engage in mental health practice.

Traditional psychotherapy has its roots in religion, magic, and science (Hogan, 1979). In many cultures, there have been "professionals" responsible for assisting individuals who were experiencing mental/emotional difficulties. Because psychotherapy has been a nonmedical treatment through most of its history, and because there have been many bizarre methods for treating mental illness (including some that were inhumane), society has a natural interest in regulating practice. It is clear that the process of helping people who are in a highly vulnerable position carries with it the potential for psychotherapists to cause harm. The circumstances most likely to result in harm to clients develop when therapists exploit the dynamics of the treatment relationship. There are incompetent, unethical therapists whose practice needs to be regulated. But it is equally true that many clients come to treatment specifically as a result of emotional difficulties and problems relating with others. Those clients who are disappointed by unmet treatment expectations or the failure of the therapeutic relationship sometimes act out their anger by filing lawsuits (Bednar, Bednar, Lambert, & Waite, 1991). Regardless of whether a lawsuit is based on legitimate grounds, clinicians need to be prepared to demonstrate that their practice was based on a standard of care for their profession.

The term *standard of care* is difficult to pin down to an exact definition. It can generally be thought of as a set of expectations governing the behavior of a professional. Standards can be developed in several ways. First, the profession can publish the standard of care in both technical and ethical areas. Guidelines for assessing a suicidal client or working through trauma survival symptoms have been developed by researchers and published by the professions. Every clinician is ex-

①

pected to be knowledgeable of relevant standards and follow them in
practice. Similarly, the professions publish written codes of ethics that
set the expectations concerning the behavior of practitioners. Another
process for the establishment of standards of care is through the judiciary, where a decision in a court case provides guidance by articulating
what the behavior of professionals should be in similar circumstances.
Finally, the state and federal legislatures are involved in passing legislation that codifies the standard of care in specific areas. The standard
② of care concept is crucial to understanding the reciprocal nature of the
relationship between the law and psychotherapy and will be revisited
throughout this book.

    As mental health services are no longer located in the institutions,
the legal risks for counselors and psychotherapists have increased dramatically. There are more individuals "in the community" who in the
past would have been maintained in a secure hospital setting. Clinicians
are being asked every day to make judgments about whether a person is
actively suicidal or homicidal, or whether an individual is competent to
take medications or live independently. In the past, a patient might have
been admitted to a psychiatric facility as a result of being "at risk." With
the increase in managed care influence on treatment decisions, psychotherapists are being asked to make more precise diagnoses at an earlier
point in the treatment relationship. Unfortunately, psychotherapy is not
an exact science and the ability to help a client is sometimes unrelated
to the degree of knowledge or skill possessed by the worker. Clinicians
will always be vulnerable to legal challenges to practice due to the
imprecise nature of therapy and the inherent difficulty of predicting,
with any degree of certainty, the behaviors and emotions of people under
stress. Simon (1991) refers to psychotherapy as an "impossible profession" because of these inherent limitations in mental health practice that
can result in unavoidable lawsuits. As workers increasingly are leaving
agency-based settings to provide services in private or group practice,
these legal issues take on added significance in terms of personal
financial exposure.

    In an epilogue to Simon's excellent text *Clinical Psychiatry and the
Law* (second edition, 1992), Jonas Rappeport uses the term *belegaled*
to refer to the plight of psychotherapists affected by the inescapable
presence of the legal system in mental health practice. What is the
balance between the guidance received from court cases or consulting
attorneys, and the practice decisions that arise from client-centered,
supervision-reinforced, clinical judgment? As Rappeport wisely com-

ments, "Good law may not be good medicine, and good medicine may not always avoid lawsuits" (p. 571). In essence, Rappeport's quote reaches to the heart of the issue. Although knowledge of the law may help mental health professionals avoid the most obvious sources of lawsuits, the best malpractice protection is not legal expertise but clinical expertise (Bednar et al., 1991). Yet even with rigorous adherence to standards, the practice of counseling/psychotherapy will remain inexorably linked to the law because of the myriad interrelationships of the two fields. And it is because of this that psychotherapists have a professional obligation to influence the legal system.

THE LAW AS AN INSTRUMENT OF SOCIETY

Lisa McIntyre (1994, p. 6), a sociologist, has expressed a view of law as a civil contract that articulates expectations about the basic rights and duties of certain individuals in certain types of relationships. It is her belief that the law permeates all relationships in modern society. From this view, the law should be examined as an unavoidable and potentially useful tool for the practice of counseling/psychotherapy. Sharing McIntyre's views is another sociologist, Larry Barnett (1993), who argues that the legal system is inherently conservative because legal decisions are reflective of societal ideals rather than being the sources of social change. This distinction is important in understanding the influence of the legal system on mental health practice. Gradually, society has begun to "officially" recognize the legitimacy and substance of counseling and psychotherapy. As part of this development, the legal system has assumed its role by clarifying the expectations for mental health practice, standardizing treatment, and regulating practitioners so as to further integrate mental health services into the mainstream of life. When society judges professional behavior to be below the minimum level of acceptable conduct, legal liability or some other form of sanction is imposed (Bisbing, 1990). Through its interventions, society's legal system is influential in shaping the development of counseling and psychotherapy.

Another component of the regulation of practice has emerged from the mental health field. The civil rights movement of the 1960s sought to protect the rights of all citizens from unwarranted government intrusions. Procedural protections and judicial oversight of commitment proceedings have increased, with the goal of protecting the rights of persons with mental illness and other disabilities. The denial of one's liberty through institutionalization should not occur where a less restrictive alternative exists (Sales & Shuman, 1996). Judicial oversight has led to expectations of clinicians that a specific process must be followed, and that the need for institutionalization must be supported by *clear and convincing evidence* concerning the client's level of functioning (*Addington v. Texas,* 1979). Improper commitment has led to civil rights lawsuits and civil cases against therapists for negligence in assessment and treatment or for false imprisonment as a result of detaining a client in a hospital setting without due cause or without ongoing treatment. This movement has led to new standards for commitment and the overall treatment of those with mental illness.

In response to society's efforts to regulate practice through the legal system, the questions for counselors, psychotherapists, and other mental health providers are how to respond and what role to play in the process. Most therapists seek to avoid interactions with the legal system until a problem arises. Having knowledge of relevant law can enable a practitioner to adjust practice policies and manage risks, but maintaining up-to-date knowledge of case law and statutes is impractical for most psychotherapists. One would quickly fall into something akin to Lewis Carroll's famous line in *Alice's Adventures in Wonderland,* "Here it takes all the running you can do, to keep in the same place." Instead, counselors and psychotherapists must understand the basic concepts of the law and the purpose or social interest served by each interaction between law and psychotherapy.

The legal system, through civil lawsuits, insurance law, licensing statutes, and other means has exerted enormous influence on the development of standards for practice, regulating the credentials of therapists and sanctioning those therapists who practice outside of ethical or legal boundaries. In recent years, the mental health professions have begun to develop more specific standards of care for various areas of practice. Many of these standards would not be articulated at this time except for the impetus of the law. It is common for a professional field to be induced to make changes by the functioning of the legal system. A comparison with another field is useful to understand the dynamics of this phenomenon. In environmental law, some regulations governing clean air and water standards have been developed under the principle of "technology-forcing." From this viewpoint, industries are held to standards that are not currently attainable (Kneese & Schultze, 1975; Pourtney, 1990). The expectation of higher standards leads to increased allocation of resources to reach the goals identified in court decisions and legislation.

In counseling and psychotherapy, the intervention of the legal system requires a similar technology-forcing. Where inadequate standards for practice are articulated for the helping professions, courts and legislators will write them and practitioners will have to deal with the results. There is an unacceptable level of intrusion that undermines the autonomy of the professions when standards arise from the law. This threat is already being perceived by workers in the controversial area of recovered memories/child sexual abuse where the legal risk of establishing a treatment relationship may discourage some therapists from taking on clients who present with these issues (Madden & Parody, 1997). A further threat to the field results from the nature of legal decision making. The focus on the individual client in a lawsuit may not produce results that are in the best interests of the majority of clients or therapists in similar situations.

What, then, is the technology that is being forced by the increasing influence of the law on mental health treatment? It is the development of published standards for practice including the standardization of policies and procedures in the practice and in the business of psychotherapy. Clinicians always have been attuned to the present, the current client. The use of the professional relationship and individualized assessment and treatment plans are at the heart of psychotherapy practice. This orientation sometimes has been at the expense of the development of practice research and professional standards. Mental health workers have been motivated to establish expectations for professional behavior, primarily in response to high-profile legal cases. Again, using the example of the recovered memory cases, several professional organizations, including the American Psychiatric Association and the American Psychological Association, developed standards for practice once therapists began to be found liable (see, e.g., National Association of Social Workers, *Practice Update: Evaluation and Treatment of Adults With the Possibility of Recovered Memories of Childhood Sexual Abuse,* 1996b).

To the extent that the court cases force psychotherapy to define practice so as to standardize expectations, the influence has been positive. However, there is a danger that the standardization of psychotherapy approaches will have a negative effect on practice by eliminating the degree of creativity and discretion required for both individual differences in clients and the development of new, more effective approaches. Relying on the legal system to set the parameters of practice is the strategy of convenience. The time has come for psychotherapists to become more active in exerting as much influence on the legal system as the law has exerted on the field of psychotherapy.

THE RESPONSE OF
MENTAL HEALTH PROFESSIONALS

Counseling and psychotherapy services are provided to a broad spectrum of individuals whose problems range from mild adjustment disorders to serious mental illness. Because these services are delivered by a diverse group of practitioners with varied educational backgrounds and treatment approaches, it is difficult to articulate standards for practice that would be universally accepted and applied. Most practitioners, regardless of their professional training, would like to be able to know how to avoid legal entanglements in their practice. One of the reasons many enter the field is the autonomy of the work. Professionals are accorded this autonomy because the nature of the work involves the individualized application of theory and practice to each client. When intimately involved with an individual, a family, or a group, therapists use a combination of personal and professional helping skills, a knowledge base derived from theory and research, and the art of practice that is nurtured through experience. The process of supervision is used to manage transference and to ensure proper assessments and treatment plans. For these reasons, most clinicians are focused on the micropractice level. Analysis of practice strategies is focused on their relevance to current cases rather than on any consideration of which strategies would be in consonance with a professionwide standard of care. It is extraordinarily difficult for the field to develop and publicize relevant standards of care, and to ensure quality control, when each case is viewed as unique.

Most recent books on the law and counseling/psychotherapy/social work have approached the subject by chronicling the important cases and identifying the guidance given by the court (Freedman, 1995), by reviewing the structures and components of the legal system and the ways therapists might interact with them (Wrightsman, Nietzel, & Fortune, 1994; Sales & Shuman, 1996), or by describing malpractice risks and strategies for avoiding lawsuits (Houston-Vega, Nuehring, & Daguio, 1997; Reamer, 1994). Each of these approaches implicitly treats the legal system as a visitor to the profession, rather than a permanent, integrated component of the practice environment and, indeed, of the whole society. Laws and the legal system exist to protect the rights of all in society. If mental health professionals adjust their perception of the legal system to see it as a purposeful tool of society to enforce certain expectations and to protect consumers, they can respond by shaping interactions with the legal system in ways that are egosyntonic to practice.

The response of psychotherapists to the law can be characterized as more reactive than proactive. Because the language and orientation of the law is foreign to the profession, many psychotherapists have avoided learning about how the law works and may be uncomfortable playing a role in the legal process. There may also be relevance to the status and prestige associated with the two fields. Just as it has been uncommon to question medical doctors concerning their opinions and diagnoses, the specialized language and approach of lawyers has resulted in discomfort that prevents most outsiders from intervening in the legal system. The perception of the power and aggressiveness of lawyers adds to the dynamic. Many see themselves as protectors of the system of government, as illustrated in the oft-quoted legal maxim, "While a physician saves a life, a lawyer is responsible for the society which makes life worth living." The myth seems to be that lawyers act alone in this regard. The reality, however, is that, to function properly, the legal system needs information from experts in various professions. Expert opinions are relied on in court cases to set the relevant standard of care. Psychotherapists and those who speak on behalf of professional organizations help to shape the development of legislation. In the late seventeenth century, Spinoza observed, "Nature abhors a vacuum." The law is similar in its functioning as it rushes to fill the voids in social relationships where there are no explicit expectations or written standards. It is only in the absence of an active presence by the field that the legal system will be inclined to set standards for the profession. The legal system is designed to be accessible to all groups. The mental health professions need to respond enthusiastically to the open invitation to participate in the legal process.

LAWSUITS AGAINST PSYCHOTHERAPISTS

It is important to note that lawsuits and legal hearings have become a part of doing business in the practice of counseling and psychotherapy.

Professionals should be prepared, at some point in their careers, to be involved in legal proceedings. Some clinicians remain in denial about the possibility of being called into court while others attempt to meticulously learn the law to limit their risk. However, it is a myth and an illusion that legal understanding creates legal invulnerability (Bednar et al., 1991). By facing the inevitability of legal involvement, mental health professionals can respond to the event in a balanced, thoughtful manner, which allows them to serve their present clients and the system more effectively. Many of the calls lawyers receive from counselors and psychotherapists can be classified as panic-driven. In one case, an experienced clinician reported to me that he would refuse to testify at a hearing on the custody of his client's child. He argued that he had not contracted with his client to provide these services and asked about stipulating in all orientation materials his refusal to participate in clients' legal proceedings. In another case, a caller confessed that she had destroyed all of her written records, except for dates of sessions, when a former client telephoned to inform her of a forthcoming subpoena.

The idea that clients might involve clinicians in a lawsuit either as a witness or as a defendant is antithetical to the foundation of trust that is crucial to the therapeutic relationship. It introduces a different role for the professional as well as a different set of expectations. In therapy, the opinions of the therapist are generally reserved for diagnostic purposes and are often not directly expressed to the client. In the courtroom, the therapist may be forced to provide answers to questions truthfully, without consideration of the relationship the worker has established with the client. Some of the responses may be against the client's interest (such as in a custody case), while other responses may not be therapeutically appropriate for the client to hear. The altered dynamics of the therapist in the courtroom are similar to those that arise when the worker inappropriately involves the client in a dual relationship. Perhaps the most disturbing aspect about being involved in a court case is the lack of control the therapist has in the process. From the formal receipt of the subpoena to the carefully prepared questioning in depositions and testimony, involvement in legal cases represents a foreign, uncomfortable experience to the autonomous, creative, emotive characteristics of most clinicians.

Beyond discomfort with the legal process, being sued can result in actual damages and harm to the practitioner. The most obvious concern is the adverse publicity that can attach to even the most frivolous claims, which could affect future client referrals and career opportunities. A related economic loss relates to the time it takes to prepare for a court hearing, to be deposed, or to go to court. This often involves the hiring of an attorney and other direct costs of protecting one's practice and reputation as well as an inevitable rise in the cost of malpractice insurance. A less obvious source of harm from being sued was reported in a small study by Charles, Wilbert, and Franke (1985). They surveyed sued and nonsued physicians and found that those who had been sued reported psychological stress symptoms including depressed mood, tension, anger, and frustration. Of interest, they also found this group to be more likely to stop seeing certain types of "high-risk" patients. One of the implications that can be drawn from this limited study is that lawsuits may have a negative effect on the quality of care provided by the individual who was sued, even while it may help to enhance the overall practice of psychotherapy by reinforcing the standards for appropriate professional behavior.

THE RATIONALE OF LIABILITY

There has been a great deal of discussion concerning illegitimate, often frivolous lawsuits and the negative effects they have on business and society. Although it is true that there are social costs to this development, there are also social gains, beyond the monetary rewards reaped by successful plaintiffs. LoPucki (1996) observes that in contemporary society, governments enforce the law (standards of behavior) through incarceration and liability. In criminal cases, individuals are controlled by the threat of jail. In noncriminal contexts, society exerts control by enabling a party, who was injured by an act of another, to receive a monetary award. The latter civil law system is called tort law. This system serves two important social purposes. First, tort law is based on the fairness rationale, which compensates injured parties to "make them whole" so that the one who caused the injury pays for the damages. Second, liability may subject the party at fault to expensive punitive damage awards that serve as deterrents to further harmful actions. This also serves notice on all those involved in similar endeavors that a particular action or behavior would subject them to potential liability.

The success of this goal of deterrence, however, is dependent on the perceptions of the professional community. If clinicians experience tort law as punishing undesirable behavior, they are more likely to shape their treatment in compliance with court decisions (Shuman, 1993a). If the perceptions of cases filed against counselors and psychotherapists are that they are mostly frivolous, lawyer-driven nuisances, the results are likely to be dismissed by the professional community. An interesting study on the *Tarasoff* decision supports this point. *Tarasoff* (1976) is the California case in which a therapist was informed by his client that he intended to harm a third party. The case established a legal duty for psychotherapists to warn or otherwise protect an identified person who is threatened with serious danger of violence by a client. Researchers found that after the well-publicized case, psychiatrists and psychologists were considerably more willing to notify people who might be in danger from clients who threatened harm (Givelber, Bowers, & Blitch, 1984). Whether one agrees with the decision or not, it is indisputable that *Tarasoff* established a new standard of care for psychotherapists. For a court decision to be an effective deterrent to undesirable professional behavior, as happened in *Tarasoff,* several conditions must be present. The essential elements that support compliance with a court-established standard of care are (a) the legitimacy of the issue to the profession, (b) widespread publicity of the case, and (c) an unacceptable risk to the psychotherapist for noncompliance.

Risk assessment is the analytical process undertaken by a professional concerning what action to take in cases where there are competing interests. If the costs are substantial (e.g., loss of license or possible imposition of punitive damages), there is increased incentive to follow the court's standard of care. The best example of why high noncompliance costs are necessary and effective is the infamous Ford Pinto case. After several lawsuits against Ford for flammable gas tanks on its Pinto model that resulted in many deaths and injuries, Ford undertook an economic analysis to determine its response. The company initially concluded that it would cost less to deny responsibility, take no action to recall the defective vehicles, and pay out damage costs to the persons who would were injured in crashes than it would be to recall all of the Pintos to fix the gas tanks (Marks, 1981). As a society, it seems clear that we do not favor this type of evasion of responsibility. Punitive damages and other high jury awards make it economically undesirable for a company or an individual to intentionally or negligently cause injury to another.

The problem with the attention garnered by the frivolous cases is that people tend to classify all suits as falling in this category. Frivolous cases do, at times, make it through the initial screening that occurs early in the life of a case. The challenge for the legal system is how to eliminate these claims while not unfairly discouraging those cases in which information to substantiate a claim is in the control of the defendant (Freedman, 1987). In these cases, the filing of the lawsuit and the discovery process may be the only way for an injured party to access the evidence to prove the merits of the case. It is important for psychotherapists to take an apolitical view of lawsuits against practitioners. If a therapist is practicing negligently or outside of the standard of care and an injury results, there should be a cause of action available to clients to receive compensation for the damages they suffer (Madden & Parody, 1997).

In many ways, the quality of life we enjoy in America has resulted from the civil law system that serves as an omnipresent quality control device. We all want safe products, doctors who don't make mistakes, lawyers who have turned over every rock, and psychotherapists who safely and effectively provide help to their clients. As in many relationships, it is the very thing that attracts us that may eventually repel us. In recent years, many high-profile cases have contributed to the notion that the pendulum has swung too far (Polinski & Rubinfeld, 1993) and too many cases seem to be examples of playing legal lottery, hoping for a huge payoff. While these cases garner headlines, the reality is that civil cases against professionals are extremely expensive to litigate for both sides. To file a lawsuit, an individual must have an attorney agree to take a case. In rare instances, a client may attempt to sue without an attorney. Civil lawsuits generally are handled on a contingency fee basis. No fees are charged to the client unless and until a damage award is won, in which case the attorney takes a percentage of the award. This means that attorneys have to put up the money to file the suit, depose witnesses, hire experts, prepare legal briefs, and spend extensive time in litigation if the case proceeds to trial. An additional protection against frivolous suits is the system of judicial penalties and fines levied against attorneys who file civil suits that have no substantive evidence to support the claims.

In cases against mental health professionals, an attorney examines the facts to determine whether the client has suffered substantial damages that would pay for the costs of pursuing a case. If the case is minor, such as a billing dispute, the lawyer may handle it for the client by charging an hourly rate. Also, if the case represents an egregious violation of professional standards, the case may be taken, on principle, even if the damages to the client are minor. Regardless, the analysis of the case rests on the degree to which the clinician acted in accordance with the standards of the profession. There are two elements to this concept that each practitioner and the field of psychotherapy as a whole must address. First, the professional organizations must work more diligently to establish foundational standards for practice that are clear, based on sound research, and made available to the practitioners. Second, each individual therapist must become informed of these standards and demonstrate compliance with generally accepted treatment approaches, practice procedures, and business practices. Attending to both levels of action will result in fewer lawsuits against practitioners, and more important, a higher standard of practice.

A RECIPROCAL RELATIONSHIP

The relationship between the law and psychotherapy is a reciprocal one that has been characterized much more by the degree to which the law has influenced psychotherapy than the degree to which psychotherapy has influenced the law. There has been some work done by the mental health disciplines to shape the law by sharing insights and educating legal professionals about the field to make legal decisions more "therapeutic" (see Wexler, 1990), but this area of scholarship is relatively new and requires far greater attention. In legal proceedings, the questions that must be addressed are specific to a case. The debate surrounding these questions is necessarily adversarial. Lawyers seek to portray evidence that supports their position as infallible while characterizing opposing viewpoints as ridiculous (Madden & Parody, 1997). When there is no clearly articulated standard of care, the court relies on experts to determine whether a professional acted reasonably. It is unlikely that the most appropriate practice standards can be developed from this type of process. Courts often create rules in the context of the dispute, in consideration of the plaintiff who may be seriously injured (Givelber et al., 1984). The courts, and especially juries, are subject to pressures stemming from sympathy for the injured party and the mistaken idea that insurance will cover the payment of damages. The subsequent decision is not analyzed with regard to how it will affect future practice in the field but only as a retrospective analysis of the behavior of the clinician in the case under consideration. As a result of a decision in a court case, new standards of care may be established through the common law process. The common law is based on a system where the findings in one case are used to help decide similar cases arising in the future. This is particularly true in cases that are decided by higher courts such as at the appellate level or the supreme courts on the state or federal level (although a similar case on the same level might be persuasive to a trial judge). When higher courts decide an issue, their holdings are binding on subsequent trial court decisions on the same issue under the legal principle known as *stare decisis*. One misinformed legal decision can have undue influence on future decisions and thus on clinicians' behavior. As a result of this process, mental health professionals have found their standard of care being defined through litigated cases rather than by serious scholarly dialogue and research-based analyses. The criticism of the results of lawsuits centers on the degree to which they reflect hindsight bias.

Frequently, no specific standard of care has been articulated for an area of practice being litigated. As a result of expert testimony and based on the facts and vagaries of the individual case, the court may retroactively establish a standard of behavior. Some see this process as inherently flawed in that it comes down to the plaintiff's experts convincing a judge what the standard of care ought to be, rather than actually reflecting current standards (Shapiro, 1990). Clinicians are justified in their fear of this type of case, as there is no rule or standard to follow prior to the imposition of liability. This is why it is crucial for psychotherapists to conduct practice research and for professional organizations to develop standards of care for more areas of practice.

Mental health clinicians are caught in the proverbial nexus between a rock and a hard place in seeking to advance practice through new techniques. If an established standard of care does not include a new approach to treatment, it is difficult for the profession to grow. In other branches of health care, experimental procedures can be tested in a laboratory or on animals to determine a baseline measure of effectiveness and safety. There is a process for federal approval that includes clinical trials before a technique, medication, or treatment can be used in practice. This process provides evidence for demonstrating that the treatment is within a standard of care. In mental health treatment, with the exception of psychotropic medications, there is no similar process for testing the efficacy of new treatment approaches prior to actually using them on clients. In this way, clinicians are discouraged from treatments that are experimental.

Lest it appear that the practice of psychotherapy is completely controlled by the decisions of the legal system, it is important to note that in most instances, the therapeutic approach of the worker is difficult to challenge. The more the treatment activity relies on the performance of technical skills (such as assessment of suicide or violence risk or the prescription of medications), the easier it will be for a court to find that the procedures should have been done in a certain way. The more intuitive the treatment, and the more individualized the therapy, the harder it is to determine the standard of care that should have been used (Stone & Mathews, 1996).

REGULATION OF
PSYCHOTHERAPY PRACTICE

Most of the discussion to this point has centered on the role of the courts and the tort law system in the regulation of psychotherapy practice. While these areas are fertile for analysis and highly unstable, it is important not to overlook the role of legislatures and professional organizations. State legislatures have passed statutes regulating the practice of various professions using a public safety rationale to justify their interventions. Statutes determine who may call themselves psychologists, social workers, and the like as well as articulating the credentials needed to practice in a given area. It is important to distinguish the type of statutory category used by the legislature to regulate each profession in each state. Saltzman and Proch (1990) provide a clear analysis of the differences in the types of regulatory schemes. Registration is the least comprehensive in that it is simply a listing of those professionals who are able to present themselves to the public using a certain title (e.g., marriage and family therapist, counselor). Certification involves a higher level of oversight by the state administrative agency assigned the task of regulating mental health professions. Certification usually requires completion of specific educational programs, the passing of an exam, and a period of supervised practice experience. Certification protects the title, as well as who can identify as a social worker, hypnotherapist, and the like, but it does not restrict an individual from engaging in the practice. A licensing statute is the most far-reaching in that it restricts the practice of the profession to those who have a license. Licensing requires documentation and testing similar to that involved in the certification statutes.

Most statutes regulate the conduct of professionals by reserving the power to revoke the credential for violation of professional standards (Cohen & Mariano, 1982) and by using criminal penalties or civil sanctions to deter unauthorized practice of an occupation. This system helps to give legitimacy to the professions and helps the public to consume services with the confidence that all professionals meet minimum standards for practice. In addition, these regulatory statutes are important because they form the basis for the inclusion of a profession in other statutory regulations. For example, every state has regulations that mandate the type of coverage that must be included in any insurance policy written in that state. The insurance statute often refers to the professional regulatory statute, requiring insurance companies to cover services provided by certified or licensed mental health practitioners. Similarly, the statutes that determine what relationships should be privileged, and thereby protected from a disclosure of information without the client's consent, generally only apply to licensed or certified mental health professions (VandeCreek, Knapp, & Herzog, 1988). State regulation of counseling and psychotherapy advances the public confidence and trust, provides a mechanism for controlling quality to protect public safety, and increases the legitimacy of the professions.

A frequently overlooked regulatory power is the system of private, voluntary regulation that occurs through professional organizations. Membership in a professional organization often lends prestige to a practitioner and usually assures the public of a certain type of training and level of experience (Greaney, 1996). Each of the major professional organizations related to psychotherapy has established a code of ethics that sets standards for practice. Procedures are in place to review complaints against members of a professional organization for alleged violations and to recommend corrective actions or sanctions if the allegations are substantiated (Houston-Vega et al., 1997). Control over the professional educational standards and curriculum is another way the professional organizations can regulate the profession. In many cases, the professional must have graduated from accredited academic or training programs to be eligible for organizational membership. Certain jobs (by regulation or tradition) specify the necessary academic preparation, ongoing professional development, or state credentialing that are required for the position. This results in another form of voluntary regulation. These private forms of regulation serve a further purpose. Most of the organizations publish materials that define practice standards and codes of conduct for the profession. These standards are, in effect, rules of conduct that govern the practice of the mental health worker. Failure to act in accordance with these standards may be considered evidence of a violation of the standard of care for the profession (Cohen & Mariano, 1982). In this way, the professional organizations and the legal system work together to regulate the profession.

The requirements for regulation of the profession differ in one significant way from the case law that has been discussed. The regulation from state agencies and professional organizations was initiated and nurtured by the mental health professions and represents a norm for each professional group, while the standards developed from case law arise out of the judge or jury deciding on a specific case. The professional standards are necessarily more vague and conservative because they reflect general policies that can be applied to a variety of situations. In specific cases, the court may find that the professional standards usual to a practice situation are insufficient to prevent a harm. In these cases, the court may rewrite professional standards and create a conflict between the legal duty and the professional duty. One example of this occurred in California following the *Tarasoff* decision. Prior to this case, the professional standard of maintaining confidentiality was the dominant consideration, even when a client was perceived to be dangerous. The California Supreme Court's decision resulted in psychotherapists changing the way they evaluate their duty to warn a third party (Givelber et al., 1984). This type of change could have occurred only in the context of a court decision of this magnitude.

The legal community has examined the issue of how to regulate legal professionals in a much more formal manner than has occurred in the mental health professions. A growing field of study called *legal process scholarship* assesses the competence of various institutions to perform regulatory tasks (Schneyer, 1996). There are benefits and limitations to the use of statutory rules, administrative agencies, professional organizations, and court decisions. It is important to understand which systems can best provide guidance to clinicians to reinforce acceptable practices and deter inappropriate professional behaviors. The mental health disciplines must begin to explore the nature and effect of the various forms of regulation in terms of their efficacy for improving practice, and actively engage in policy making and political activities to this end.

THE LAW, SOCIAL CONTROL,
AND PSYCHOTHERAPY

The message of society seems clear. There needs to be more standardization and quality control in the practice of psychotherapy. If
psychotherapists are unable or unwilling to develop these standards, the
standards will evolve gradually as a result of the adversarial process of
court cases. When this occurs, mental health professionals respond,
often giving more power to the court's decision than it warrants. There
frequently is a political agenda associated with the most high-profile
cases that further clouds the clinical issue with the rhetoric of politics.
The process becomes what Hirshman (1991) termed the "protracted and
perilous seesawing of action and reaction" (p. 3). If a prominent court
case results in a decision against a therapist, the profession has tended
to adjust practices to abide by the court's guidance. This results in
defensive practice and, at times, the avoidance of those client problems
that might give rise to legal actions. Defensive psychotherapy can be
defined as an act or omission by a therapist that is performed not for the
benefit of the patient but solely to avoid malpractice liability or to
provide a legal defense against a malpractice claim (Simon, 1992).
Often it results in more liability, rather than less, because the therapist
is acting from an inappropriate orientation, prioritizing self-interest
over client interest.

Society, through the law, has an interest in controlling certain aspects
in the practice of psychotherapy. The first area concerns the standards
governing practice policies and procedures. How do professionals maintain records and protect confidentiality? These and other issues will be
developed in Chapter 2 of this book. When psychotherapists understand
the basis of society's expectations, clear practice policies will be more
thoughtfully developed to meet the needs of clients and workers. The
practitioner can then use these policies as a basis for fair and ethical
treatment of clients, which not only is the best strategy for reducing the
risk of being sued but also is the best defense.

Clients and practitioners have an expectation that the sanctity of the
counseling relationship will be supported by society and preserved by
the courts. The outcome of cases would suggest the following answer
to a client's questions about confidentiality: "It depends." There are two
major types of cases related to the disclosure of confidential information. Some mental health workers have been sued or otherwise sanc-

tioned for the improper release of information to third parties. In other cases, the issue for the court is whether to compel the release of information against the wishes of the client or worker. Chapter 3 analyzes these cases and provides guidance as to the values that drive the courts' decisions.

The second area of focus for this book is the clinical standard of care. In handling certain types of client situations and presenting problems, clinicians need to know about the major practice guidelines and standards for care. Because any action for malpractice will analyze the degree to which the professional acted reasonably, given the circumstances (*Black's Law Dictionary,* 1983), it is imperative that the therapist act within established parameters. Chapter 4 will explore legal issues that arise in managing the treatment relationship. What constitutes informed consent to treatment? How do clients and therapists contract for services, interact with managed care companies, and develop and implement treatment plans and evaluation designs? How does the treatment relationship end? How does a worker decide whether to take a certain case and what constitutes a dual relationship? Chapter 5 of the book looks with increased depth at some of these clinical standards for practice and how they have developed in response to important cases. Recent case law will be analyzed to determine the treatment issues that will be litigated in the future and what the mental health fields need to do in preparation and response. This chapter will provide a detailed analysis of three areas of practice that have generated a large number of lawsuits against mental health clinicians: misdiagnosis/incorrect treatment, duty to protect (suicide assessment), and recovered memory/false memory of child sexual abuse.

There are some circumstances in which a therapist is involved in the legal system by "invitation." One may be subpoenaed as a witness, become a party to a legal action as plaintiff or defendant, or testify as an expert witness. Each of these situations holds opportunities for practitioners to use their knowledge base to educate and inform courts so that legal decisions are more relevant to the needs of both clients and therapists. Each of these situations also holds potential risks for the clinician. Once again, if the purpose of the interaction with the legal system is understood, the worker will be able to respond more confidently and competently. Increasingly, mental health professionals are being asked to educate the courts and legislatures as cases or bills are being considered. The social science data and insights into the field of psychotherapy provided in testimony not only have persuasive power relevant to the issue of the hearing (Loewen, 1982), but also tend to have a broader influence on the legal system. Chapter 6 of the book will explore these issues and will discuss the ways in which the mental health professions can further their efforts to educate and influence the legal systems and its decisions. This chapter will also discuss the importance of consultations with an attorney whenever a legal issue arises in the practice or business of psychotherapy.

There are recurring situations in practice involving the legal problems of clients. Many of these legal issues are related to treatment. Clinicians need to be knowledgeable about the basic elements of the law to assist clients by providing support, information, and advocacy when necessary. The most common areas of legal entanglement are cases involving divorce/custody, child welfare/protective services, civil commitment proceedings, and various probate court actions including adoptions, wills, guardianships, and other transferrals of decision-making authority. Chapter 7 reviews the basic legal concepts in these areas and suggests ways for professionals to ease the burden of the process for clients.

This book will examine legal issues in counseling and psychotherapy practice by reviewing recent cases and relevant statutes. The goal is to examine the motives and rationale of the courts and legislatures to develop an understanding of the guidance being given to the professional community. The examination of each area will focus on the purpose and function of a decision/law for the client. Too often, the analysis of legal trends has been elitist, taken from the perspective of the therapist rather than the client (Shuman, 1993b). As a result, the literature reads like a lecture, warning of what not to do in practice. If therapists become aware of what protections are extended to clients, they will conform practice to meet society's expectations of the therapeutic relationship and professional behavior. However, in those cases where court decisions conflict with professional principles, the various professional organizations and academic communities should accept these results as a mandate to publish and publicize research-based standards to the membership and to the larger community. These profession-generated standards are necessary to refute any illegitimate court-established standards.

Viewing lawsuits by clients only as an attack on the profession leads to the circle-the-wagon phenomena that does nothing to improve practice. The courts and legislatures are outsiders examining the practice of psychotherapy with a very different lens than practitioners use. It is not surprising that the lens may be more focused on the needs and vulner-abilities of clients as a result of the advocacy role of the attorneys and the fault-based tort law system. There is much that the mental health professions can learn from interactions with the legal system if clinicians are open to hearing the message. At the same time, there is a need to educate legal professionals about mental health practice to create an environment that supports the shared goals of improving practice and protecting consumers.

CONCLUSION

Mental health professionals can be described as being anxious-avoidant when it comes to interactions with the law. Instead of reacting to the legal state defensively, this book argues for the mental health professions to engage with the legal systems to promote good clinical practice and sound business operations. The legal influence on counseling and psychotherapy will not diminish, so clinicians must learn to embrace it. There are several things practitioners can do to begin the process of creating more productive relationships with the legal system. Given that the threat of legal action against therapists is a constant reality, part of the overhead of a professional practice must be adequate malpractice insurance and regular supervision and/or consultation. Each practitioner should identify an area of expertise and make use of professional development opportunities to master the standards of care for that field—to be well prepared for legal challenges to practice.

Clinicians need to be vigilant about developing clear assessments as well as treatment plans with a theoretical foundation, and they must maintain high-quality, timely, written records. Each practitioner should be attuned to individual client concerns (Charles, 1993) and ensure that clients understand the treatment and give legitimate informed consent. Frequently, bad feelings about the therapist and bad endings of treatment relationships feed the client's anger and hurt emotions, leading clients to file suits against therapists (Korner, 1995). Managing these conflicts as they arise may reduce the risks of lawsuits as much as any strategy adopted in practice.

Finally, there are myriad opportunities for counselors and psycho-therapists to shape their own future through improved interactions with the legal system. As the mental health professions become more active in producing and publishing practice research, setting standards for practice, and agreeing on standards of care for critical areas, there will be a well-established set of parameters for the courts to consider. It is clear that therapists and clients believe in the efficacy of treatment but there is very little research to back up the claims of success (Jacobson, 1995). Clinicians and researchers who serve as expert witnesses must keep in mind their important role in the development of practice standards. Their testimony must reflect the research rather than the interests of their employers (one of the parties of a lawsuit). Counselors and psychotherapists must also be active participants in the legal system to change laws that affect both professional interests and the conditions of practice such as commitment procedures, competency, guardianship, professional regulation, insurance laws, and many other areas.

As the professionalization and standardization of counseling and psychotherapy evolve, there will be increasing demands for formal written guidelines and standards for practice. In some areas, this is already under way. In other areas, definition of a standard of care will continue to be elusive. Mental health clinicians probably never will have the predictive ability to assess suicide and dangerousness so as to prevent all harm. But the public does have the right to expect competent, careful practitioners who refrain from the iatrogenic creation of illnesses and who adhere to ethical principles. In *The Common Law*, Oliver Wendell Holmes Jr. wrote, "The first requirement of a sound body of law is, that it should correspond with the actual feelings and demands of the community whether right or wrong" (1881/1982, p. 36). The community has spoken through the proliferation of lawsuits and the development of statutes and regulations governing clinical practice. It is time for the profession to express its needs and demands to influence the legal system and thereby shape the future.

Chapter 2

STANDARDIZATION OF PRACTICE POLICIES AND PROCEDURES

It was early on a July morning when Ernie approached his super-visor at the plant. Ernie confided that he was depressed and would like to talk with someone from the agency that provided mental health services to the company's employees. His supervisor arranged for Ernie to meet with a clinical social worker later that morning. After evaluating Ernie's mental status, the social worker assessed him as depressed and highly suicidal. He recommended that Ernie check into the hospital immediately. Ernie was concerned that the company not find out about his condition and later testified that he specifically asked the social worker to keep everything he said in strict confidence. The social worker called the company and (a jury subsequently determined) he informed them that Ernie was in the hospital due to his suicide threat and would not be returning to work. The company called Ernie's wife to let her know about the situation. Ernie returned to work five days later only to be reassigned to a different job. Some time later, he sued the social worker for violating his privilege by disclosing information concerning the hospitalization and suicidal tendencies. The jury found the social worker liable and seemed to put a great deal of credence in the testimony of a psychologist who testified that the breach of confidentiality was a major factor in Ernie's ongoing depression. The jury awarded Ernie $60,000 in actual damages and an additional $100,000 in punitive damages. The appeals court reluctantly upheld the decision, commenting that it was clear the social worker was attempting to help and was not purposeful in causing harm to Ernie. The court did reduce the punitive damage award to $20,000 (*Davison v. Tangari,* 1989).

In some cases, psychotherapists clearly act outside of the scope of professional expectations such as in cases of sexual relations with clients, insurance fraud, or other serious malfeasance. However, mental health professionals are most often confronted by the legal system in cases where they tried to do the right thing. In this chapter, the focus is on the development of and adherence to practice policies and procedures. It is rare that a professional's policies are malicious or so removed from the standard of care that they require action by the systems that enforce professional standards. More often it is the case that the psychotherapist failed to consider the ramifications of a particular action or failed to adhere to basic practice management policies. In the case of Ernie, the social worker should have understood the inherent client concerns when providing services in an employee assistance program. In this crisis situation, the worker was most interested in securing help for the client and protecting his job by letting the supervisor know that the worker would not be returning. Unfortunately, despite good intentions, his actions violated a basic expectation of every client who approaches a therapist for service: the right to keep all information about the client confidential. One would need to examine the procedures of the agency to determine if there was adequate attention to protecting client confidentiality. The agency providing the employee assistance services should have had policies in place regarding communication with the company. The presence of clear, consistent policies minimizes the mistakes that occur through reaction to events. This problem is especially acute for mental health workers who see themselves as advocates. There is a tendency to allow conviction to drive judgment, which sometimes results in unintended harm to the client.

When a court, administrative agency, or professional organization is hearing a complaint against a practitioner, the case record and standardized practices/procedures provide exceptional witnesses to the treatment in question. The record can demonstrate the contemporaneous thoughts and actions of the therapist during treatment as his or her adherence to professional standards is evaluated. Given this, there is a strong temptation to think about clinical record keeping as a means of defending oneself from future questions about practice decisions. Although this is a powerful incentive to maintain good records, in the end, it is an insufficient perspective. Instead, the policies and procedures of one's practice must be looked at as a reflection of personal and professional values. For example, a psychotherapist who is committed to the value of privacy would be likely to develop and follow strong policies on confidentiality. An agency that values professional development and expertise in its staff would require consistent clinical record keeping and regular supervision. When and if retrospective analysis of clinical behavior occurs, the record will stand as an embodiment of good practice, not because the policy is technically correct but because it truly represents professional standards and values.

At times, the practice of psychotherapy requires practitioners to make difficult decisions among competing interests. Other times, therapists are involved in the human drama and may react without having carefully considered the ramifications of a particular course of behavior. There is no single strategy for standardizing practice policies and procedures that is completely effective in preventing lawsuits. However, therapists who develop an understanding of general expectations of clients and society will be more likely to act in ways that reduce the threat of legal action. Clients usually come to psychotherapy full of trepidation. The dominant issue early in treatment is the development of a trusting relationship with the worker. This trust is based on the expectation of privacy and the client's perception that the therapist is a competent professional who can be helpful. When viewed from the client's perspective (rather than a self-interest-driven focus on malpractice risk reduction), a therapist's response to practice dilemmas is more likely to be in consonance with the interests of the client.

The client's perspective, however, is only one part of the analysis. In addition to the client's view, society expects psychotherapists to maintain certain practice standards that, at times, may conflict with the desire of an individual client. For example, a client who expresses a desire to commit suicide may prefer that the therapist not divulge this information or take any action to prevent the completion of the suicide. Society, however, could judge a therapist on whether there was opportunity to stop the suicide if the family were to bring a malpractice lawsuit. Does the worker risk being sued for breaching confidentiality or failure to prevent a suicide? What practice policies would assist a worker in responding to this sort of dilemma? The balancing of the interests of the individual client and the expectations placed on the practice of psychotherapy by the general public is extraordinarily complicated. At times these duties are mutually exclusive. Satisfying one causes a breach of the other. This is why the idea of completely shielding oneself from lawsuits is impossible. The judgment of a clinician's behavior rests on an analysis of whether professional standards were followed and whether the therapist acted reasonably, given the circumstances.

The following case provides a useful example of the necessity for maintaining clear vision as to professional responsibility. A clinical social worker brought an action in small claims court for the purpose of collecting a $220 debt for professional services (*Creamer v. Danks,* 1988). His client contested the bill and in the process of finding out the facts, the judge asked some questions concerning the treatment. The social worker testified that the client had a diagnosis of depression. The client later sued, alleging that the therapist's comments in court regarding his mental condition constituted slander, invasion of privacy, intentional infliction of mental distress, and professional negligence. Although the therapist was not found liable (because the disclosure of the diagnosis occurred as a relevant part of a response to judicial questioning in a court action), this case illustrates the point that therapists must be vigilant in maintaining policies in all settings. In many of the cases reviewed for this chapter, therapists found themselves in unusual circumstances where breaches of procedure occurred. The real test of whether a psychotherapist has violated a professional standard with respect to information management may ultimately be made in a jury deliberation room. There, the therapist's sincerity and trust are evaluated on the basis of the evidence of adherence to "authentic" policies that are designed to be in the best interest of the client.

The standardization of practice policies and procedures involves the effective management of information and clear communication with clients. Clinicians need to become aware of the expectations society places on practice so as to appreciate the demands for various types of documentation and service delivery. These expectations are oriented toward the protection of the public. Case records must reflect competent practice. Information that arises out of the treatment relationship must be kept confidential and the conditions under which information may be released must be clarified to clients in advance. Clients must be informed of the parameters of the treatment and consent to the methods to be used by the therapist. Care must be taken to craft agreements with clients and third-party payers concerning the scope of treatment and the communication about the client's presenting symptoms and diagnosis. If a therapist constructs practice management principles that are client-centered and within generally accepted professional behavior, it will be obvious both to current clients (minimizing "bad experience" complaints) and to any third party who examines the records of a case.

RECORD KEEPING

In the 1930s, when the practice of psychotherapy was in its infancy, Margaret Cochran Bristol (1936) wrote one of the first books on case recording. Bristol documented problems in information management that still resonate with the modern practitioner. She argued for techniques to increase the relevancy of the task to practice goals.

> The worker of the future will doubtless practice severe selection of material for the record and will be enabled to do this more satisfactorily than at present because she will be better equipped with a knowledge of the factors which are likely to prove to be the essential determining elements in the situation. . . . Record writing will be looked upon more as a part of the art of case work and less as a mechanical process of reproducing accurately the objective data in case situations. (p. 78)

Perhaps the practice of psychotherapy has not advanced as rapidly as Bristol envisioned as the struggle to identify the causal factors in emotional and mental health cases is still under way. The issues for today's practitioners are similar to Bristol's concerns. Mental health workers are typically people-oriented and many denounce the paperwork that is required by agency policies or third-party payers to be a loathsome task and a necessary evil. Each of the mental health professions deserves blame for failing to educate and monitor practitioners adequately concerning opportunities to improve practice through purposeful record keeping. As a result, many workers either avoid the task or create sparse records that add little to the clinical process (Gelman, 1992).

Kagle (1991, p. 141) identifies three competing goals of record keeping: (a) accountability, (b) efficiency, and (c) client privacy. She believes these can be reconciled when records of service are focused on documenting the purpose of the treatment (including assessment, diagnosis, and the resulting treatment plan), the process of the treatment (information that demonstrates that services were appropriate to the client's evolving needs and that supports the decisions made by the practitioner), and the impact of treatment (evaluation of the treatment for the client). The clinical reasons for having quality records are numerous. Most important, the process of writing about therapy provides an opportunity for increasing the depth of thinking about a client and the therapeutic process. Some authors have suggested that by writing out and reflecting on each session, clinical understanding is enhanced (Kagle, 1991; Simon, 1991). It is also very useful for clinicians to review a client record prior to a session, so as to be oriented to any unresolved or ongoing issues for the client. Periodic reviews of a case record by the therapist may yield interesting patterns or recurring themes. Further, the records can supply a therapist with the information necessary for effective evaluation and supervision. Case records also serve an administrative purpose as they are used to submit claims for reimbursement from third-party payers, to justify funding requests, to evaluate the agency functioning, and to supervise the performance of workers.

Maintaining adequate treatment records is an expectation of professional behavior and should be considered part of the standard of care for all psychotherapists (Houston-Vega et al., 1997; Reamer, 1994; Simon, 1991). What is the expectation of psychotherapists in terms of record keeping? There are few cases that specifically address the legal requirements of case records (Austin, Moline, & Williams, 1990) and none could be found in which the issue of records was the primary complaint. Generally a case is brought about negligent treatment, malpractice, or some other complaint, and the absence of adequate records is used as evidence against the therapist. Clinical record keeping is one area of practice in which the courts have not established a clear standard of care. The professional expectation has been set by the literature and ethical codes of the mental health professions. The requirements include

> maintaining records that are adequate, accurate, complete, and timely (Roach, Chernoff, & Esley, 1985);
>
> detailing an account of the therapeutic process;
>
> documenting evidence of reasonable, professional practice; and
>
> demonstrating competency in following an accepted treatment approach.

Case records are a way of providing a history of the work, and documenting the clinical process provides evidence as to how the standard of care was met (Houston-Vega et al., 1997).

Many recent texts have attempted to identify the elements necessary for a clinical case record (e.g., Austin et al., 1990; Houston-Vega et al., 1997). Kagle (1991, p. 16) makes the most sense when she advises that form should follow function. Each psychotherapist must consider the purpose of the treatment and the methodology being used when determining what form of case record and documentation is necessary to serve the interest of the process. It is also very important to include a record of any consultations or supervisory sessions in which the case was discussed. The documentation of these efforts by the therapist is important if professional standards are questioned or the case becomes contested in court. Finally, any referral that was given to the client should be documented in the record as well as in the follow-up information as to whether the client accessed the service.

A service-centered approach enables the practitioner to keep records relevant to the treatment and thus keep out information that is extraneous. The increase in managed care and use of insurance to pay for mental health services has brought new attention to the content of records and, as will be discussed in a later section, concerns about the privacy issues that accompany this development. Corcoran and Vandiver (1996) recommend that the therapist consider record keeping from the position of what is in the client's best interest. This includes maintaining concise and topical notes and submitting to the managed care organization only the information relevant to the authorization of services.

The increased scrutiny into the therapeutic relationship by those managing and paying for the care has resulted in some improvements in clinical record keeping. A therapist will not get reimbursed unless the record documents a problem and a valid treatment approach. As a result, more therapists are vigilant about record keeping. Unfortunately, when a case record is narrowly focused only to justify the need for treatment, a great deal of clinical information that might be relevant to a complete understanding of the client could be left out.

Sometimes information about a client is obtained from other persons, often under the condition that the information not be disclosed to the client. Other times, clients may disclose information to the therapist that would be injurious to the client's relationship with another person. The therapist may also be conflicted about writing diagnostic impressions about a client, fearing that the client would be harmed by the information if the client exercised the right to access the information in the files. Many therapists wonder about the legality of keeping two sets of records, the official record, and a second file including personal notes, hypotheses, subjective comments, or other information not directly relevant to the reason for treatment. Although a few states do allow separate working notes (see, e.g., Illinois Mental Health and Developmental Disabilities Confidentiality Act, 1996), this practice is generally discouraged. Except where protected by statute, personal notes are subject to a subpoena and lawyers routinely include reference to personal notes when requesting client records. These subjective or speculative notes may contain information that can be used to undercut the conclusions in the formal file. If case notes are carefully written, there should be no reason to keep a separate set of notes. One exception to the discouragement of unofficial notes involves process recording or other written notes made for the purposes of supervision or education/training. In these documents, therapists and students should be careful not to include any identifying information about the client and to maintain these notes in a separate location from the client's official file.

Another concern with maintaining personal notes or with including extraneous detail in official notes has to do with defamation problems. *Defamation* is defined as any communication that tends to harm the reputation of another as to lower him or her in the estimation of the community or that deters third persons from associating or dealing with the person (*Black's*, 1983). In a defamation action, the truth of the published statement is an absolute defense to the allegation. Even though there may not have been intent to harm or even intent to have the record become public, a therapist could be sued for statements made in the case record or personal notes that subsequently were made public. An example of this type of situation occurred in a case where a doctor sent a letter to a patient with the results of a physical examination. The letter stated that the patient had a venereal disease in 1985, at which time he was married. In fact, he had contracted it years earlier. The patient's wife opened the letter, which caused considerable marital discord. The defamation claim in this case failed because the letter was not "published" as it was addressed to the patient (*Dowell v. Cleveland Clinic Foundation*, 1992). In another unreported case, a therapist was accused of defamation by a man whom the therapist identified as a perpetrator of sexual abuse in a newspaper interview about a related criminal case. If the disclosure of information about an individual occurs in the context of a legal proceeding, the professional is given absolute privilege and cannot be sued for defamation related to records or testimony (Roach et al., 1985).

Although these situations are not common, it is recommended that psychotherapists not put anything in the records about a third party because it is rarely, if ever, necessary for the purposes of treatment, and should the record ever be released, the therapist might be held liable for publishing the defamatory comments (Simon, 1992). In some cases, it is important for a practitioner to document suspicions in the case record. In cases such as possible child abuse or drug addiction, there is a need to document the suspicion to show how subsequent interactions affirmed or refuted this suspicion. This should not be considered defamation even if it is part of a record that is released to third parties (Roach et al., 1985). The important distinction is in how the entry is written. Clinicians must be careful to identify the source of the information and the relevance of the material to the treatment (Kagle, 1991). Rather than writing that a person is the perpetrator of abuse, a therapist should document that "the client stated her belief" that the person was the perpetrator. If professionals keep in mind the source of the note (i.e., Is it directly observed, reported by the client, reported by a third party, or speculation of the worker?), the decision about including the item in the case record should be clarified. The use of supervision to discuss questions of how to document suspicions is strongly recommended.

Perhaps the most effective way to think about clinical records is to maintain them with an understanding that others may someday need to examine the record, or, as Barker (1987) writes, "Prepare every record as though it was certain to be reviewed in courtrooms" (p. 5). Case notes are substantively different from a diary of the interactions with the client or a report of the client's topics in each session. The notes need to be purposeful in exploring the therapeutic process and connecting the treatment to the evaluation and assessment. The client record also needs to include documentation concerning the policies and procedures of practice including confidentiality information, policies on missed appointments, informed consent forms, billing policies and contracts, release of information forms, and other practice management documents. Some practitioners and agencies preload new client files with a checklist and prepared forms detailing practice policies, ensuring that they discuss all policies with each new client. Evidence of this type of procedure can be very useful should questions arise about whether a client was aware of an agency policy.

The ability of a therapist to know what elements to include in a case record has legal implications in addition to the clinical ones. In the legal environment it has been said, That which is not written is not done. If a psychotherapist is challenged in court concerning treatment decisions, a case record helps to provide evidence of reasonable behavior. Well-written records enhance the credibility of the worker. On the stand at trial, it would be easy to make a therapist look unprofessional and incompetent if insufficient records are retained. If an expert witness testified about the professional standard of care, the absence of case records by itself constitutes a violation of the standard.

As discussed previously, adopting a client's perspective can be useful to psychotherapists in developing policies and procedures about clinical records. Clients expect that their therapists will maintain notes summarizing client information and the content of sessions. If a client is referred for an evaluation, for hospitalization, or begins treatment with another therapist, there is an expectation that case records will be available to be sent to the other professional. If a treating professional becomes incapacitated, clients expect that their records will be sent to a professional who is covering the practice. If records that contain inaccurate information or negligently prepared evaluations are forwarded to a third party who relies on them to make treatment decisions, both parties might be liable to the client who suffers an injury as a result. By the same theory, if a psychotherapist relies on information from a previous therapist or an old evaluation, liability might accrue for failing to adequately check on the validity of the clinical information. In these types of circumstances, the lack of adequate records or reliance on inaccurate records may subject a worker to an administrative complaint or even a lawsuit.

When considering clinical record keeping procedures from the client's perspective, it is important to think about a full range of practice situations including the "worst-case scenario." For example, in one litigated case, a counseling agency was treating a young man with a history of impulsive, aggressive behaviors. The man had been seen by staff physicians for medication over a long period of time but was currently being seen by a mental health counselor for acute outpatient treatment. The case primarily concerned whether the agency had a duty to warn the man's parents about a threat of harm. However, part of the case dealt with policies on intra-agency communication. The complaint identified the lack of procedures for consultation between therapists and physicians in the agency who were treating the same client. Essentially, the court affirmed the expectation that the therapist should work with the physician and share records to better assess the dangerousness of the situation. Had this consultation occurred, medication or hospitalization might have prevented the harm (*Peck v. Counseling Service of Addison County,* 1985). The development of procedures governing case records is time-consuming and often requires strong agency management or self-discipline in private practice to ensure that policies are followed consistently. However, strong policies have the potential for preventing some harms that can result from the absence of quality case records or the failure to follow a basic procedure.

Psychotherapy records are considered medical records and most states have statutes governing the handling and disposal of these records. (For a good summary of the elements of medical record statutes and specific cites for each state, see Roach et al., 1985.) There are varying opinions as to how long to retain records beyond the statutory minimum (usually five to seven years, or in some cases it is specified that the amount of time be equal to the statute of limitations for a tort action). Whatever the decision made about retention of records, it is important to follow the policy closely. Given the ease with which records can be scanned onto disks, the storage of files is becoming less of a problem for agencies and individual practitioners. Because of the variety of situations in which it would be advantageous for a client or professional to have future access to records, it is recmmended that they be retained in perpetuity or for a minimum of 15 years. Malpractice cases frequently are not litigated until two to five years after the treatment that is the source of the legal complaint. In that time period, a clinician may have seen hundreds of clients and may have difficulty recalling specific facts. The case record provides the only detailed account of what actually occurred. If a practitioner has maintained professional-quality records, it is better to have the documents available to answer any future questions.

A case example is useful to illustrate the benefit of this policy recommendation. A 7-year-old girl is seen in therapy with a primary diagnosis of adjustment disorder. She subsequently enters treatment as an adult at age 22 when she is diagnosed with post-traumatic stress disorder as a result of sexual abuse occurring when she was a young child. She files a suit against you for failure to recognize the cause of her symptoms and intervene appropriately. Normally, a lawsuit must be filed within a limited time period after an incident (the statute of limitations). In this type of lawsuit, each state determines the appropriate time limit, usually three to five years. However, a child is unable to file suit as a minor, and thus the statute does not begin to run until the client reaches the age of majority in that state. Without the case record, it would be extraordinarily difficult to defend one's practice decisions in a case that occurred more than 15 years in the past.

Therapists may be tempted to alter records, destroy files, or create historical documents where none existed in response to a request for records from a client or the court. Under no circumstances should a professional do this because it may result in more problems than it solves. If there is a mistake in the records, a therapist should leave the original record intact but a dated notation may be added in the margin to achieve accuracy. If this is done, it should be noted in the record chronologically as well, to avoid accusations of record tampering (Simon, 1992). It is acceptable to create a treatment summary or other similar document but care should be taken to identify its date of production. A worker's alteration of a document may constitute a felony in some states (Austin et al., 1990). There are many ways to discover alterations of records such as testimony from other agency personnel or the presence of unaltered copies of the original records. The alterations may subject a worker to civil suit or to disciplinary action by the agency, professional organization, or state administrative agency. Also, even if no direct disciplinary ramifications result, the worker's credibility in testimony will be destroyed.

Medical records, and specifically mental health records, should be considered the property of the agency or professional in private practice. The client has an interest in the information in the files and in most cases would be deemed to have a right of inspection and opportunity to copy these records. A reasonable fee can be charged for the actual cost of copying the record. But because the actual files belong to the professional or agency, clients cannot take possession of the original file, nor can they require that a file be destroyed. Some clients have sought to "correct" inaccuracies in the clinical record (*Foster v. Plaut,* 1993). Some states grant this right in the law, but, regardless, it is difficult to identify any harm from including a client's written statement of correction in the case file. In fact, some have argued that the best strategy for ensuring high-quality records is to encourage regular client access to case records (Gelman, 1992).

In some states, and in many programs that receive federal funds or are covered by federal regulations (such as alcohol and drug programs or educational settings), the right of client access to clinical files is granted specifically by statute. Some states permit guardians, physicians, or attorneys, but not the patient, to gain access to mental health records (Simon, 1991). The rationale for those statutes that exclude clients is that, in some cases, viewing a file could be detrimental to a client. In general, it is sound practice to examine the case file in supervision prior to allowing the client to view it and to sit with the client while the record is reviewed to provide clarification, explanation, and support. Where a professional believes that client access to information would result in an injury to the client, the release of records is not required. One solution to this dilemma may be to use a court-appointed guardian or legal representative as the party to whom the information is released.

Psychotherapy is a profession that is based on instinct and skill (the art of practice) at the same time that it attempts to follow research and theory (the science of practice). The dilemmas involved in record keeping mirror the professional challenges posed by this duality. Clients expect records that are accurate, unbiased, up to date, and reflective of their experience in treatment. Society, especially through the legal system, expects records that are able to elucidate what occurred in the therapeutic process so that accurate judgments can be made about the conduct of the professional or about the mental and emotional condition of the client. Professional organizations expect records that are in keeping with the basic standards of the profession as defined in published standards and codes of ethics. Yet psychotherapists often feel conflicted about documenting the subtle dance that is therapy. Despite the orientation toward the individual client, psychotherapists must be able to explain the goals and outcomes of treatment. Psychotherapy records can do this if they include information that allows one to understand the process and effectiveness of the interventions. The more sophisticated clinical records become, and the more clinicians are able to produce high-quality, relevant documentation of the work, the status of the profession will continue to increase in the eyes of the legal system. In this way, the profession can have a proactive influence on how the legal system handles cases involving psychotherapists.

PRIVACY

In January 1997, the embattled Speaker of the House, Newt Gingrich, was in the midst of a controversy over alleged ethics violations. During the negotiations over how the House Ethics Committee would proceed, Gingrich publicly pledged not to meet with Republican leaders, prior to the hearings on the committee report, to plan political and media damage control. Later in the same week, Representative John Boehner was in his car in Florida when he and other House Republicans held a conference call with Mr. Gingrich in which the ethics case was discussed. The conversation was overheard and taped by a Florida couple who were listening to an adapted police scanner in their car (Yang, 1997).

The controversy during the next several days centered almost exclusively on the invasion of privacy and the violation of federal laws prohibiting such eavesdropping. The public scrutiny and outrage were much greater over the violation of the privacy than the propriety of the political activity. One of the most interesting features of the Gingrich eavesdropping case was the behavior of the Democratic representative who received the tapes and brought them to the attention of the public. Representative James McDermott eventually had to recuse himself from the committee for his role in furthering the privacy breach. McDermott is a psychiatrist by profession. Although this fact was not discussed widely in the media reports, it is ironic that a psychiatrist, for whom privacy should be a deeply understood and valued concept, would be the one to publicize the private conversations. The case provides an example of how psychotherapists find themselves in trouble with confidentiality. McDermott's actions likely were motivated by the value of exposing a perceived wrong. One could argue that he reacted by selecting the priority of politics over principles. It is in similar contexts that psychotherapists may act to breach the confidences of a client by releasing information or discussing a case without the consent of the client. The general concept of privacy has strong roots in the American value system. These societal convictions about privacy have direct applications to the practice of psychotherapy and the behavior of practitioners.

The concept of privacy may have roots dating back to the earliest civilizations (Gurry, 1984), but it is especially significant in this increasingly complex, technologically advanced, modern society. Other social and political concepts such as freedom and liberty have been debated and analyzed for centuries. But the concept of "legal privacy" is comparatively young. The noted legal scholars Samual Warren and Louis Brandeis wrote an essay in 1890 that sparked debate concerning the privacy protections that should be developed by the legal system. This debate has grown to include a range of definitions of privacy (including those that focus on intrusions into a person's seclusion or private affairs, public disclosures of private information, and appropriations of a person's ideas, designs, or expressions; Schoeman, 1984, p. 16). Privacy rights under the U.S. Constitution have been similarly broad, including the right of the individual to be free from government intrusion and surveillance; the right of an individual not to have private affairs made public by the government; and the right of an individual to be free in action, thought, experience, and belief from governmental compulsion (*Whalen v. Roe,* 1976).

Warren and Brandeis (1890) argued for creating a legal remedy to control the unauthorized disclosure of private information. As a starting point, they identified the right of each individual to determine to what extent thoughts, sentiments, and emotions should be communicated to others. The corollary of this right is the premise that no one has the right to publish private information without consent. Warren and Brandeis identified private thoughts, feelings, images, and the like as a type of property. Thus to violate someone's privacy is to take something of value. In modern society, this right to privacy has become nearly sacred. Privacy has a direct impact on an individual's dignity and autonomy and, as such, engenders strong emotions when it is violated. If privacy is violated, the breach should be considered a legal injury for which damages are possible. As discussed in Chapter 1, when violation of a standard of conduct results in substantial consequences, professional behavior can be influenced.

Privacy concerns have increased with the growth of technology. One of the occurrences that sparked the Warren and Brandeis essay was the unauthorized publication of a photograph, a new technology in the late 1800s. Today, similar concerns confront the widespread use of technology to communicate and store information. Strong emotions are connected to the value of privacy because of its implications for individual control. The more bureaucratic and complex society has become, the more people need the right of privacy (McLean, 1995). The historic American value of individualism is triggered by the implicit threat to autonomy in this environment. Faden (1993) calls attention to the emotional linguistics of the issue in the use of the powerful, value-laden term *invasion of privacy* rather than merely a *loss* or a *violation of privacy.* Also, the high level of emotion attached to the privacy issue results in the use of the terms *rights* and *obligations* rather than the less emotional concept of a *duty*.

The legal system has been slow to react to privacy protection because the area is full of conflicting values and emotions. In one of the most ironic occurrences in recent legal history, Judge Robert Bork, a noted opponent of constitutional protection of privacy rights (Moore, 1989), was indirectly responsible for the establishment of the most effective privacy protection law on the books. It was 1987 when Judge Bork was nominated to serve on the U.S. Supreme Court. He was a controversial selection due to his views on the Constitution. The hearings were contentious and various political groups lined up for or against the nomination. The media actively reported the unfolding story. Who was this man and what did he believe in? An enterprising reporter for a Washington weekly newspaper accessed the records of a video store and published a list of the movies Judge Bork had rented. The outrage was immediate, nonpartisan, and powerful. All seemed in agreement that this constituted an unacceptable level of intrusion into a private life. It raised the same level of anxiety that Warren and Brandeis (1890) felt almost 100 years earlier when they argued for a standard of "the right to be let alone" (p. 75). In response to the Bork disclosures, Congress unanimously supported and passed the Video Privacy Protection Act, restricting the release of information by movie rental outlets (Goldman, 1993, p. 76).

It is difficult to understand why there would be more outrage and immediate legislative action for information about one's video viewing habits while unauthorized releases of medical records, credit reports, and other private information fail to generate much attention from either the public or the legislature. Perhaps the risks will not become part of the collective understanding until a notorious case is publicized. What the Bork case does illustrate is the visceral level of emotion that is engendered by a violation of privacy (Goldman, 1993). The response was so strong because of the revulsion each person felt at the idea of being assaulted in this way. Psychotherapists must bear in mind the effects of the unauthorized disclosure of information so as to develop policies and practices that will prioritize the sanctity of confidentiality in the therapeutic relationship. When an individual discloses personal information to a mental health professional, there is a faith and reliance on the professional to protect the information. The next section will explore the concept of confidentiality and the limited situations in which the therapist may share details of the work with others.

CONFIDENTIALITY

Whatsoever things I see or hear concerning the life of men, in my attendance on the sick or even apart therefrom, which ought not be noised abroad, I will keep silence thereon, counting such things to be as sacred secrets.

The "oath" of Hypocrites
(as cited in *United States v. Willis*, 1990)

Dr. Roe was a physician who had practiced psychiatry for more than 50 years. As an experienced clinician, she frequently shared her knowledge with other professionals. There is a tradition in psychoanalysis, dating back to Freud, of publishing case studies to illustrate how the client and therapist proceeded through the treatment. Eight years after the termination of treatment with one couple, Mr. and Mrs. D., Dr. Roe and her husband published a book that reported, verbatim and extensively, the patients' thoughts, feelings, and emotions; their sexual fantasies; their most intimate personal relationships; and the disintegration of their marriage. Interspersed among the footnotes of the study were the authors' diagnoses of the disorders suffered by the patients and one of their children. Mrs. D. was enormously upset by the publication of this book and filed suit, seeking damages and the right to block further distribution of the book. Although no names were used, Mrs. D. felt her privacy was shattered given that the details of the portrayed case made her easily identified by anyone who was associated with her or her family.

In the lawsuit, she claimed that she had been damaged as a consequence of this publication. She reportedly suffered acute embarrassment on learning the extent to which friends, colleagues, employer, students, and others had read, or read of, the book. Mrs. D. believed that this contributed to her health problems. She had insomnia and nightmares. She became reclusive as a consequence of the shame and humiliation induced by the book's publication, and her well-being and emotional health were significantly impaired for three years. Dr. Roe answered the lawsuit by arguing that Mrs. D. consented to this publication. Consent had been sought while the plaintiff was still in therapy. It was never obtained in writing. In Dr. Roe's own words, consent "was there one day and not there another day. That was the nature of the illness I was treating, unreliable."

The court rejected the argument that the value of the book as clinical research for educating other analysts justified the publication. They concluded that not only did Dr. Roe fail to obtain Mrs. D.'s effective consent, she was well aware there was none when she published the book. The court awarded Mrs. D. $20,000 in damages and issued an injunction from further violating the plaintiff's right to privacy, whether by circulating this book or by otherwise disclosing any of the matters revealed by the plaintiff to Dr. Roe. Mrs. D. sought punitive damages for this violation of her privacy but the court rejected further punishment. The judge found that Dr. Roe's actions were not willful, malicious, or wanton but merely "stupid" (*Doe v. Roe*, 1977).

Had Dr. Roe started from the client's perspective, she would have developed an understanding of the expectation of confidentiality that clients have as a necessary prerequisite for psychotherapy. In retrospect, it is not difficult to imagine Dr. Roe's thought process. It had been eight years since therapy had ended. The book was intended for a professional audience and was a way of publishing important clinical information to further the knowledge base of the field. Because no names were used, there was no real danger of violating confidentiality. The crucial error in judgment that was made by Dr. Roe was the same one that gets many therapists in trouble with confidentiality. Her analysis was from the perspective of the professional, not the client who might come to read this book or otherwise suffer emotionally from its contents.

Confidentiality has been referred to as the foundation of the therapeutic relationship (Watkins, 1989). Simon (1992) defines *confidentiality* as "the ethical duty of the psychiatrist not to disclose information obtained in the course of evaluating or treating the patient to any other individual without the express permission of the patient" (p. 52). The concept of confidentiality in psychotherapy is tied to the characteristics of the professional relationship, particularly intimacy and trust, and the commitment of the professional to the client. If a client does not have complete confidence in the sanctity of the psychotherapist's office, the degree to which the client is able to relax defenses and display vulnerabilities or explore troubling thoughts and emotions is limited. Although the research is sparse to confirm the absolutely critical nature of confidentiality to the therapeutic process, it has been internalized as a norm, relied on by both clients and therapists (Stromberg et al., 1988, p. 387).

The question of confidentiality generally arises in one of several areas. First, there are times in which confidentiality is breached accidentally or as a result of a negligent act by the therapist. In other cases, the therapist judges that the breach of confidentiality is justified given the circumstances. If the client signs a release of information form, the therapist may be authorized to share information with a third party. Also, in cases of a guardian or legally authorized representative, the access to case records and information may be allowed. In other cases, the client may refuse to authorize disclosure of information but the therapist may have a compelling professional reason to do so, such as the prevention of a harm to the client or another individual. A professional's discretion may also be overridden by an order of a court requiring testimony and the submission of case records.

Some authors have expressed growing concerns over the erosion of confidentiality in recent years (Bollas & Sundelson, 1995; Kopels & Kagle, 1994). Much of the change is traceable directly to the influence of the legal system. Court rulings such as those requiring mental health professionals to warn third parties of danger from clients (*Tarasoff,* 1976), to take actions to protect a potentially suicidal person (*Meier v. Ross General Hospital,* 1968), or to report suspected abuse (*Landeros v. Flood,* 1976) have resulted in the opening of exceptions to the historical "absolute" confidentiality between client and psychotherapist. These exceptions to confidentiality have become part of the accepted standard of practice without a great deal of debate.

The legitimate exceptions are easy to follow in the clear cases and are detailed below. The situations that confront practitioners, however, are seldom in this category. Psychotherapists find themselves on the edges of the exceptions, usually making decisions based on personal values that assess the societally imposed responsibility for protection against the duty to protect the client's interests. Because the mental health professions have not assumed a more definitive position concerning when confidentiality can be breached, high-profile court cases have intimidated the field and inappropriately influenced practice by weakening the commitment to confidentiality. The broadly written codes of ethics of the mental health professions are useful only to find justification for whichever side a professional takes on confidentiality exceptions. Reliance on the courts to set standards in this area is a mistake. Courts, as discussed in Chapter 1, are primarily concerned with the facts of the case being litigated. The analysis of a clinician's judgment is made with benefit of hindsight and sometimes as a result of sympathy for a plaintiff. The truth is that clear rules would make clinicians and courts happy, but because of the unique facts of each case, it is unrealistic to assume that rules will be able to guide decisions outside of the few "bright-line" situations (e.g., child abuse, violent threat to a known third party). Psychotherapists should learn these exceptions and follow clear practice policies to reduce the likelihood of inadvertent or unintentional breaches of confidentiality. However, the best protection for clients, the public, and practitioners is to act reasonably in making decisions about confidential communications. This includes obtaining consultation and supervision as well as documenting the decision-making process.

The decision to release information about a client or otherwise to violate confidentiality may be analyzed differentially based on the characteristics of the client and the role perspective of the professional. The more the behavior of the client is considered antisocial, the more likely it will be that the therapist will be able to justify the breach of confidentiality (Kopels & Kagle, 1994). The popularization of psychotherapy during the past 30 years may also have had a subtle effect on the erosion of confidentiality. The varied roots of the profession include the long-term, elite treatment of the wealthy in psychoanalysis and the short-term, behaviorally oriented treatment in the public sector. The allegiance to absolute confidentiality is strongest in psychoanalysis because the psychoanalyst's primary duty is to the client who is paying for the services. In addition, the nature of psychoanalytic treatment includes creating an environment in which the unconscious may emerge, in whatever form. The presence of absolute confidentiality is a necessary component of that environment given that it is not possible to filter material (i.e., to be unconsciously selective) to avoid issues that could force a therapist to breach confidentiality (Bollas & Sundelson, 1995).

When psychotherapists perceive their role as being agents of social control, it becomes easier to justify the breach of confidentiality. The idea of psychotherapists as agents of social control has been expanded in the courts' treatment of confidentiality cases. The nature of the legal system is to judge behavior on the facts of an individual case. For every wrong, there is analysis of whether the wrong could have been pre-vented. In cases involving confidentiality, there is always a balancing of interests between the need to protect client confidence and the opportunity to prevent a harm. The worse the harm, the easier it is for a court to conclude that its prevention would outweigh the damages of breaching confidentiality. It is important that the professions have a thorough debate concerning this development. Are the exceptions harm-ful to all therapeutic relationships by sending the message that the sanctity of the counseling room is conditional on the content? What is the role of the individual therapist in controlling the behavior of the client?

Perhaps the standards will never be agreed upon by psychotherapists as a group because the fields of practice, roles, and orientations are so diverse within the profession. For example, social work, with its focus on the environment, results in interventions that are directed at multiple systems, often using a collaborative approach. This inevitably leads to problems as to who the client is and what duty of confidentiality is owed in various treatment situations. Bollas and Sundelson (1995) argue that we may need different forms of psychotherapy with different rules of confidentiality for different practice settings. Should practitioners who are in clinical private practice have a more stringent duty to maintain confidentiality than a psychotherapist working at a state mental institu-tion? The establishment of this type of tiered system of expectation would result in a furtherance of the discrimination against some groups who are more likely to have confidences violated. Instead, psycho-therapists need to accept the imprecision of the rules, guard confidenti-ality with vigor, and narrowly construe the exceptions.

Legal Bases of the Confidentiality Duty

Confidentiality in psychotherapy is an expectation that is expressed in the ethical codes of all the professions, in many state statutes, and in the case law that has developed over time. One of the earliest cases to find a professional duty of confidentiality was a Scottish case, *A. B. v. C. D.* (1851). The court found that a doctor had violated an implied contract with his patient when he revealed the apparent premarital conception of a child to a minister, which caused the patient to be expelled from the church. In this country, there have been attempts to link the right of client confidentiality to the constitutional right to privacy (see *In re Zuniga,* 1983). However, there are many limitations to this approach. Many cases have explored the question as to which legal theory would constitute the most appropriate basis to enforce the duty, including a reliance on a public policy rationale, privacy rights, breach of contract, and violation of a fiduciary trust. In the majority of cases, courts have recognized a legally compensable injury when an unauthorized disclosure of information occurs. A New York case, *MacDonald v. Clinger* (1982), explored these issues and concluded "it will be assumed that, for so palpable a wrong, the law provides a remedy" (p. 803, citing *Smith v. Driscoll*). In cases since *MacDonald,* public policy and privacy arguments have provided the rationale for the decisions against therapists. Regardless of the theory, courts have strongly backed the expectation of confidentiality.

The word that seems most appropriate to use in the analysis of confidentiality in the psychotherapy relationship is *covenant. Black's Law Dictionary* (1983) defines *covenant* using descriptors such as "promise" and "pledge." It goes beyond a simple contract concept, where one party agrees to do something in exchange for receiving something of value from the other party. In a basic contract, if one party breaches the contract by failing to fulfill one part of the agreement, the other party can void the deal and seek damages for unfulfilled actions. The concept of covenant, however, carries with it a special duty or relationship that supersedes the mere performance of the contract. The promise of secrecy is as much an express warranty as the advertisement of a commercial entrepreneur (*Doe v. Roe,* 1977). The expectation of confidentiality is considered such an integral part of the service agreement that it would be implied even if it were not written out or discussed between the client and worker.

As a result, when a client begins treatment with a psychotherapist, the legal system assumes that the promise of confidentiality is present as a matter of public policy. If a therapist breaches the duty, the contract will be considered breached. This allows a client to go to court to seek damages in the same way a person would if a carpenter had failed to put doors or windows on a home addition as contracted with the owner. It is similar, in theory, to a warranty on a product, guaranteeing that it will work for a specified period of time. The confidentiality guarantee, however, is not time limited. Every client has a right to rely upon this warranty of silence, and society has an interest in enforcing this guarantee. Unfortunately, while the contract theory helps clients to show a legal cause of action, damages are limited to what was expected in the contract. This model doesn't translate well to the damages suffered by a client who has had confidentiality breached. For example, refunding the fees paid for psychotherapy service would do little to satisfy the damages suffered by a client who has had sensitive information released by a therapist.

In a contract, it is characteristic to have both parties assume a mutuality of obligation. In other words, each party is on equal footing with respect to the commitment of something of value to the agreement. In a standard contract, money may be exchanged for goods or services. In a counseling relationship, this mutuality is not always in place and doesn't account for the unilateral expectation of maintaining confidentiality that is placed on the therapist. The legal concept of a *fiduciary relationship* has been used to sustain this legal right to expect confidentiality. Some relationships, by their very nature, require one party to act for the benefit of the other as to matters within the scope of that relationship (DeMott, 1988). Examples of fiduciary relationships include guardian-ward, attorney-client, and director-shareholder. The common characteristic in these relationships is the trust that is implicitly given to the party who holds a degree of control over the decision making. The case example of Dr. Roe described at the start of this section is a good example of a breach of a fiduciary duty. Dr. Roe had control over sensitive information about the client and her family but did not act for the client's benefit when she published the case study.

A *tort,* the breach of an expected standard of behavior, is the main legal theory relied upon by those bringing suit against psychotherapists (Madden & Parody, 1997). A tort is a private or civil wrong for which the court provides a remedy in the form of an action for damages. Every tort action must show a duty owed by the professional, a breach of that duty, and an injury sustained as a result of the breach (*Black's,* 1983). In the case of confidentiality, the landmark case *MacDonald v. Clinger* (1982) established that the character of the therapeutic relationship creates an automatic duty of confidentiality. For a case to proceed, a client must show that the therapist had a duty to keep information private (i.e., existence of a treatment relationship) and evidence as to the breach of confidentiality. Finally, the client must demonstrate that an injury resulted from the breach. If the actions of the therapist reached the level of willful, wanton, or malicious, the client may also be able to collect punitive damages against the therapist. The question of justification for breaching confidentiality is usually at the heart of the analysis. The cases turn on the issue of whether the breach of confidentiality was wrongful, that is, without justification. The duty of confidentiality is not absolute because there is a public interest in some unauthorized disclosures, especially in limited circumstances involving protection of a person (*MacDonald v. Clinger,* 1982). The court will usually allow a jury to determine whether the balancing weighs on the side of the therapist's decision to breach or the client's right to keep the information private.

An important concern for the psychotherapy community is whether the tort action for breach of fiduciary duty to maintain confidentiality is the most appropriate remedy. If *MacDonald,* a New York case, continues to be relied on to provide the standard for how breach of confidentiality cases are tried, then the standard of care as to whether the assessment and subsequent actions of the therapist were reasonable would be determined by the jury. In *MacDonald* (1982), one judge expressed concerns in a concurring opinion that deserve attention. The judge argued that the review of the therapist's clinical judgment should be evaluated in the context of a *malpractice* tort action. In this type of trial, the jury hears evidence presented by expert witnesses from the field of psychotherapy and must analyze whether the therapist acted within the scope of "reasonable professional behavior." (For a complete discussion of malpractice and standards for professional practice, see Chapter 4.) This is one area the profession may be able to use influence to shape the development of the law. If research yields better standards for practice, guiding therapists as to when it is appropriate to act to protect a client or other individual, it will be easier to argue to the courts that this is a question of professional practice, and the appropriate way to assess the reasonableness of a psychotherapist's decision to breach confidentiality is by the evaluation of other professionals. Making it a lay opinion, rather than an expert determination, devalues the level of knowledge and skill required to undertake an assessment of dangerousness in a clinical situation.

PRIVILEGE

When an individual walks into a doctor's office and opens his mouth, everything spilling out of it, whether it be his identity or false teeth, is presumptively privileged and beyond the scope of discovery.

Sarchie v. Roe (1993, p. 908)

In most states, confidentiality guarantees have been strengthened by the passage of privileged communication statutes covering psychotherapists. All 50 states have enacted into law some form of psychotherapist privilege (for citation to each state's privilege statutes, see *Jaffe v. Redmond,* 1996, p. 1929). These recent legal changes have been misunderstood in professional circles so it is important to clarify the nature and scope of the protections and obligations created by these statutes. Privilege is the client's legal right to keep certain communications private and not available as evidence in legal proceedings (Polowy & Gorenberg, 1995). The privilege to maintain the confidentiality of information from a psychotherapy relationship belongs to the client. When information is being sought about a client who has been in treatment, therapists have an obligation, both ethical and legal, to assert this privilege on the client's behalf, unless the client or legal representative waives the privilege. The privilege generally covers all information learned by a therapist in the course of a treatment relationship, including the diagnoses and treatment plans, even though they may not directly reveal client communications (Kendrick, Tsakonas, & Smith, 1993).

The idea of granting a privilege is not embraced by the legal system. Judges and attorneys value the accessibility of all available information so that each case can be decided on its merits, with consideration of all facts. The influential legal scholar Professor Wigmore termed *privilege* "an indefensible obstruction to truth in practice" (Wigmore, 1961, p. 221). He was committed to the legal maxim, "The public has a right to every man's evidence," which has guided courts for three centuries (*Jaffe v. Redmond,* 1996). Supreme Court Justice Scalia, writing a dissenting opinion in *Jaffe,* considered the Court's decision offensive to the principle that "testimonial privileges . . . 'are not lightly created nor expansively construed, for they are in derogation of the search for truth' " (p. 1933, quoting *United States v. Nixon,* 1974). Testimonial exclusionary rules and privileges contravene this fundamental principle of full disclosure. As such, the legal system strictly interprets the scope of a privilege and accepts "only to the very limited extent that permitting a refusal to testify or excluding relevant evidence has a public good transcending the normally predominant principle of utilizing all rational means for ascertaining truth" (*Elkins v. United States,* 1960; J. Frankfurter dissenting).

Unfortunately, professionals whose education or experience is not covered within the privileged communication statutes have little recourse when faced with a legal demand to surrender confidential information. Many privilege statutes include only those clinicians who are certified or licensed as well as those who work under the direct supervision of these professionals. It is advisable for these professionals to communicate with their clients as to the limits of the protections at the beginning of the counseling relationship. Courts may still choose to exclude such confidential information on public policy grounds or because the information is not relevant, but the lack of a statutory protection for the communications lessens the power of the argument to keep the records confidential.

A testimonial privilege for psychotherapists is one of few exceptions to this general rule. Many state laws have been passed granting statutory privileges to psychotherapists, which indicates the legislature's recognition of society's need for confidentiality in the psychotherapy relationship. Courts that have ruled in favor of granting privilege for psychotherapists have relied on what the Supreme Court has described as a "public good that transcends the normally predominant principle of using all rational means for ascertaining the truth" (*Elkins v. United States,* 1960). There are only a few areas of the law in which the public good rationale outweighs the consideration of all evidence. In the criminal context, for example, evidence or testimony may be kept out of a trial to protect an individual's constitutional rights. Here the analysis is similar. The good that comes from keeping out the evidence outweighs the harm that results from proceeding in a case without the excluded information.

Courts have defended the public good of the psychotherapy privilege as enabling the effective treatment of the mental and emotional health of citizens. The Supreme Court recently referred to this as "a public good of transcendent importance" (*Jaffe v. Redmond,* 1996) and indicated that not supporting this privilege would lead to a chilling effect on the discussion of issues by clients involved in a legal proceeding. For example, if a client was in the process of a divorce and a potential custody battle, she might not engage in a discussion of the degree to which her emotions were affecting daily living activities, fearing that the information might hurt the chances of being named custodial parent. In addition to the chilling effect, several courts have questioned the value of a therapist's testimony. Clients in counseling may share thoughts and feelings that are intended to be private and may or may not be based on actual occurrences. When a therapist is required to testify about what a client said, it is a fundamentally different context in which to view the client's reports than the counseling room. Also, courts have questioned the exclusive nature of the information the therapist might possess. Many courts have required a showing of the relevancy and necessity of the evidence as well as proof that the same information is not available through other sources prior to considering overriding the testimonial privilege.

Although the psychotherapist-client privilege has been supported in federal courts and in most state courts, there is universal agreement that the privilege is not absolute (Baumoel, 1992). The conditional nature of the privilege exists despite the use of the term *absolute privilege* in some state statutes regarding communications made to qualified sexual assault counselors. The same public good rationale that supports the privilege supports the exceptions to the privilege. Most of the cases involving breach of confidentiality occur in the context of a privilege statute because these laws provide a clear statement of public policy supporting confidentiality, with some limitations. Generally, courts have compelled testimony when the public interest outweighs the violation of a client's privacy. Many therapists are troubled by the relative nature of the privilege and argue that allowing any exceptions to confidentiality renders it a sham and functionally useless, once clients learn of the limitations (Bollas & Sundelson, 1995). As pointed out in a well-known California case, *in re Lifschutz* (1970), a large segment of the profession practicing analytic psychotherapy concurs in the belief that an absolute privilege of confidentiality is essential to the effective practice of psychotherapy. In other practice environments, the commitment to absolute confidentiality is not as pronounced. In fact, Anderson (1996) goes so far as to say that one of the primary duties of a professional counselor is "to protect the client and others from harm" (p. 25).

Neither side of the argument about exceptions to the general rule of confidentiality supports themselves with well-constructed analyses. Those who say the existence of any exception means that clients will view the contents of therapy sessions as open to public scrutiny overstate the scope of the exceptions, the frequency of their use, and the deterrent effect on client trust. Those who argue on the social good side are usually arguing that nothing should interfere with a trial and that all available evidence should be produced. The legal professionals who make this argument are generally overzealous in their assessment of the value of the evidence that psychotherapists can offer to their case and underestimate the availability of other sources of nonprivileged evidence that could be used to prove the point being litigated. Others who share the public good rationale support their position by arguing that the prevention of harm should be a higher rated value than maintaining confidentiality in a therapy relationship. A legitimate standard of care lies somewhere between the extremes. Once again, it is up to the professions to determine the standard of care that defines for practitioners when it is appropriate to breach confidentiality. Given the diversity of the profession, the standard may be different for social workers than it is for psychiatrists. But if therapists are provided with a standard of care, such as exists in *Tarasoff's* duty to warn a *known third party* of *imminent risk of physical harm,* decision making can become more standardized and practitioners can become more confident and comfortable in the factors used for the analysis.

Legal challenges to breach of confidentiality or violation of a client's statutory privilege may take one of two forms. First, the therapist may be sued for breaching the confidentiality of a client and causing damages to that person. Second, a client, third party, or the estate of a deceased victim may sue a therapist for failure to breach confidentiality, thereby acting to avoid a "preventable" harm caused by the client. The following chapter will break down the situations in which a breach of confidentiality occurs, both authorized and unauthorized, and will explore the legal principles that can guide the decision-making process in these cases. In most situations, the cases involve breach of legal privilege. Although professionals not protected by a privilege statute do have cases go to court, the existence of the legal sanction for upholding confidentiality in the face of a legal demand to produce evidence results in more frequent and detailed litigation.

Chapter 3

DISCLOSURE OF CONFIDENTIAL INFORMATION

AUTHORIZED DISCLOSURES

Release of Information

The most obvious way for psychotherapists to be authorized to share information about a client is to receive a written release. The literature and the case law are clear about the requirements for a release to be fully effective in protecting the rights of all parties. Therapists should be aware that some states have formally codified the requirements in legal statutes (See, e.g., 110 Illinois General Statutes 5(b), 1996). As an initial consideration, clients must be competent to effect the release. The law requires that anyone entering into a legal agreement must be able to understand the nature and scope of the agreement. Absent the competency to truly consent, a legally authorized representative such as a parent, a guardian, or an executor may authorize disclosure of medical records to a third party. It is important to use a written release form for several reasons. A standardized form can include the conditions for the release and a listing of the material to be shared. (Several high-quality forms are available on disk from practice software companies and others are included with legal/mental health texts such as Houston-Vega et al., 1997.) The therapist should review the form with each client, carefully discuss the content of the information, and invite the client to inspect materials prior to release.

The release form must be signed by the client to be effective. It should include a clearly defined scope of what information is to be released.

This information should be selective and specific to the purpose (Houston-Vega et al., 1997) rather than a blanket release. Clients should be informed about their rights to inspect the records to be sent and to revoke their consent at any time. Irrespective of the right to revoke the consent, the form should contain an expiration date, generally linked to the purpose of the disclosure. For example, if the information is to go to an inpatient facility, the records should be sent on a one-time basis and this should be reflected on the form. If the information is being sent to an insurance company, the content should be relevant to the authorization of service, and the time restrictions should correspond to the available benefits. If possible, the release should identify the person to whom the information will go, and the case materials should be mailed or hand delivered rather than sent by fax or computer file transfer. The form should remind recipients that redisclosure of any information being forwarded about the client is prohibited.

It is suggested that a client sign a general release form at the start of treatment that lists the colleagues and special conditions under which the therapist will share information. This general release form is separate from any forms to obtain or release information to an outside agency or professional, which must meet the criteria outlined above. In the initial consent, the therapist should explain the requirements of releasing information to the insurance company as well as identify the supervisor used by the worker and the limitations of confidentiality that have been discussed concerning the prevention of harm. If a question arises at a later date concerning the propriety of the release, having a standard procedure and written evidence of the agreement will be beneficial to the therapist. More important, careful adherence to acquiring legitimate consent gives the message to clients that their privacy is respected and helps clinicians avoid misunderstandings and careless mistakes in disclosures.

Therapists must be cognizant of the legal protections concerning confidential information when on the receiving end of a release form. When requesting information from an agency or another professional, the therapist has a duty to follow the same guidelines as when releasing information. Therapists should be alert to forms that are inadequate for releasing the information being sought. For example, there is a federal law that protects records of substance abuse treatment in agencies that receive federal assistance. It requires that records of this treatment be kept separate from records of mental health treatment or other services

(Code of Federal Regulations 42, Part 2). If a therapist requests specific mental health treatment records but gets a whole file including inappropriate material on the client's substance abuse treatment, the therapist has a duty to return those files to the sending agency.

Questions often arise as to whether information can be shared with agency colleagues, supervisors, consultants, and family members without obtaining a release from the client. It is useful to think about clinical information as belonging to the client. If the information is being used internally, that is, within the worker's usual cadre of treatment resources (those who share the professional duty to maintain strict confidentiality), there is no need to obtain a specific release from the client. It is reasonable to assume that a client accepts the presence of professional support: A worker receives supervision; a secretary maintains communications and files; and cases are reviewed by colleagues. In these circumstances, the therapist should reveal only as much information about the person as is necessary to gain the insights and support of the supervision process. If an outside consultant is used, or if a therapist wishes to discuss a case with a client's family or friends, it is necessary to obtain written client permission. Client information used in research studies or program evaluation must be effectively coded to protect the privacy of the individual clients. It is not considered a breach of confidentiality to use client files for these purposes, although due care needs to be exercised to ensure that clients' characteristics aren't divulged in such a way as to ostensibly identify them.

If a client is seeking to have services covered by an insurance company, there is generally a release included on the insurance form. Clients are not aware of the extent to which their signature enables the insurer to access case records so this must be discussed during the initial session. Therapists are often faced with uncertainty about how to respond to insurers or managed care companies when the requested information exceeds the authorization or seems overly broad to the purpose of utilization review. It is interesting that authors writing about managed care issues advocate maintaining case records that are relevant to the authorization of services (Corcoran & Vandiver, 1996), while more general psychotherapy references suggest the importance of including all information relevant to the treatment (Epstein, 1985). There is something illegitimate about keeping records with a purpose of satisfying insurance carriers rather than producing records for significant practice benefits. For example, what does one do in a case where a therapist has suspicions of possible drug abuse symptoms? If this information is put into the client's record for utilization review/record review, the information may reach the client's employer and jeopardize the individual's job. If the issue is not mentioned, and the client later causes an injury while under the influence, a therapist might be named as a negligent party for failure to recognize symptoms of addiction and take steps to get the individual into treatment. On the other hand, it is unlikely the client has understood that the signing of the insurance form gave the therapist permission to share information about possible drug addiction if the treatment was commenced around a different issue. Clinicians should release only that information relevant to the payment of a claim. All other information should be documented in the case file but, ethically and legally, client consent is required before a clinician releases sensitive information.

Legally Mandated Reports

Despite the views of the minority of therapists who advocate absolute confidentiality, most therapists are in agreement with the need to require the reporting of abuse. These mandatory reporting laws, which now exist in every state (Polowy & Gorenberg, 1995), generally cover reasonable suspicions of abuse against children or persons who are elderly or have a disability. Sometimes therapists are reluctant to report abuse when the abuse occurred in the past and the therapist is currently engaged in treatment that includes the alleged perpetrator. The rationale is that the therapeutic relationship may be compromised by a referral to protective services and cause the family to discontinue treatment. With concerns about the effectiveness of many public agencies to provide effective interventions, a referral might mean that a family will be isolated from services.

There are two basic legal issues related to mandated reports. If a therapist fails to report a reasonable suspicion of abuse, most state statutes provide for a penalty, usually in the form of a fine that can be assessed against the therapist. In addition, should abuse subsequently occur and an individual suffer damages as a result, the therapist could be sued for negligence in failing to report. Finally, the professional organization or state administrative agency could initiate disciplinary procedures against a therapist for failure to report an incident of abuse. Some cases have addressed the question of whether a therapist can be sued for making an abuse report. In most states, there is an immunity clause in the mandated reporter law that protects any professional who makes a "good faith" report. However, a more difficult question arises when the complaint against the therapist is that the assessment leading to the decision to report was not done with due care. In essence, this type of complaint is a malpractice claim and, as such, may enable a lawsuit to be filed despite the statutory immunity. The psychotherapy profession and the legal system should be quick to condemn this effort to circumvent public policy.

Nontreatment Relationships/Evaluations

The requirements for releasing information are different when a therapist is conducting an evaluation for court or other party. In these cases, the duty of the therapist to seek specific permission from the client to release information is not clear. It is an obvious implication that a court-ordered evaluation would not be privileged. Courts have found that the expectation of privacy is an important component in the analysis of whether a communication should be protected. In the case of evaluations done in connection with a court action such as a custody case or an employment-related evaluation, therapists should give prior warning to the individual about the absence of confidentiality. In most cases, the court, the other parties in a case, and their lawyers are all provided with access to the documents and the therapist is not prohibited from testifying. There are some limits to the general rule that no privilege or confidentiality attaches to evaluations. A recent California case illustrates the problems with the expectations of the person being evaluated and the role of the clinician as an agent of the organization seeking the information rather than the person being evaluated.

Pettus v. Cole (1996, opinion of the court). Louis Pettus appealed from a final judgment entered in favor of two psychiatrists, Drs. Unger and Cole, as to his claims of unauthorized release of medical information in violation of the Confidentiality of Medical Information Act (hereinafter CMIA) and invasion of his constitutional right of privacy. The issues presented in these consolidated appeals include whether and to what extent medical information compiled during the psychiatric examination of an employee may be disclosed to the employer (Du Pont) without employee authorization or consent where the employee has requested leave from work because of a stress-related disability, the examination is required under the employer's short-term disability policy, and the examination has been arranged and paid for by the employer.

We conclude as a matter of law that Drs. Cole and Unger violated the CMIA by providing Du Pont a detailed report of their psychiatric examinations of Pettus without a specific written authorization for such disclosure. The material facts of this case are essentially undisputed. Louis Pettus had been working for Du Pont for 22 years when, in June 1988, he sought to take time off from work because he was suffering from a disabling stress-related condition. Before requesting disability leave, Pettus sought medical help for his stress condition from his personal physician and from an outpatient psychological counseling program at the Sierra Clinic. Both recommended to Du Pont that Pettus's stress condition warranted a disability leave. Under Du Pont's short-term disability leave policy, Pettus was required to submit to an examination by a Du Pont-selected doctor for verification of his need for disability leave.

In the course of having his disability verified, Pettus submitted to three medical examinations arranged and paid for by Du Pont. The first examination was with Dr. Collins, a physician under contract with Du Pont to provide general medical services for Du Pont employees. Dr. Collins verified Pettus's stress condition, and his need for time off, but believed a psychiatric evaluation was necessary. She recommended to Du Pont that Pettus should see Dr. Cole, who verified Pettus's stress condition and agreed that he had a legitimate medical need for time off work. Finally, Pettus underwent another psychiatric evaluation by Dr. Unger. Du Pont arranged for Pettus to see Dr. Unger, a specialist in chemical dependency cases, after Dr. Cole reported that Pettus's stress condition might be linked to an alcohol abuse problem.

Pettus was terminated from his job at Du Pont on September 21, 1988, because he refused to enter a 30-day inpatient alcohol rehabilitation program that Du Pont required as a condition of continued employment. Pettus's alcohol consumption became a matter of concern to Du Pont when Drs. Cole and Unger disclosed to Du Pont in their disability evaluation reports that his stress condition might be caused or exacerbated by misuse of alcohol. Pettus first contends that, as a matter of law, Drs. Unger and Cole violated the CMIA when they disclosed to his supervisors at Du Pont the detailed reports of his psychiatric evaluations. For reasons we will elaborate, we agree. The list of permissive exceptions is lengthy. Under section 56.10, subdivision (c)(8), a "provider of health care that has created medical information as a result of employment-related health care services to an employee conducted at the specific prior written request and expense of the employer may disclose to the employer that part of the information which is relevant in a lawsuit, arbitration, grievance, or other claim or challenge to which the employer and the employee are parties and in which the patient has placed in issue his or her medical history, mental or physical condition, or treatment, provided it may only be used or disclosed in connection with that proceeding."

Dr. Cole contends that no health care services were provided to or received by Pettus, and that therefore he was not a "patient" under section 56.10. In support of this contention, Dr. Cole claims that the psychiatric evaluation he performed was for the sole purpose of advising Pettus's employer of his findings with respect to appellant's disability claim, not to advise Pettus. The language employed in section 56.10, subdivision (c)(8)(B), specifically restricts permissible disclosure to an employer to a description of the "functional limitations" of the employee who has been examined. The disclosures made by Drs. Cole and Unger to Du Pont describing in detail Pettus's hostility toward the company and a coworker, his drinking habits, and other details about his personal life go well beyond a description of "functional limitations."

There are, of course, good policy reasons for such a conclusion. If a health care professional were free to give an employer all the details of an employee's personal life and physical and mental health as revealed during a disability evaluation, there would be a great disincentive to full and honest disclosure by the employee. Indeed, in many cases of psychological disability, there would be a strong disincentive for the employee to seek professional help at all. Neither employees nor employers would be well served by such a rule.

We have no doubt, and determine as a matter of law, that Pettus had a legally cognizable interest in maintaining the privacy of the detailed medical information he conveyed to Drs. Cole and Unger. Informational privacy is the core value furthered by the Privacy Initiative and it is well settled that the zone of privacy created by that provision extends to the details of a patient's medical and psychiatric history. As the *Cutter* court explained, "The right to control circulation of personal information is fundamental. . . . If there is a quintessential zone of human privacy it is the mind."

A review of Dr. Cole's and Dr. Unger's written reports clearly demonstrates the private nature of the information transmitted to Du Pont. These reports were quite thorough and detailed in their discussion of the rash that covered Pettus's body, the medication he was using to treat it, and his fears about that medication causing cancer; his sleep patterns and sex drive; his hostile feelings toward certain current and former coworkers and supervisors; past suicidal feelings; his smoking and drinking patterns; a social history of his life from the time of his birth, with his family of origin, through a marriage and divorce, to the present; and his anxious and highly emotional behavior during the interview (crying, wringing his hands, burying his face in his hands, jumping out of his chair, and removing his shirt to reveal the marks on his skin from the rash medicine). Certainly, this is the type of "sensitive personal information" the California voters had in mind when they adopted the constitutional privacy guarantee, expressly limiting the freedom of both government and business entities to obtain, disseminate, and use such data.

A reasonable expectation of privacy is an objective entitlement founded on broadly based and widely accepted community norms. Various factors such as advance notice, customs, practices, justification, physical settings, and the presence of an opportunity to consent may inhibit or diminish reasonable expectations of privacy. The detailed psychiatric information Du Pont requested and obtained from Drs. Cole and Unger, ultimately used to make adverse personnel decisions about Pettus, was far more than the employer needed to accomplish its legitimate objectives.

In sum, based on the evidence presented in Pettus's case-in-chief, we hold that the disclosures by Drs. Cole and Unger of detailed medical and psychiatric information about Pettus to his direct supervisors were a serious violation of Pettus's reasonable expectations that the psychiatrists would maintain the confidentiality of such highly sensitive information. We further conclude that the justifications offered by respondents do not outweigh Pettus's informational privacy interests, and that there were less intrusive alternatives to full disclosure that would have equally well served the psychiatrists' and Du Pont's interests. [Citations omitted; text edited for style and readability.]

The *Pettus* case illustrates the vagaries of the legal system's retrospective process of judging clinical decisions. In most cases, the rule is that no confidentiality attaches to evaluations done as part of a court hearing or as required in employment settings. Clinicians who conduct these assessments need to be aware of the limits of this general rule. If an evaluatee discusses concerns that are tangential to the purpose of the evaluation, the individual may have the right to confidentiality with respect to these issues. The court in *Pettus* was clearly focused on the violation of privacy and did not accept the argument of the doctors that the information concerning Pettus's substance abuse or potential for violence was relevant to their role in assessing eligibility for medical leave. This is the classic legal second-guess scenario in which mental health professionals receive no clear guidance. Had the psychiatrists maintained confidentiality concerning the substance abuse and violence, and Pettus subsequently caused injury to others as a result of that behavior, the same court with the same jury would likely reach the opposite conclusion: that Drs. Cole and Unger should have informed the company so that action could be taken to prevent the harm. When assuming a role in evaluating clients, clinicians need to articulate the boundaries and limits of confidentiality to the client so that the sharing of information is predicated on true informed consent. If a client is so informed, the argument that there was an expectation of privacy for certain information is more difficult to support.

Given that few therapists have legitimate prescient abilities, the standard of care may be unknowable at the time the decisions must be made. It is only after the case evolves and someone suffers damages that the judgment of the therapist is undertaken. This leaves clinicians in perpetual threat of a lawsuit over confidentiality decisions. Despite this reality, therapists need to act in a principled manner, remaining true to personal and professional values. In fact, the lack of standards is liberating in that regard. Each professional must maintain a clear vision of the primacy of the rights of the individual, the conditions under which information may be released without the client's consent, and the perspective to prepare reports that are specific to the referral questions. Clinicians engaged in evaluations should remain focused on that role and, as both a clinical and a legal strategy, ancillary issues should be referred to another professional for treatment.

Child Custody Cases

One of the most difficult legal questions involves the treatment of privileged communications in child custody cases in which the courts must maintain a unique perspective. The standard for courts to follow is, foremost, to act in the best interests of the child. In other legal contexts, courts may determine the balance of rights in any way that serves the interest of fairness. In custody and other child-centered litigation, the courts lean heavily in the direction of protecting a child's interests and thus would be more likely to require testimony or the production of clinical records, even when protected by a statutory privilege. For example, in a Wisconsin case, a psychologist was retained by the court to conduct an evaluation of each member of a family as a result of a request for visitation rights by the father. The psychologist was an employee of a psychology group practice. During the course of her evaluation, the psychologist learned that the mother had engaged in therapy sessions several years previously with another clinician in the group practice. The psychologist examined the records from these counseling sessions and included information from them in her report to the court. The mother brought suit, claiming that reports of the previous counseling contained personal information from her past that she did not want revealed. She claimed the release of this information to her ex-husband caused her physical and psychological damage (*Snow v. Koeppel,* 1990). The therapist in this case clearly exceeded the scope of proper professional behavior when she used the agency files without the permission of the client. Clearly there was no implied or explicit consent to release this information. The court, however, chose to prioritize the importance of the child's interest in evaluating whether the therapist's conduct was culpable. The judge reasoned that because the evaluation was ordered by the court, the therapist was acting as a "quasi-judicial officer" and thus was immune from liability. It was clear in the handling of this issue that the need to have all potentially relevant information available to the judge deciding on visitation rights took priority over the violation of privacy and the misuse of privileged information. The same reasoning has guided family courts in other jurisdictions. If the information under the control of a mental health practitioner is deemed potentially relevant by a court, clinicians can expect that they will be asked to divulge it. The mistake made by many practitioners is assuming the role of advocate, usually for the child. Many therapists feel strongly about the custody arrangements for a child. Often, judgments about an adult caregiver and emotional attachment to the child lead practitioners to use any means to influence the outcome.

In an Illinois case, the therapist was found liable for inappropriate release of information in a custody case (*Renzi v. Morrison,* 1993). The mother initially entered into treatment with this therapist to discuss marital difficulties. The therapist conducted an assessment and later, without permission, shared the contents of the evaluation with her client's husband. The couple proceeded with a divorce in which the custody of their 2-year-old daughter was contested. The mother contacted the therapist and demanded that she not disclose any further confidential information to the father (as the therapist had previously). The father subpoenaed the therapist, who willingly agreed to testify and was allowed to do so over the objections of the mother, who argued that the information was privileged. Because the therapist felt strongly about the outcome of the custody case, she did not act to protect the confidentiality of her client. The mother filed suit against the therapist for violation of the privilege statute. Despite being given clearance by the trial judge to testify, the therapist was found liable. The court distinguished those cases where the therapist was being asked by the court to evaluate both parents; in those cases, there was no privilege or expectation of confidentiality. Here the mother had contracted for therapy, and the release of information without her consent was inappropriate.

The *Renzi* case appears to have conflicting findings. One could argue that the family court judge, by rejecting the mother's objections to the testimony, was giving legal permission to the therapist to breach the confidence. However, this decision was reached in the context of the child's best interest. The court that established liability for the breach of confidentiality was not under the same constraints and could evaluate the alleged breach on its own merits. It was reasonable for this court to conclude that the real breach of confidentiality occurred when the therapist initially consulted with the husband and shared her evaluation with him. Therefore, the later testimony was irrelevant to the question of whether the therapist had breached confidentiality.

The preceding cases are instructive concerning the way the courts analyze the question of confidentiality and privilege. Therapists should remain clear about the role they play in any case. The duty of confidentiality is determined by the expectations of the client, and clinicians will be held to the demands of their role. In *Pettus,* although the psychiatrists were retained by the employer, when Pettus shared sensitive information beyond the scope of the requested evaluation, a duty of confidentiality concerning that information was implied by the court. In *Snow,* the clinician was acting as an agent of the court in conducting an evaluation, while in *Renzi,* the clinician was in a treatment relationship. In these cases, the court predicated liability on the issue of whether the client was implicitly waiving any right to keep information private by agreeing to a certain type of relationship with a therapist. In practice, clients often don't make this sophisticated distinction. Therapists must use consistent release-of-information forms and clearly inform clients as to the confidentiality of information prior to the initiation of treatment or evaluation.

Dangerous Client Exceptions

The relative nature of the psychotherapist-client privilege means that confidentiality may be broken under certain circumstances. It is a well-established principle that an individual is under no obligation either to come to the aid of someone in need or to control the dangerous conduct of another (*Hallet v. United States Department of the Navy,* 1994). An exception to this rule arises in cases where the defendant bears some special relationship to the dangerous person or to the potential victim (*Tarasoff v. Regents of University of California,* 1976). In cases where a therapist has an opportunity to prevent a serious harm from occurring, the law instructs that protection of an individual supersedes the duty of confidentiality. On paper, the duty to prevent serious harm is acceptable to most therapists. Few question the need to take action to warn a third party who might be endangered or to attempt to restrain someone from committing suicide. The difficulty for most therapists comes in the assessment of a particular case as to whether it reaches the level of seriousness and imminence to allow for a breach of the duty of confidentiality. A reading of the law provides little useful guidance. For example, in *Alberts v. Devine* (1985), the Massachusetts Supreme Judicial Court stated,

> In this Commonwealth all physicians owe their patients a duty, for violation of which the law provides a remedy, not to disclose without the patient's consent medical information about that patient, *except to meet a serious danger to the patient or to others.* (pp. 119-120, emphasis added)

Joe, a 49-year-old man, sought treatment at your counseling agency for depression after losing his job as an automobile salesman. He has discussed suicide in sessions but admits that he probably doesn't have the nerve to end his life violently. In the past two weeks, he shared with you that he has been taking his car out to the mountain roads outside the city and driving as fast as he can. He has received two speeding tickets, including one for traveling 85 miles per hour in a 30-mile-per-hour zone. If you assess Joe to be actively suicidal, but he is unwilling to get a psychiatric evaluation, take medication, or enter a hospital, do you have a duty to act to protect Joe and anyone he may injure in his car? Are you allowed to contact his wife?

Stacey, a 19-year-old student at a local university, has been in treatment with you in your private practice for several weeks, having been referred by the dean of students. She presents as angry, and themes of violence dominate her discussions. She has a history of assaultive behavior, interpersonal conflicts, and limited family support. In her fourth session, Stacey tells you that she has been engaged in a conflict with several other students in her dorm concerning recent thefts. She has been blamed and is now the subject of harassing phone calls; ugly epithets have been written on her door. Stacey tells you about her plan to set fire to the dorm some night when everyone is asleep. You believe she is capable of this act but remain uncertain about whether the threat is imminent or legitimate. Do you have a duty to let the dean of students know of this threat?

<hr>

As these cases illustrate, the analysis of when a dangerous threat reaches the level to trigger the duty to warn or protect is fraught with difficulty. If a therapist decides to breach confidentiality, it probably will result in the end of the treatment relationship and possibly impair the client's ability to trust a therapist in the future. If a therapist does not breach confidentiality, the threatened behaviors may result in serious harm to the client and/or other persons. Neither of the cases described above provides sufficient data on which to base a decision conclusively as to whether to breach confidentiality, but, in practice, such a decision would have to be made. In the sections that follow, the leading cases in dangerous client and suicidal client situations will be explored. The cases suggest a balancing of interests test that involves an independent evaluation of each set of facts. The most critical part of the analysis is to follow a professionally accepted standard of care that delineates the assessment criteria. After the assessment, psychotherapists must conduct a duty/risk assessment similar to traditional cost/benefit approaches in economics. A therapist must evaluate whether the risk of not breaching confidentiality is greater than the ethical and therapeutic duty to keep information confidential.

The assessment of risk is the crucial element although the weight accorded to the duty of confidentiality by the individual therapist may vary with training and role. Unlike in many areas of practice, the standards for the assessment of dangerousness are relatively well defined. If a particular case meets the criteria that have been established by the line of cases and the professional literature, a therapist should feel justified in breaching confidentiality. This determination should be undertaken only with extensive input from peers, supervisors, and, if necessary, legal or clinical consultation. Further, clients should be notified of the impending breach of confidence, unless it would increase the danger in that particular situation to an unmanageable degree.

The professional literature has yet to develop a rationale for examining the issues involved in the dangerous client exception to the usual rule of confidentiality. The issue has been aptly described and cases have been analyzed and criticized, but there has not been a conceptual model for analysis of when the duty to warn or protect is triggered. The most important concept to organize professional thinking should be *competency*. In a therapeutic relationship, the fiduciary duty to maintain confidentiality should be upheld unless the client is judged to be incompetent to make the decision that has generated the potential danger. In those cases, the therapist has an obligation to employ substituted judgment to protect the client or another individual from serious harm.

Competence is usually thought of as a broad concept. If someone is deemed incompetent to stand trial or make life decisions, the deficits are generally pervasive. Simon (1992) argues that the competence of a person should be determined with reference to a particular issue at hand (p.126). A person would not need to be judged incompetent in all areas of life for a finding that the individual is incompetent to make decisions concerning the dangerous conduct. Mishkin (cited in Simon, 1992) distinguishes competency from incapacity. This distinction may be useful in this context. If a client is overwhelmed by rage or depression, or seriously impaired due to chronic or situational psychiatric problems, the person may be assessed as not being *capable* of making a rational decision and thereby could put someone at risk of harm. In this context, the therapist has a conceptually supportable rationale for breaching the usual duty of confidentiality. The focus on the client's ability to act rationally helps clinicians to make decisions outside of the political ramifications of civil rights or the philosophical nuances of self-determination. It is not therapeutic for a client to be left alone to act in a way that is both unsafe and irrational. But it is also not therapeutic to breach a client's confidence without the justification of an assessment of imminent danger that the client is incapable of managing.

The psychotherapy community has had to respond to the guidance of the courts and legislatures in various state and federal jurisdictions on the question of what to do when a client threatens harm. The results have been an unwieldy mix of standards. The statutes and case law of some states require that very serious harm has been explicitly threatened, against a specific victim, and the therapist has a very strong belief that it will occur (Massachusetts General Laws Annotated, 1991). Other states have allowed therapists to breach confidentiality with much less certainty as to the threat, for example, when the identity of the victim is not known to the therapist (*Lipari v. Sears,* 1980) or even when the threat is to property (*Peck v. Counseling Service of Addison County,* 1985). The following cases illustrate the different standards. It is interesting to read them with attention to the inconsistent expectations for the therapist. The courts seem to decide each case based on how sympathetic they find the victim rather than by evaluating the level of professional competence in assessing dangerousness or the reasonableness of the therapist's behavior, given the circumstances.

Duty to Warn

Therapists sometimes are determined to have a duty to warn an individual who has been threatened by a client. The specific conditions under which this duty arises vary from state to state. Because of the way these cases are litigated, a plaintiff usually can establish enough evidence to get a case to trial. A clinician's justification for the decision to disclose confidential information must be based upon a showing of circumstances and competing interests that support the need to warn. Because such a showing is a matter of affirmative defense (i.e., a therapist admits to the breach of confidentiality but offers a rationale supporting the decision), a jury is needed to assess the reasonableness of the action (*Chizmar v. Mackie,* 1995).

A series of recent cases have provided clarification as to the duty to warn. These cases involve outpatient therapy in which there is no identifiable victim but the client is perceived by the therapist to be dangerous. There has been confusion as to the type of duty owed, with some arguing that a therapist has a duty to control the client. Three of the recent decisions involve clients who were being treated by the Veterans' Administration in outpatient facilities. In each case, the client committed a violent act that resulted in a lawsuit against the therapist. In each of these cases, the court distinguished between duty to warn and duty to control. The duty to control a client arises in the context of a special relationship such as a patient who is committed to a mental health institution (*Fraser v. United States,* 1996). Here, the psychotherapist may be found to have a duty to control the confinement of the client to prevent the discharge of a potentially dangerous person (*Rousey v. United States,* 1996). The theory that drives this type of case is more appropriately grouped with the negligent treatment or malpractice cases because the complained-of behavior is negligence in carrying out a professional activity. In the case where the patient is in outpatient therapy, the therapist has an obligation arising from the duty to warn only when the precedent conditions are met (i.e., a specific, very serious threat directed against an identifiable victim; *Lacock v. United States,* 1997).

The injured parties in these cases primarily relied on one rogue case, *Lipari v. Sears, Roebuck & Co.* (1980). In *Lipari,* the client was voluntarily committed to a mental health institution and was being treated at a Veterans' Hospital. Against his doctor's advice, the client left the facility and refused further treatment. Two months later, the client fired a shotgun into a crowded room, killing one man and seriously injuring the dead man's wife. The wife brought suit and argued that the Veterans' Administration facility failed to take reasonable measures to prevent the incident. The federal district court, applying Nebraska law, specifically rejected the standard that the therapist only owes a duty to warn readily identifiable potential victims, and instead found that a psychotherapist has a duty to warn when he could "reasonably foresee that the risk engendered by his patient's condition would endanger other persons" (pp. 187-193). The *Lipari* decision has been criticized by later court decisions (*Rousey v. United States,* 1996). It is unworkable in practice because it places an impossible burden on psychotherapists' ability to predict general dangerousness, to control clients outside of the agency, and to protect unknown individuals in the community. No states currently impose a duty to warn when there is not at least a reasonably identifiable victim (*Lacock v. United States,* 1997).

In those cases where the client is committed to a mental health institution, there is a special relationship that enables a facility to control the release of a dangerous client. Here, violent threats, even when the victim is not identified, could create a duty to control the client to prevent the harm. Many of these cases have involved psychotherapists who have attempted to get the client committed but the legal or mental health system denied the admission. In these cases, the therapist would be seen as having taken reasonable steps to fulfill the duty and would have a strong defense to any legal action. The recent case law cited above has drawn a clear distinction between duty-to-control cases and duty-to-warn cases. In the latter situations, the requirement that there be a specific victim remains the standard.

The *duty to warn* is a misnomer. In reality, the courts have found that a warning is merely one option that a therapist can take to prevent the harm threatened by a client. Perhaps the requirement should be renamed the *duty to intervene.* Obviously, the most helpful intervention is a clinical one that reduces the client's impulse to commit the violent act (Kopels & Kagle, 1994). Therapists should not respond to all threats of violence with panic but, instead, seek to conduct a thorough evaluation to assess the level of dangerousness and immediately involve supervisory personnel and other professionals in the deliberations about what action to take. Recent cases have established that the harm caused by a client must be foreseeable to the worker for any liability to attach *(Fraser v. United States,* 1996). If therapists remain clear about the need to conduct regular assessments of potentially violent clients, the question of forseeability can be defensible. Once the worker has some indication of dangerousness, a protocol for how to respond should be followed. The following case provides a clear example of one agency's response to a dangerous client situation. It illustrates a well-conceived, careful handling of this practice dilemma.

Ms. B. v. Montgomery County Emergency Services (1992, opinion of the court). In this action, Ms. B. filed suit against Montgomery County Emergency Services, an institution at which she received psychiatric treatment, and against individual defendants who participated in her treatment there. The basis of Ms. B.'s claim is the defendants' disclosure, to law enforcement personnel and to her supervisor, of threats she made during the course of her treatment. Ms. B. alleged that this disclosure was in violation of the Pennsylvania Mental Health Procedures Act (hereinafter MHPA), which protects the confidentiality of a mental patient's treatment records. Ms. B. is a former postal worker. She was referred to the agency by her attorney, who felt she needed psychiatric treatment. During the course of the initial evaluation, Ms. B. informed the therapist that she was preoccupied with thoughts of killing her supervisor and two coworkers. She further stated that she owned a 9mm Uzi semiautomatic pistol, that she had previously stalked her supervisor and the two workers, that she knew where they lived, and that if she returned to work, she would shoot them. Ms. B. declined to admit herself voluntarily for treatment. After the evaluation, the therapist submitted an application for involuntary emergency examination and treatment (the Pennsylvania statute authorizes holding a dangerous client for involuntary treatment for 120 hours pending an application for extended involuntary emergency treatment).

On January 7, during the course of an interview with a counselor and social worker, Ms. B. repeated her explicit threats to kill her coworkers. Ms. B. also met with her treating psychiatrist and expressed strong anger at her coworkers concerning the manner in which she perceived they had wronged her and her desire for revenge. The psychiatrist thereafter completed an application to retain Ms. B. for extended involuntary treatment. On January 9, after a hearing, the Mental Health Review Officer denied the application for extended involuntary treatment. At the conclusion of the hearing, the psychiatrist met with another doctor, the agency's counsel, and the agency's criminal justice liaison. The four agreed that Ms. B.'s threats were serious and that the intended victims and law enforcement authorities should be warned of Ms. B.'s threats and imminent discharge.

The therapist then telephoned Ms. B.'s supervisor, the FBI, and the relevant local police departments. He informed these individuals of Ms. B.'s identity, of the nature of her threats, and of the fact that she was about to be released from the program. The therapist said nothing of the nature of Ms. B.'s mental illness and did not reveal any communications she had made during the course of her treatment, other than the explicit threats against the three individuals. Prior to release, Ms. B. met once more with the psychiatrist. At the meeting, Ms. B. once again voiced her threats. The psychiatrist told Ms. B. that the threats would be disclosed to the threatened individuals and to appropriate law enforcement agencies. Ms. B. was then released. On January 10, officers of the Tredyffrin Township Police Department arrested Ms. B. She was subsequently convicted of making terroristic threats.

The sole issue before the court was whether the defendants' actions deprived Ms. B. of any rights, privileges, or immunities secured by the Constitution or laws of the United States. As the defendants note, the MHPA's implementing regulations provide for nonconsensual release of confidential information "in response to an emergency medical situation when release of information is necessary to prevent serious risk of bodily harm or death." While the statute does not define the phrase *emergency medical situation,* it does not purport to restrict disclosure to situations where the patient herself is at serious risk of bodily harm or death; it may plausibly be read to encompass situations in which the threat is to a third party.

The court must engage in a balancing of interests, weighing the individual's interest in nondisclosure against the state interests that are furthered by the disclosure. In the present case, the type of record involved and the information contained therein are deserving of a high degree of protection. In the process of undergoing psychiatric treatment, a patient is expected to lay bare his inner self, to reveal thoughts and feelings that are highly personal and that are often painful and embarrassing to confront. Indeed, the success of psychiatric treatment depends on the patient's ability and willingness to reveal his innermost thoughts, desires, and fears. A patient cannot and should not be expected to submit to such a process without strong assurances that what he says in the course of treatment will be kept confidential.

Breaches of confidentiality create several types of harm. First, the breach may produce direct negative consequences for the patient. Such was the case here, as Ms. B., as a result of the defendants' communication, was arrested and ultimately convicted of making terroristic threats. Second, the patient may suffer harm simply from knowing that elements of the intimate details of his life have been laid bare for the uninvited viewer. Third, the patient may suffer harm to his public image that, if the public disclosures are true, cannot be rehabilitated through legal action. Finally, the patient-doctor relationship, founded as it is on trust, may be irredeemably shattered. It is evident that only a strong state interest could outweigh Ms. B.'s interest in maintaining the confidentiality of her psychiatric records. It is likewise evident, however, that the state interest in protecting citizens from violent assault is a sufficiently strong state interest. Most jurisdictions that have considered the issue have concurred with the *Tarasoff* court in finding that a mental health professional has a duty to take reasonable steps to avert harm to others threatened by her patient.

Defendants in the present case found themselves in an extraordinarily delicate position. On the one hand, they were bound by their ethical and statutory duty to maintain the confidentiality of Ms. B.'s communications to them. On the other hand, they were aware, based on Ms. B.'s repeated threats, of a grave danger to the individuals who were the targets of Ms. B.'s threats. Once they decided to act, defendants limited their disclosure only to the fact that Ms. B. had made the threats and apparently had the means to carry them out, and they communicated the threats only to law enforcement personnel and one of the individuals threatened. Given the extensive judicial recognition of a common-law duty to warn and the limits placed on the ethical duty of confidentiality, I cannot conclude that the defendants' acts improperly infringed on Ms. B.'s Fourteenth Amendment right to privacy. On the undisputed facts before the court on the defendants' motion for summary judgment, I have concluded that no such injury exists. Accordingly, the defendants' motion for summary judgment will be granted. [Citations omitted; text edited for style and readability.]

The staff at the agency dealing with Ms. B. followed the professional standard of care. The clinical assessment of the client appeared to have been thorough and involved psychiatric consultation and input from supervisors and peers. The interventions attempted by the agency were relevant and progressive. Significantly, the first action of the therapist was to seek temporary commitment to restrict Ms. B.'s ability to carry out her threats. When that was not successful, the staff reevaluated the danger, finally deciding that the situation activated their duty to warn. At that point, the warning was limited in scope to the information needed by the authorities and the intended victims. The therapists chose the least intrusive means available and thus did not infringe on Ms. B.'s right of confidentiality any more than was necessary.

The range of interventions in dangerous client cases may be limited, dependent on the degree of control a therapist has over the client and whether the client is mentally ill. Clearly, the opportunity to seek commitment is appropriate only when mental illness is documented. If the therapist determines that an involuntary commitment is required, there is an exception in most state privilege statutes that allows the mental health worker to release the client's information to protect the person from harm. However, there is no clear guidance as to whether a therapist has a duty to seek commitment for a potentially dangerous client. Some courts have found that there is no affirmative obligation for a professional to initiate hospitalization or involuntary commitment proceedings (*Paddock v. Chacko,* 1989), while others have found such a legal obligation (*Currie v. United States,* 1987). The implications of an evolving duty to commit will be explored in Chapter 4. In domestic violence cases, the warning of a victim and notification of police may be insufficient to prevent the harm, but these may be the only interventions available to a therapist (*Egley & Ben-Ari,* 1994). In cases where the threat of harm is against a public figure, the courts have found that notification of the police is an important element of discharging the duty (see, e.g., the *Brady v. Hopper,* 1983, suit against the psychiatrist who was treating David Hinkley, the man who attempted to assassinate President Reagan).

Many therapists have become overly concerned with the duty to warn. Following *Tarasoff,* there seems to be a perception that there is an unconditional duty to warn third parties when clients threaten harm (Kagle & Kopels, 1994). In reality, the duty has always been fairly limited and standardized across jurisdictions. The duty to warn includes only cases with identifiable victims within a recognizable zone of danger and does not commit therapists to a general responsibility for all of the conduct of their clients. Despite this, in some circumstances, a court could still find that the therapist should have known the client was dangerous and should have intervened. In one case, a court went so far as to find a duty to the 8-year-old son of an intended victim. The boy witnessed the violent assault on his mother and suffered emotional injuries from the experience. In that case, the court reasoned that a close family member could be considered a readily identifiable victim (*Hedlund v. Superior Court of Orange County,* 1983). But most of the "extreme" decisions holding therapists to higher levels of responsibility occurred during the 10 years following the *Tarasoff* decision. Since then, the decisions have been more realistic in establishing the duty of a psychotherapist.

A New York court recently stated its standard for review in a way that reflects the majority of cases decided in the past few years. The court stated,

A physician, after learning of a patient's violent propensities, owes a duty neither to the public at large nor to a specific individual absent a particularized threat or danger presented by the patient to such individual, particularly where, as here, the injured third person had been aware of the patient's bizarre behavior. (*Adams v. Elgart,* 1995, p. 639)

As a result of the increasing uniformity of decisions, it is important to tailor practice to the majority view. Therapists should resist premature and/or unnecessary breaches of confidentiality and honor the values of psychotherapy that stress the sanctity of client confidentiality. At the same time, professional organizations and academic institutions must continue to sponsor rigorous practice research to extend the ability of therapists to predict dangerousness while publicizing appropriate standards of care to members and students.

The question of the balancing of the duty to protect with the commitment to client confidentiality is a policy determination. As such, the courts are probably the worst places in which to decide on standards. The legislature, with a view of the policy issues outside of the emotions of a single case, should be the place where the standards are articulated. The courts should be the place where the individual cases are evaluated according to whether the professionals followed the standards appropriately. Mental health workers have the opportunity to write legislation to include language in "confidentiality of medical records" or "privilege" statutes that would codify the expectations. Although some therapists would favor language that relieved them of any duty to breach confidentiality, the political reality precludes such a development. The Massachusetts statutory language (1991) seems to be most in line with the professional standards as it requires severity of harm, specificity of victim, and an assessment of likelihood that the client will carry out the threat, prior to a duty to warn. If the professional organizations take a proactive role in advocating for statutory language to this effect, the courts will be required to judge a therapist's behavior against a legitimate standard. In the absence of such statutory language, decisions like *Lipari* are possible, and therapists will be vulnerable despite "reasonable" professional practice.

Prevention of Harm

When a therapist is confronted with a client who is suicidal or otherwise presenting a danger to him- or herself, a dilemma arises that is, in most respects, the same as is faced in duty-to-warn cases. The primary consideration is the nature and quality of the clinical assessment that provides the mental health worker with information concerning the competency of the client. There is no general duty to protect a client from self-harm. In fact, some mental health professionals have argued for a right of individuals to commit suicide (Knuth, 1979). Even for those who take the self-determination position, the legal analysis rests on whether the reasonable actions of the professional could have prevented the harm. When a client is evaluated as needing protection due to age or mental disability, the duty to intervene so as to prevent the harm is implicated most strongly. The legal issues that therapists face are related to the quality and thoroughness of the evaluation as well as the degree of control the worker maintained over the client. Just as in duty-to-warn cases, the therapist duty is greater when the client is in a controlled, residential, or institutional setting than when he or she is in an outpatient clinic.

The standard on which the duty to protect is assessed is whether the person was in imminent danger that was known or should have been known by the therapist and whether the therapist was in a special or custodial relationship with the person. The duty to protect is equated in the literature with the duty to warn, but it is more appropriately handled as a professional malpractice action. In a duty-to-warn case, the opportunity to prevent harm requires a breach of the client's confidentiality to protect a nonclient. The value issue of self-determination and the social value of protection of an "innocent" party make the analysis of the duty quite different. In the duty-to-protect cases, the prevention of harm involves an action to protect a client from self-harm. It is foremost a question as to the duty of care owed to a potentially suicidal client. The duty of care arises out of three factors. First, was there a special relationship between the suicidal person and the professional? Second, was the possibility of suicide reasonably foreseeable? Finally, if the first two questions are answered affirmatively, did the professional's conduct fall below the standard of care and result in a failure to take proper precautionary steps (Knuth, 1979)?

The duty to prevent a client from harming him- or herself is limited in scope and defined by the circumstances including the type of relationship, the setting, and the degree of control the professional has over the client's environment. There are fewer cases that charge mental health workers with failure to prevent harm than there are cases involving failure to warn third parties. The former cases are more difficult to prove and there is generally less external blame. In violence cases against third parties, the natural question asked by family and friends of the victim is whether anyone could have prevented it. In suicide cases, that question tends to be asked only in cases in which the family and friends perceived the victim as being in need of protection such as in the case of children and persons in the care of a treatment facility. In other cases, both loved ones and society in general tend to place the responsibility of the suicide on the person committing the act. Recent cases seem to show a growing awareness of the difficulty for a therapist to predict the eventual actions of a potentially dangerous client.

Tara Ann was in crisis related to her mental illness during late spring 1983. Beginning in April, she was admitted to a state hospital for five days, followed, about a month later, by an admission to a county hospital, where she remained for one week. From there, she was admitted for additional therapy at a private community mental health center before once again being discharged about two weeks later. In each of these hospitalizations, suicidal ideation was present and was a focus of the treatment. In July, Tara was readmitted to the county hospital. During the intake process, workers at the hospital found a receipt from a gun store for a handgun. Tara had attempted to purchase the gun the day before admission but was waiting for the mandatory background check prior to taking possession of the weapon. This stay at the hospital lasted another two weeks followed by another round of follow-up evaluation and treatment at the private hospital for a few more days.

The day after her latest discharge, Tara borrowed a gun from a friend, attempted suicide, and injured herself, but not fatally. Once again she was admitted for treatment, this time at the state hospital. One day before her scheduled release, her mother telephoned the gun store and informed an employee that Tara had recently made a down payment on a handgun and that she was currently a mental patient after attempting to take her own life. The facts are disputed but it appears the staff at the county hospital had informed the parents of finding the sales receipt from the gun shop, which precipitated the mother's call. On September 14, Tara was released from the hospital, visited the gun store, and was allowed to complete her purchase. The next day Tara used the gun to commit suicide.

The parents filed suit arguing that the mental health staff at the county hospital where the gun receipt had been found, alleging that they negligently failed to inform either the state administrative agency that issues gun permits or the gun store. Further, the complaint alleged the county hospital had not fully informed the staff at the state hospital where she had most recently been treated. (The gun store was also sued in a separate action.) The question for the California Court of Appeals was whether the duty to warn, established in the *Tarasoff* case, applied to the facts of this case. In other words, was there a duty to breach confidentiality to ensure that the client not gain access to a gun? The court found that the incident occurred six weeks after Tara's last treatment at the county hospital, limiting their obligation and their opportunity to control her actions. No legal duty was found under the *Tarasoff* doctrine that could require the warning of the administrative agency or the gun dealer directly. The court acknowledged that there may have been a duty to inform the parents of the attempt to purchase the gun, but, in this case, the mother was apparently informed, or already was aware, of the danger (*Katona v. County of Los Angeles*, 1985).

The *Katona* result is consistent with other cases that have found no duty to disclose confidential communications when the risk of harm is self-inflicted injury. The question in these cases is whether the therapist should have taken precautionary steps, consonant with good mental health practice (i.e., malpractice standards). Another California case, *Bellah v. Greenson* (1978), distinguished the duty of care from the *Tarasoff* duty to breach confidentiality so as to warn a third party. The court in *Bellah* declined to extend the duty to warn to suicide cases, reasoning that the social benefits of keeping the treatment relationship free from legally mandated intrusions was of paramount importance. When a client is potentially suicidal, the psychotherapist has a range of interventions that are available, perhaps including a warning to family or others who may be able to prevent the client from self-harm. The option of breaching confidentiality when clinically indicated is quite different from having an affirmative duty to warn in all cases of threatened suicide. A duty to warn to prevent suicides would result in serious harm to the therapeutic relationship.

Several courts have begun to apply the *professional judgment rule* in cases where a client is dangerous to self or others. *Lorenzo v. Fuerst* (1997) is an Ohio case that found the rationale of the rule persuasive. The court examined the question of predictive ability and commented that a mental health professional's ability to predict violent behavior is "probably better than a lay person's" and identified some agreed-upon factors in the assessment of violence. But the court acknowledged that diagnosing both the existence and the severity of violent propensities is still a "highly subjective undertaking." The court was refreshingly realistic in its analysis of dangerous client situations. Rather than second-guessing based on a bad outcome, the court expressed its understanding of the dilemma. First, the setting and degree of control a mental health professional has over a client varies widely. Then, if violent propensities are confirmed, the treatment options are not fully under the control of the assessing professional either.

> The patient's right to good medical care, including freedom from unnecessary confinement and unwarranted breaches of confidentiality, must be balanced against the need to protect potential victims. Courts, with the benefit of hindsight, should not be allowed to second-guess a psychiatrist's professional judgment. (pp. 11-12)

Although it is too early to determine whether the professional judgment rule will become the dominant view, this case represents a good example of how a realistic standard for the profession can be developed by a legal system when it understands the complexities of evaluating and predicting human behavior and emotions. In its application, this rule would not be a bar to a malpractice suit. If the therapist's evaluation was incomplete or incompetent, liability would attach. What the professional judgment rule does is to take away a results-oriented analysis while maintaining an expectation of professional competence. Mental health professionals should be proactive in attempting to initiate legislation that would codify this standard in cases of dangerous clients.

Reporting Past Criminal Acts

Kevin was a young boy who had lived a troubled life. At one point, a court sentenced him to a residential drug/alcohol treatment program. Soon after admission, Kevin admitted to his counselor that he had once set fire to a house knowing that people were inside. He also talked about his fascination with fire. When the residential facility experienced a fire in one of its bathrooms, Kevin was suspected. The therapist revealed Kevin's fire-setting confession to the boy's probation officer. Subsequently, charges were brought against Kevin for arson. The only substantive evidence presented at trial was the testimony of the therapist concerning the confession. Kevin's attorney sought to have the testimony barred on the basis of psychotherapist-client privilege. The appellate court held that the confession was admissible because the therapist had reason to believe that Kevin presented a danger to the other residents of the treatment program (*In re Kevin F.,* 1989).

The general rule is that mental health workers are not required to report past criminal acts of a client. There is no compelling public policy rationale comparable to the protection of public safety in the duty-to-warn cases. In the case described above, it is possible to analyze the facts as a duty to warn. The therapist believed that the fire-setting behavior constituted a direct threat to the other residents, who could be classified as identifiable victims. Another example of reporting of past criminal acts is the category of legally mandated reports such as those made when evidence of child abuse is discovered by the therapist. It is only in cases like these, with facts that provide a compelling professional reason justifying the breach of confidentiality, that past criminal acts can be reported. It is important to distinguish the personal discomfort one might feel at being informed by a client about a past crime from the duty to nonetheless maintain the client's confidentiality expectations. Some state statutes, such as in South Dakota (1996), contain specific language stating a licensed social worker shall *not be required* to treat as confidential a communication that reveals the contemplation of a crime or a harmful act. However, even in states with this type of exception to privileged communications, the decision to breach confidentiality is only supportable where it may accomplish prevention of a serious harm.

Client Waivers

There are some situations that arise in the legal system where the actions of a person are deemed to have effected a waiver of the right to privilege. The most common form of waiver is the previously discussed release-of-information form. Although it is generally assumed that a client must "knowingly" wish to end the privilege and to be aware of the consequences (Dickson, 1995), some cases have interpreted client actions as waivers when there is considerable doubt concerning the client's intent. The following sections explore the client actions that may serve as a waiver of privilege.

Client-as-Litigant Exception

The legal system is often represented by the symbol of the scales of justice. The balancing of rights is an important element in the effective administration of the law. In cases where a participant in a lawsuit puts an issue before the court to help prove an element of a case, the rules of the court are that the person cannot assert privilege to block the opposing side from access to the otherwise confidential material. This situation most frequently arises during child custody and personal injury litigation. In these types of cases, the individual's emotional condition or mental health diagnosis may be an important component of a party's offer of proof. Where it is injected into the court hearing by the person, the law does not allow a claim of privilege to block the opponent's access to the testimony and records of the therapist. Most likely, the mental health worker is the only source of information on these issues except for the client. The court will consider the privilege waived in the interest of fairness to the opposing side in the litigation when the party attempts to use privileged information both as a sword and as a shield (Slovenko, 1966).

The first category of cases to assume a waiver based on the client's mental or emotional condition was discussed earlier in this chapter. In a child custody hearing, the very act of seeking custody would effectively seem to make a parent's mental and emotional condition subject to scrutiny. Courts have found that when the protected information is *necessary* and *material* to a determination as to the custody of a child, the rule of privilege had to yield to the dominant duty of the court to protect the welfare of the child (*Perry v. Fiumano*, 1978). The court in *Perry* recognized the potential "chilling effects" such a rule could have on the willingness of parents to seek professional counseling when they may be facing a custody hearing. The court stated that the privileges may not "cavalierly be ignored or lightly cast aside" (p. 518). There first must be a showing that resolution of the custody issue *requires* production of the privileged information.

Although the *Perry* court was sensitive to the effect of its ruling on psychotherapy and counseling, not all of these cases require a factual showing by the party seeking to compel the disclosure of the information. Mental health professionals often find themselves in a complicated situation of having been subpoenaed to testify and to submit records, but the client refuses to waive the privilege voluntarily. (This situation, and the range of responses for the worker, will be discussed in more detail in Chapter 5.) Judges may use different rationales for the same result: requiring the testimony. This can be accomplished in either of two ways: (a) by ruling that the placement of one's mental or emotional health at issue is assumed from the contesting of the custody, leading the court to interpret this action as a waiver of privilege, or, similarly, (b) ruling that the *best interest of the child* requires the court to compel the testimony and production of the privileged communications.

Disclosures to Third Parties

Because of the legal system's view that privileges are to be construed narrowly due to the value of having access to all available relevant evidence, waivers of privilege have been inferred from the actions of clients and therapists. For example, courts have been consistent in finding that statements that originated in a confidential communication in a privileged relationship, when revealed to a third person, are no longer confidential (*People v. Clark*, 1990). The rationale for this view is based on the idea that a client must intend the interaction to have been private. Once a third party is privy to the content of the communication, the law essentially implies a waiver of privilege. In those cases where the client is the source, sharing information about therapy with a third party, the implied waiver rulings are logical and supportable. The most interesting, and somewhat disturbing, trend in the cases on third-party disclosures is that when the client is sympathetic or the victim of a crime, the privilege tends to be upheld. When the client is someone who has committed a crime or is otherwise blameworthy, courts have found rationales for ruling the privilege to be waived.

Duty-to-warn disclosures. Two recent cases have explored the question of whether the warning issued by therapists to intended victims of a potentially dangerous client results in the abrogation of privilege. In *People v. Clark* (1990), this issue arose during the trial of a man accused, among other crimes, of killing his former therapist's husband in revenge for her decision to terminate the treatment relationship. In preparation for the trial, defense lawyers retained a psychiatrist to evaluate the man and to serve as an expert witness. During discussions with the psychiatrist, the man made threats to kill other family members and friends of his former therapist. The psychiatrist eventually warned the intended victims based on his assessment of the seriousness of the threats.

The defendant sought to keep out the statements made to the psychiatrist on the grounds that they were privileged. The court ruled that because the communications had already been revealed to third parties outside of the therapeutic relationship, they were no longer privileged. The court justified its ruling by stating, "The reason for the privilege—protecting the patient's right to privacy and promoting the therapeutic relationship—and thus the privilege itself, disappear once the communication is no longer confidential" (p. 151).

In the highly publicized murder trial of Lyle and Eric Menendez, a similar issue arose (*Menendez v. Superior Court,* 1992). A psychotherapist was treating the two brothers prior to and following the murders of their parents. The brothers were suspects in the murders. As part of the police investigation, a warrant was issued to search the office and home of the psychotherapist. The audiotapes of three counseling sessions were seized. Upon the request of the psychotherapist, the records were sealed until it could be determined whether the information was privileged. At a hearing, the superior court rejected the claim of privilege, allowing all three tapes to be introduced as evidence. The Menendez brothers appealed the decision to the California Supreme Court.

During the sessions on tape, the brothers allegedly had made some admissions concerning their involvement in the murders. They also made explicit threats against the therapist, his estranged wife, and his current girlfriend, apparently in an attempt to intimidate him into maintaining secrecy. The therapist subsequently warned the two women of the threats. His girlfriend reportedly eavesdropped on a couple of the sessions and obtained copies of the tapes. The Supreme Court was asked to rule on the question of whether the privilege was waived, given the circumstances.

The court found that the presence of the "eavesdropper" did not affect the privilege because it was not relevant to the intent of the parties to keep the communications private. However, the court (relying on another recent California case, *People v. Wharton,* 1991) ruled that the psychotherapist-client privilege is inoperative when the dangerous client exception applies. The ruling did not limit the nonprivileged status just to the specific words that threatened harm. The court allowed the tapes of the two sessions in which the duty-to-warn facts arose to be introduced as evidence, thus abrogating the privilege. The legal ruling was based on the third-party disclosure concept that once the confidential communications are shared with a third party, they lose their legal protection.

The question of how to balance the mandated child abuse reporting law (a variation of the duty to warn) with the concept of privilege arose in an Indiana case (*Daymude v. State,* 1989). A family was court-ordered to participate in treatment after their 13-year-old daughter began to experience serious problems. The state was involved due to previous reports of sexual abuse by the father. During the family therapy, the father made admissions concerning instances of sexual abuse. The father subsequently was charged with child abuse and the state sought to question the therapist concerning the family therapy sessions. The father acknowledged the mandatory reporting law but argued that the privilege is abrogated only in the reporting of child abuse, but not for communications made during court-ordered counseling. The Indiana court ruled that the reporting statute's purpose was served by the fact that the abuse had already been reported. The court stated, "The central purpose of the child abuse reporting statute is the protection of children, not the punishment of those who mistreat them" (p. 1266). The court found that there was no abrogation of the privileged communication stemming from the child abuse reporting statute.

Group and family therapy. Many of the disclosure-to-third-party cases examine the issue of whether privilege exists in group and family therapy when the therapeutic conversations are not made in the privacy of a one-to-one relationship. Commentators in the 1960s and 1970s issued dire warnings about the apparent lack of legal recognition for the privileged nature of communications made in the course of group and family therapy (see, e.g., Slovenko, 1966, pp. 118-119). Some practitioners consciously refrained from keeping notes of group sessions because the sanctity of the therapy could not be ensured. The idea that a client was somehow giving up the expectation of confidentiality by participating in a multiperson therapeutic method convincingly demonstrates the lack of understanding the legal system has had about mental health practice. In recent years, however, the case law seems to have evolved. The tendency today is to recognize that an otherwise privileged communication remains privileged when the presence of a third party is necessary and integral to the client's diagnosis and treatment (*State v. Andring,* 1984).

The important concept for the courts should be whether the therapeutic disclosures were made in such a way as to render the communication public (Kendrick et al., 1993). In a treatment modality that involves family members or persons with similar concerns in a group, the client has not consciously waived confidentiality or given permission for the therapist to testify in a future court proceeding. The expectation of the client is for the communication to remain private, an expectation shared with all of those in the room. The Supreme Court of Minnesota articulated this notion in an influential case. In *Andring,* the court was ruling on a defendant's attempt to access the records of group therapy sessions. In a group setting, each client was said to be the therapeutic agent of the other and thus the presence of third parties was essential to accomplish the special goals of group therapy. The court reasoned that to find otherwise would seriously limit the effectiveness of this valuable treatment method.

Four years later, an appellate court in California heard a similar case brought by a father accused of sexually assaulting his teenage daughter (*Lovett v. Superior Court,* 1988). The father sought to question members of a support group the daughter was in to cope with her trauma. In rejecting the father's claim, the court relied on the language of the California privilege statute, which plainly indicates that communications made by patients to persons who are present to further the interests of the patient comes within the privilege (citing California Evidence Code, section 1012). The court, however, did indicate that group communications are like any other privileged communication in that the privilege is not absolute. The obligation is on the defendant to show a good cause for the court to conduct an *in camera* review of the records. In this case, the court found no such evidence and upheld the privilege.

Some states have language in their statutes that protects the privileged content of group sessions (see, e.g., Colorado privilege statute, 1985; New Jersey Statutes, 1992). Other statutes specifically protect group or family members from having to testify (Massachusetts General Laws, 1992). The latter statutory language is significant. In many cases, therapists will be found to have a legal protection from being forced to testify or produce records if the client does not give permission. There is no explicit statutory language in most states that includes group members. Courts could find that the therapist cannot testify but could allow group members to be subpoenaed. This would circumvent the intent of the privilege statutes, which are based on the social utility of promoting mental health counseling by protecting confidentiality. In most cases, courts have not made this distinction between professional and group members. If the communication was privileged when made in a one-to-one relationship, courts have extended the privilege to cover group and family therapy under the treatment of the professional (*Hosey v. the Presbyterian Church,* 1995). No cases could be found where the presence of third parties in these sessions was judged to be a waiver of privilege.

There have been a number of cases in which group and family members have been required to testify about the content of therapy sessions. In these cases, the analysis has rested on some key issues that provide an encouraging picture of the legal system's growing support for the psychotherapist-client privilege. In each of the cases that allowed group or family members to testify, there were facts that took the case outside of the privilege statutes. In a Maine case, a court allowed testimony from a man who was in a therapy group with a defendant while they were residing together in a substance abuse treatment center. The court ruled that the conversations about which the man could testify had occurred outside of the therapy group and thus were not protected by statute (*State v. Boucher,* 1994).

In a notorious New York case, the participants in an Alcoholics Anonymous (A.A.) meeting were issued a subpoena to testify. The case involved a group member accused of brutally murdering two people during an alcohol-induced blackout. The group members argued that they were bound by the organization's rules to keep all group inter-actions strictly confidential. The judge rejected this argument, finding that a legal privilege was not present given that the self-help group was not facilitated by a mental health professional (Weiner, 1995). Although the court did protect the confidentiality of the members by shielding them from media and not requiring them to use their complete names, there was no protection of the accused man's confidentiality in this setting. The expectation of confidentiality is clearly not the same as the legal protection afforded by privilege statutes.

Clinicians should require all group members to sign a confidentiality agreement prior to the first session. Guaranteeing confidentiality in a group is beyond the physical control of the professional. As such, group members should be apprised of the potential for confidentiality breaches by other group members to obtain effective informed consent for participation in the group (Roback, Moore, Bloch, & Shelton, 1996). The District of Columbia (1996) has an ordinance that specifically prohibits group members from divulging mental health information regarding another client in a group. Although this may not result in any realistic limits on clients, the language of the statute may be persuasive to judges in the district who consider the question of whether to compel or allow the testimony of a group member concerning in-group communications.

In family/couples counseling, communications made in therapy usually have been shielded from judicial disclosure. The exceptions have been in cases where the purpose of the proceeding was to decide on the care and custody of a child. As previously discussed, in these hearings, the usual rules are subjugated to the best interests of the child. Otherwise, courts have had no difficulty finding the involvement of family members to be necessary and integral to the treatment of a client and have extended the privilege to communications made in the course of family therapy. Therapists face a difficult dilemma when confronted with requests for information by one family member. The most prudent action is to gain the written consent of all of the parties prior to releasing the records. Also, the informed consent to treatment in family therapy should include a discussion of the confidentiality issues.

Limited disclosures. The theoretical analysis of privilege rests on the notion that there is a secret communication that should be left private to further the interests of society. When a client or therapist discloses a part of a confidential communication to a third party, courts have had to decide whether to protect the remainder of the content. In one recent case, a federal court ruled a complete waiver resulting from a partial disclosure of privileged information. A Presbyterian minister accused of inappropriate conduct with children from his church entered a treatment program at the Menninger Clinic (*Hosey v. the Presbyterian Church,* 1995). Families of the children filed suit against the minister and the church. They sought access to the treatment records, arguing that the minister had waived his privilege by disclosing details of his diagnosis and treatment to church officials. The court agreed that Kansas law explicitly states that privilege is waived if the client discloses any part of the matter in question. The Menninger Clinic was ordered to produce the requested information.

Although some courts see any disclosure as constituting a complete waiver of privilege, a more appropriate remedy is to consider the privilege to be waived for only the limited subject of the actual disclosure. In the highly publicized case below, the court's analysis of the effect of a limited disclosure is clear and seems to be a more balanced approach to this situation.

Farrow v. Allen (1993, opinion of the court). At issue in this appeal is the scope of a waiver of the physician-patient privilege. The underlying proceeding in this case seeks to vacate Woody Allen's adoption of two children, who are also the adopted children of Mia Farrow. Farrow sought to compel the depositions of several non-party psychiatrists, including Dr. Kass, one of whose patients is another child of Farrow, Soon-Yi Previn. It is claimed that Soon-Yi communicated information to Dr. Kass that is material and relevant to the current proceeding. While Kass resisted deposition on the ground that his testimony was protected by the physician-patient privilege, Farrow contends that any such privilege was waived by the psychiatrist's release, with his patient's authorization, of a letter dated January 26, 1993, which dealt with certain matters revealed to him by his patient during the course of treatment. Dr. Kass does not deny that he sent the letter, with his patient's authorization, but argues that this limited disclosure did not act as a waiver of the physician-patient privilege in the present context. The Surrogate (trial judge) found that because Dr. Kass's patient had partially waived the privilege by publication, Kass could be deposed but only concerning "the area of communications contained in the letter." It is that order that is the subject of this appeal.

In this case, consideration of whether the privilege existing between Dr. Kass and his patient Soon-Yi Previn was to any degree waived must necessarily start with the letter of January 26, 1993.

Kass asserts that his patient authorized him to prepare and submit the letter to the Yale/New Haven Sexual Abuse Clinic, an agency that was working at the behest of the State of Connecticut to prepare a report in relation to a criminal investigation (with which neither Dr. Kass nor his patient had any direct involvement). Kass claims that the letter was a confidential communication intended only for the mental health professionals at the clinic and that he so informed the clinic. Farrow, however, vigorously disputes that the permission given by Ms. Previn regarding the letter's distribution was of so narrow a scope, and there is some evidence supporting that position, including the fact that the letter was captioned solely "To whom it may concern," was not addressed to the clinic, and did not itself contain any indication as to the persons to whom its release was authorized. Moreover, it is clear that the letter was not kept confidential and that it has in fact come into the hands of attorneys for both parties to the proceeding.

Whatever limits on disclosure of the letter may have been intended by Dr. Kass's patient, the very fact of such disclosure foreclosed any claim of privilege as to the information contained in the letter itself. As already noted, the physician-patient privilege only applies to protect communications that have been made in confidence as well as in the context of the physician-patient relationship. It follows therefore that, even if the information was intended to remain confidential when it was communicated, once a patient puts the information into the hands of a third party who is completely unconnected to his or her treatment and who is not subject to any privilege, it can no longer be considered a confidence, and the privilege must be deemed to have been waived as to that information. Thus, even assuming that Dr. Kass and his patient reasonably, if incorrectly, anticipated that the letter and its contents would go no further, its release to clinicians at the Yale/New Haven clinic, who had no relationship to the treatment of Ms. Previn, is sufficient to waive the privilege as to the information contained in the letter itself.

Notwithstanding our conclusion that the physician-patient privilege is unavailable here to shield the contents of the letter, we find that this does not imply a waiver as to other normally privileged communications made to Dr. Kass, even if they concern the subject areas involved in the letter, and that, as a result, no deposition may be compelled.

In determining the scope of a waiver effected by a patient's disclosure, there must be some consideration of the circumstances under which the disclosure took place and its impact on the opposing party. In any situation of this type, it is recognized that it is unfair for the opposing party in a litigated controversy to have the patient use this privilege both as a sword and a shield, to waive when it enures to her advantage and wield when it does not.

Thus, once the patient has voluntarily presented a picture of his or her medical condition to the court in a particular court proceeding, it is only fair to permit the opposing party to obtain whatever information is necessary to present a full and fair picture of that condition. In such a situation, the type of broad waiver argued for by Farrow is appropriate, and the opposing party may generally obtain and introduce any other evidence in the possession of the physician that is material and necessary. However, that is not the setting in which the subject information is sought. Here, the release of the January 26, 1993, letter was completely extrajudicial and the information contained in it was not released in connection with this proceeding. Its release to the Yale/New Haven clinic did not operate in any way to put the medical condition of Ms. Previn before a court in a manner that would prejudice an opposing party. Significantly, there has been no attempt whatsoever to affirmatively use the information in the letter against Farrow or to her disadvantage. As Farrow has suffered no prejudice, fairness does not demand the suspension of the physician-patient privilege as to other information obtained by Dr. Kass in the course of treatment. [Citations omitted; text edited for style and readability.]

Partial testimony. In some court hearings, a client voluntarily answers questions concerning privileged information. Once the client does so, the privilege is deemed by the court to have been waived and, usually, the opposing side is provided with the opportunity to ask questions concerning the full extent of the otherwise privileged information. The same may be true in cases where the disclosure resulted from the testimony of the therapist. Courts have found that the testimony of mental health professionals, even when the professionals were unaware of the protected nature of the communication, serves as a waiver of the privilege. When the source of the disclosure of the privileged information is the therapist, it seems particularly unfair to the client to rule that the privilege has been abrogated. The recourse for the client is to sue or to file an administrative complaint against the practitioner. This remedy does not result in protection of the client's privacy interests. Mental health professionals need to be aware of the partial testimony rule so as not to attempt to give partial testimony, such as including only that information that favors their client's interest, naively believing that privilege will protect the full disclosure of the complete record.

Summary of Client Waivers

Mental health professionals need to be aware of the situations that courts may construe as creating a waiver to the privileged status of confidential communications. The conceptual basis for the finding of waivers rests on the idea that when a communication is divulged outside of the therapy room, there is a loss of the expectation of privacy. Clients and professionals are often surprised at the "intent" that is inferred from their actions. As a result, special care must be taken to analyze the ramifications of all releases of information. Clients may request that a professional write a letter or testify for them in a legal proceeding without understanding the concept of waiver of privilege. Prior to any action regarding privileged communications, therapists should consider the legal effects of the disclosure. The questions that must be addressed include the following:

- What is the nature of the treatment relationship? Does privilege exist in the setting?
- Is there any person in a dangerous situation that would trigger a statutory duty or the common law prevention-of-harm duty?
- Has the court issued a ruling compelling testimony or production of records?
- Is there justification for seeking an in camera review of the records prior to a court hearing?

- Has the client put his or her mental health or emotional condition at issue in a legal proceeding?
- Has there been a disclosure to a third party of the confidential information?

COMPELLED DISCLOSURES

In some circumstances, therapists are required to disclose confidential information in a court proceeding. It is important to distinguish between a subpoena to testify that is issued by one of the attorneys in a case (see Chapter 4 for a detailed discussion of responding to a subpoena) from the order of a judge. A therapist may be compelled to testify when the court rules that the need for the information is greater than the damage to the client and the treatment community from disclosure. Because the privilege belongs to the client, it is likely that the attorney for the client in the legal action will be the one to raise the appropriate objections and argue the legal points of compelled disclosures. However, in these cases, it is important for the mental health worker to discuss the potential liabilities with a personal attorney who can protect the interests of the therapist. The following sections describe conditions under which a court might compel disclosure of confidential information. The decisions are usually made on the facts of the particular case and are influenced by the judge's views on the importance of the value of confidentiality in counseling relationships.

Testimonial Privilege

The issue of testimonial privilege is often raised by a therapist who is sued for breaching confidentiality or breaking privilege by providing testimony in court. It has long been established that there is an absolute privilege for statements made in judicial proceedings, as long as the statements are in some way pertinent to the subject matter of the controversy (*Doe v. Blake,* 1992). In the *Renzi* case discussed previously, the therapist who voluntarily testified in a custody hearing without the consent of her client argued that she should be protected from liability based on witness immunity (testimonial privilege). This principle is an important policy instrument developed in common law so that individuals may present information unencumbered by the threat of retaliation. Witness immunity means that a witness cannot be sued for any comments made during the course of testifying. The policy underlying the privilege is that in certain situations, the public interest in having people speak freely outweighs the risk that individuals will occasionally abuse the privilege by making false and malicious statements (*Petyan v. Ellis*, 1986).

Courts have reasoned that it would be an unfair burden on a witness, who most often would not be trained in legal matters and who may be intimidated by the experience, to speak freely if worried about the threat of being sued for speaking falsely (*O'coin v. Woonsocket Institution Trust Co.*, 1988). One court opined that such a duty would be "onerous in the extreme and would undoubtedly create costly and unnecessary delays in discovery and prosecutions as doctors delayed in complying with valid court orders out of fear that they might incur civil liability" (*Arnett v. Baskous*, 1993). Despite these considerable policy arguments in support of the testimonial privilege, the court in *Renzi* rejected this argument without much discussion although in other cases it has provided the rationale for dismissing lawsuits against psychotherapists. The analysis in *Renzi* seemed to focus more on her inattention to her confidentiality duty leading up to the hearing rather than her actual testimony.

In a Tennessee case, the issue of witness immunity was used to shield a therapist from liability. The clinical psychologist saw a married couple in therapy for more than a year. Most of the sessions were joint, although each person was seen individually at times. In the course of the divorce litigation, the wife called the psychologist as a witness. The husband objected on the grounds of privilege. The trial judge wrongly instructed the psychologist to testify only about joint sessions because the wife was present and thus there was no privilege for those sessions (see the section on the presence of a third party and privilege, above, for a correct reading on this point). The appeals court found that the psychologist had objected to the order to testify but had been compelled by the court, even if for erroneous reasons. If the therapist had declined to answer questions, he would have been found in contempt of court. Therefore, the court concluded that the therapist should be protected by witness immunity and not be liable for his compelled testimony (*Guity v. Kandilakis*, 1991).

Criminal Proceedings

Constitutional Issues

The confrontation and compulsory process clauses of the Sixth Amendment provide that "in all criminal prosecutions, the accused shall enjoy the right . . . to be confronted with the witnesses against him [and] to have compulsory process for obtaining witnesses in his favor." The constitutional protections afforded to those accused of criminal wrong-doing have a high value in American law and tend to trump other societal values when cases are being reviewed by courts. For example, when evidence is illegally seized by police, even if it points to the certain guilt of the accused, courts will exclude the evidence from the criminal trial as being in violation of the individual's constitutional rights. When an individual is charged with a crime, there is powerful precedent to allow access to all relevant evidence and witnesses needed by the accused in building a defense. Like any rule that excludes evidence, psycho-therapist-client privilege raises difficult choices between a person's right to a fair trial and the protection of confidential communications (Podgers, 1995).

The Sixth Amendment right of confrontation permits a defendant to cross-examine witnesses to test the believability of the witness and the truth of his or her testimony (*Davis v. Alaska,* 1974). In some cases, a defendant may wish to access the medical and psychotherapy records of a witness to obtain information that may be used to impeach the witness in the eyes of the jury. For example, if a witness to a murder has a history of psychiatric treatment for a thought disorder and delusional episodes, the accused would want the opportunity to introduce treatment records and the testimony of the therapist to provide the jury with information on which to judge the testimony. In cases like this example, courts support the inclusion of evidence, as long as the information provides some significant help to the jury in its efforts to evaluate the witness's ability to perceive or to recall events or to testify accurately (*United States v. Butt,* 1992).

Courts have struggled to find a balance of rights by the development of standard procedures for deciding whether to compel testimony and the production of records, despite the privilege, or to support the privilege and order the information to be kept confidential. Often, judges have used a process called in camera review in which sealed records are provided to the judge. These are reviewed in private to determine if they contain information that is relevant and that is not available through any other nonprivileged witness. Courts have found this process to be a useful intermediate step between full disclosure and total nondisclosure (*United States v. Gambino,* 1990). Recent case law has helped to articulate the process of in camera review, but the decision as to whether to admit privileged information and compel the testimony of the therapist remains subject to the needs of the case and the orientation of the judge.

Many of the cases in which a defendant has sought access to privileged counseling information involve rape trials. A sexual assault trial requires a court to balance evidentiary privileges for sexual assault counselors that have been enacted by state legislatures, against a criminal defendant's constitutional rights. State privileged communication statutes reflect a policy decision to encourage treatment by protecting "couch confidences" from unwarranted public scrutiny. The goal is to encourage treatment by ensuring confidentiality. When a defendant who is charged with sexual assault seeks to compel discovery of the victim's privileged medical, psychiatric, or counseling records, a conflict inevitably arises. It is common in sexual assault trials to have the defense attempt to put the alleged victim on trial by raising questions about the individual's moral character or mental health. Treatment records are routinely sought to this end. Clients argue that courts must respect statutory assurances of confidentiality while defendants argue that their right to a fair trial requires disclosure. Courts have struggled to create rules by which the defendant's need for the information is balanced against the victim's need to keep the information private. Recent court rulings have resulted in a standardized review process that occurs on a case-by-case basis. Mental health workers should be familiar with the guidelines so that clients may be assisted in asserting their rights when asked to submit evidence of this sort. Although the prosecutor is likely to fight the release of therapy records, it is not the same as having a personal advocate, and the client may feel intimidated by the process.

Crowley (1995) summarized the current state of in camera inspections as they have been applied both federally and in Massachusetts. In *Pennsylvania v. Ritchie* (1987), the U.S. Supreme Court developed the conditions under which privileged records could be evaluated in criminal cases. The court held that a judicial in camera inspection of privileged records strikes a constitutional balance between the defendant's and the state's competing interests. Under *Ritchie,* if a defendant asserts a need to review a victim's privileged records, the federal in camera approach empowers a judge to inspect the requested records first—alone in chambers. The judge will then allow the defense and prosecution to review information deemed material. *Commonwealth v. Bishop* (1993) was a decision by the Massachusetts Supreme Judicial Court that established a systematic approach to the in camera review process. The court recognized the defendant's right to prepare an informed defense, but it emphasized that a defendant may have access to a victim's privileged communications only in certain circumstances. The court articulated a five-part test to clarify when and how the trial court should review privileged records as well as when and why the trial court should deny disclosure to the defense.

The five-part *Bishop* test begins with a determination of whether a statutory privilege exists. Second, if a privilege is found, the court will require the defense to submit a written statement as to why the specific records are relevant to the case. Upon ruling that privileged records are relevant, the judge provides these parts of the record to the defense counsel and the prosecutor for review. The access is limited only to the designated attorneys conditioned on strict confidentiality. The defendant's attorney then must make an argument to the court as to why the information is fundamental to a fair trial. Finally, the judge determines the admissibility of the records. The main difference between the federal standard and the Massachusetts standard is that *Bishop* only requires the information to be *relevant* to be admissible while *Ritchie* required a showing that the information would affect the outcome of the trial (Crowley, 1995). The *Bishop* test resulted in a rape crisis hot line being fined $500 per day for contempt of court when it refused to deliver its rape counseling records to a court for in camera review (*YWCA-ARCH v. Commonwealth,* 1994).

The rulings in various states have produced standardized procedures but the cases have also varied in their results. In Colorado, for example, the Supreme Court voiced a strong commitment to uphold statutory privileges and restrict the use of in camera inspections. In two recent Michigan cases, however, the court established a standard that was less concerned with protecting privilege (*Michigan v. Stanaway & Michigan v. Caruso,* 1994). These cases (consolidated for this appeal) involved two defendants charged with criminal sexual misconduct against minor children. The court was asked to rule on whether they could get access to the counseling records of the victims. The court required a defendant to establish a reasonable probability that the privileged records were likely to contain material information necessary to his defense before an in camera review would be conducted. In the two cases, the court reached different conclusions. In one, the judge found the defendant's "generalized assertions of a need to attack the credibility of his accuser" were insufficient to overcome the statutory privilege (p. 649). In the other case, however, the defendant argued that the counseling information was relevant to specific points of his defense, which led the judge to rule that an in camera review was warranted.

Some of the courts that have examined the compelled disclosure of confidential records have distinguished between absolute privileges and qualified privileges. Most psychotherapy privileges are the latter type while some sexual assault and domestic violence statutes have language that deems the privilege absolute. Counselors should be aware of the variety of state opinions on these statutes. The Rhode Island Supreme Court, for example, has ruled that the creation of an absolute evidentiary privilege would violate the constitutional rights of the defendant (Rhode Island Supreme Court Advisory Opinion, 1983). However, Illinois (*People v. Foggy,* 1988) and Pennsylvania (*Commonwealth v. Wilson,* 1992) have refused to disclose records where the statutory privilege was determined to be absolute. Similarly, the Michigan Supreme Court found that an absolute privilege could be waived only by the party holding the privilege. But if the person refused to waive the privilege and allow access to counseling records, the court should refuse to allow the individual to testify at all (*Michigan v. Stanaway & Michigan v. Caruso,* 1994).

The line of cases that set the rules for when privileged information must be disclosed to a court share some common procedures but the emphasis on which rights to balance varies by state. Some states protect the criminal defendant's rights by requiring the production of confidential material either to the court alone or to the attorneys. Other states read the legislative intent in creating the privilege statutes as supporting the value of protecting client confidentiality in psychotherapy and counseling relationships. The trend of the law is difficult to predict, but the language and reasoning from the recent Supreme Court decision in *Jaffe v. Redmond* (1996) should be persuasive to judges deciding these cases.

> Making the promise of confidentiality contingent upon a trial judge's later evaluation of the relative importance of the patient's interest in privacy and the evidentiary need for disclosure would eviscerate the effectiveness of the privilege . . . [P]articipants [in therapy] must be able to predict with some degree of certainty whether particular discussions will be protected. An uncertain privilege, or one which purports to be certain but results in widely varying applications by the courts, is little better than no privilege at all. (p. 1932)

The mental health community needs to assume a leadership role in writing amicus briefs and supporting the litigation of cases that have the potential to affirm the sanctity of the psychotherapy relationship. Although the value of the rights of the accused is significant, the harm that results from the erosion of confidentiality protections is likely to have vastly greater social consequences.

Therapist as Defendant

Courts have been asked to compel the production of confidential psychotherapy records in cases where the therapist is the defendant in either a criminal or a civil case. The issue in these cases is whether the objection to revealing confidential information has a basis in protection of the clients' right to confidentiality, or whether the objection is an attempt by the therapist to keep potentially incriminating evidence out of the trial. The courts have had to balance the rights and, when they have allowed privileged information to be admitted, they have also had to decide on the scope of information that could be released.

Weisbeck v. Hess (1994, opinion of the court). In this case, the therapist was charged with misconduct with a female client. The ex-husband of the woman filed suit and sought to obtain a client list from the therapist. His attorney wanted to question these clients to see if there were other instances of sexual relationships between the therapist and his clients. Also, the plaintiff sought to have access to the counseling records of the therapist.

James Weisbeck brought suit against Dr. James Hess, sole owner of Mountain Plains Counseling Center, alleging professional negligence. During discovery, Weisbeck requested that Hess produce a list of his patients from the previous seven years. Weisbeck also sought the right to depose Hess's personal counselor, Tom Terry. Hess refused both requests on numerous grounds, including the claim that compliance would violate psychologist-patient privilege. On October 1, 1993, the trial court issued an order requiring Hess to turn over his client lists to the court, where they would be kept sealed until further order. Permission was also given by the trial court to depose the counselor with the admissibility of his testimony to be determined at a later date.

We address the following issues in this appeal: I. Did the trial court abuse its discretion by ordering Hess to divulge his list of patients? We hold that it did. II. Did the trial court abuse its discretion in allowing Weisbeck to depose Hess's counselor, Tom Terry? We hold that it did. Because the trial court's order would require an improper violation of privileged medical confidentiality, we reverse said order.

Facts: During November 1986, Weisbeck's wife of 12 years, Cindy, began counseling sessions with Hess, a licensed psychologist and psychology professor. After June 1987, when Cindy began seeing other counselors at Mountain Plains, Hess claimed to have stopped counseling her. However, that following September, Hess hired her as a part-time secretary. Hess has since admitted to having sexual relations with Cindy during 1989, all of this having occurred while Cindy and Weisbeck were still married. The two subsequently divorced in 1990. That same year, Hess, who was also married during these events, divorced his third wife and began counseling with a Mr. Terry.

Alleging breach of fiduciary duty, fraud, and seduction, Weisbeck filed a complaint in June 1992 against Hess and Mountain Plains seeking damages for Hess's romantic relationship with Cindy, which may have begun while Cindy was under Hess's direct professional care. During discovery, Weisbeck requested a list of Hess's clients from both his private practice and at the college where he taught, during the previous seven years. He also sought to question Terry about Hess's relationship with Cindy. Hess maintains that he did not begin his relationship with Cindy until 20 months after their counseling sessions ended, and refuses to produce the requested information, asserting that it is protected privileged information.

I. Hess's patient list is privileged: It is settled law that "all relevant matters are discoverable unless privileged." It is understood, per state statute, that the patient's psychotherapist at the time of the communication has the authority to claim the privilege but only on behalf of the patient. A communication is "confidential" if not intended to be disclosed to third persons, except persons present to further the interest of the patient, persons reasonably necessary for the transmission of the communication, or persons who are participating in the diagnosis and treatment under the direction of the psychotherapist, including members of the patient's family. Hess asserts such communication embodies his list of patients who, in the course of seeking his care, divulge private and personal information. To compel disclosure of a psychotherapy patient's identity is to directly harm her privacy interests. This harm is exacerbated by the stigma that society often attaches to mental illness. If a patient knows that the privilege is fraught with exceptions, she is liable to withhold information or avoid therapy altogether.

Weisbeck wants the list so he can question Hess's former female patients to bolster his claim that his marriage fell victim to Hess's (alleged) usual ploy of taking advantage of vulnerable female patients. However, this discovery fishing expedition does not provide the facts or rationale necessary to violate the privacy of uninterested parties. Releasing the names of these clients would directly discourage uninhibited communication, due to Weisbeck's mere suspicion that such information may possibly contain relevant evidence. This plan is not reasonably calculated to lead to the discovery of admissible evidence. Nor is it enough to set aside the privilege.

II. Hess's sessions with Terry qualify as privileged communications. It is not enough that Weisbeck seeks the names of those who have revealed their innermost personal thoughts; he also desires to further violate the privilege by requesting the innermost personal thoughts that Hess divulged to his own counselor, Tom Terry. Weisbeck believes that Terry may have counseled Hess about Cindy and whether Hess should stop dating her because of professional ethics. Gleaning the record herein, it is apparent that Weisbeck is also hopeful that Terry, via the counseling sessions, has knowledge of other women whom Hess allegedly victimized. Regardless of what was revealed during counseling, Weisbeck is, once again, merely fishing. It is not our intention to validate Hess's actions, whatever they may be; rather, this Court seeks to protect the sanctity of the privilege. As such, the trial court's ruling was clearly against reason and evidence and was an abuse of discretion. [Citations omitted; text edited for style and readability.]

The *Weisbeck* decision has been criticized by some who see the case as wrongly allowing a therapist to hide behind privilege, which results in a step backward in the efforts to combat sexual exploitation by therapists (Slaughter, 1996). Although the exclusion of evidence in this case seems to have fulfilled a questionable purpose, the underlying analysis by the court was correct. The decision protected the class of individuals who had been treated by Dr. Hess rather than allowing a "fishing expedition" that would yield questionable evidence. If Weisbeck had been able to show a specific relationship between the information sought and an element of needed proof, with no other way to discover the information, the decision might have come out in favor of compelling disclosure.

There have been other cases against therapists where the courts have moved quickly to compel the disclosure of confidential information. Most of these decisions have occurred in cases where the therapist was charged with criminal fraud for billing insurance companies and Medicaid. The information that has been sought by prosecutors in these cases is client lists and dates of sessions. Clients would be contacted to determine if the dates and treatment information were fraudulent. The highest courts of some states have declined to apply the psychotherapist-client privilege to bar state grand jury subpoenas of patient records. The Massachusetts Supreme Judicial Court considered the interrelationship between Medicaid record keeping and reporting requirements and the Massachusetts statutory psychotherapist-patient privilege (*Commonwealth v. Kobrin*, 1985). The *Kobrin* court declined to approve the compelled "wholesale production" of patient records before a grand jury without regard to their relevance to the critical issue in a Medicaid fraud investigation. The court held that the state grand jury could properly demand "those portions of [the psychiatrist's] records documenting the times and lengths of patient appointments, fees, patient diagnoses, treatment plans and recommendations, and somatic therapies" but that "those portions of the records . . . which reflect patients' thoughts, feelings, and impressions, or contain the substance of the psychotherapeutic dialogue are protected and need not be produced" (p. 681).

In *In re Pebsworth* (1983), the Seventh Circuit held that a grand jury subpoena seeking patient names, diagnoses, and lists of visits was enforceable because "any arguable psychotherapist-patient privilege as to these specific kinds of billing and administrative records was intentionally and knowingly relinquished through the patients' assent to the publicizing aspect of the reimbursement and claims procedure" (p. 262). The language of *Pebsworth* has been quoted by other courts to justify the compelled production of confidential information. The idea that submitting an insurance claim negates privilege by involving a third party is conceptually weak. The court seems to be interpreting the forwarding of the insurance claim as an explicit waiver of privilege. But because insurance companies are subject to the same confidentiality of medical records as psychotherapists, that conclusion seems contrived. The message from this line of cases is that in cases where the mental health worker is charged with a criminal offense, the courts will usually find a way to compel the release of confidential records by minimizing the consideration of damage to the clients. The exception to this is where the court is not convinced of the necessity or the relevance of the request to the case.

UNAUTHORIZED DISCLOSURES

Purposeful Self-Interest

Dr. Willis, a psychiatrist, was charged with securities fraud and mail fraud in connection with his purchases of stock of Bank America in 1986 (*United States v. Willis,* 1990). The indictment charged that Dr. Willis breached the physician's traditional duty of confidentiality, on which his patient was entitled to rely, when he misappropriated for his personal profit, nonpublic, business information confided to him by his patient. Thereafter, when Dr. Willis purchased Bank America securities on the basis of his patient's confidential information, he defrauded his patient and violated Securities laws.

In 1981, Mr. Weill sold his controlling interest in Shearson to the American Express Company, and between 1981 and 1985, he served as president of American Express. He secured a commitment from Shearson to invest $1 billion in Bank America if he was successful in his negotiations with Bank America. In January 1986, Mr. Weill attempted to meet with several of the directors of Bank America to discuss his proposals, but these contacts were not disclosed publicly. Public information regarding Bank America was generally unfavorable at this time, including news reports that Bank America had incurred a loss of more than $300 million in 1985.

Mr. Weill discussed his effort to become CEO of Bank America with his wife, who was a patient of Dr. Willis at that time. Mrs. Weill discussed her husband's business activities in therapy. Dr. Willis disclosed this information to his broker and purchased Bank America stock. Dr. Willis purchased a total of 13,000 shares and sold them after Mr. Weill had become CEO and Shearson announced their investment in his company. His profit from this transaction was approximately $27,500. The court found that by not advising his patient of his intention to disclose her confidential information and to profit personally from it, Dr. Willis fraudulently induced his patient to confide in him in connection with his purchase and sale of stock.

Dr. Willis was convicted of having violated the sanctity of the professional relationship for personal gain. Although this type of case is rare, there have been other, similar instances where a mental health worker has put self-interest ahead of the duty to maintain confidentiality. The most troubling aspect of these cases is the damage they do to public trust in the profession. It is difficult to quantify a dollar amount of damage suffered by the client when the breach of confidentiality involves financial information mentioned by the client rather than any direct clinical information affecting the client's reputation. In these cases, it is more likely that a legal action would be instituted for a violation of a law, such as illegal trading in securities or larceny. The most likely legal ramification is for the therapist to be charged with violating the state statute on confidentiality, with possible loss of professional license or sanction imposed by a professional organization.

There are times when a therapist will be inclined to breach a confidential communication as a result of a strong personal conviction about an issue. Such was the case in the public disclosure of confidential information by the therapist who had been treating Nicole Brown Simpson. Susan Forward, the noted author and clinician, was among the first to reveal the murdered woman's history of abuse at the hands of O. J. Simpson when she appeared on several national interview programs. Although it is unclear whether her motives were personal exposure or true outrage, it is clear that her discussion of the details of Nicole Brown Simpson's treatment violated professional standards. The duty to maintain confidentiality survives the death of a client. A proper release would need to have been signed and executed by the person who was the legal representative of the estate. Ms. Forward's license was suspended by the state of California and she was barred from seeing clients for three months; she also agreed to serve three years' probation (Saavedra, 1995).

In a similar unpublished case, a therapist was interviewed by a magazine reporter who was writing a story about the short life of a murdered child. The therapist was charged with slander for naming the child's biological father as having sexually abused the child. Deeply upset by the horrible crime and the atrocities endured by the child, the therapist spoke to the reporter from her heart but, in doing so, improperly published information she had obtained in the course of treating the child. In the wake of tragedies, therapists often feel a need to reveal information about their clients who became victims. It is important to be aware of the legal ramifications of any disclosures, regardless of positive intentions. In one recent case from Texas, the parents of a client who recanted claims of sexual abuse succeeded in proving slander against their daughter's therapist (*Khatain v. Jones,* 1995). The therapist republished the allegations of sexual abuse to the woman's husband and four daughters, aged 17 to 23, in the context of a family meeting with them, causing estrangement between the daughters and their grandparents. When the client herself recanted some time later, her parents sued the therapist for slander and obtained a $350,000 jury verdict against him.

Accidental or Negligent Breach

The unauthorized release of privileged information frequently occurs outside of the glare of court challenges, media coverage, or other trappings of the high-profile cases. The lack of vigilance in maintaining practice policies results in many negligent or accidental breaches of confidentiality. Most of these breaches have no legal action and, in some cases, clients do not even report the situation to the agency or their own counselors. Instead, clients may lose trust in the individual worker, drop out of treatment, and become disillusioned with the field. The development of and adherence to strong policies protecting confidentiality will reduce the chances of avoidable errors.

Accidental breaches of confidentiality include such problems as poorly designed rooms where clinical conversations can be overheard or client identities are widely exposed; lunch room or coffee break conversations by clinical staff using client names; poorly trained support staff who fail to maintain client privacy in face-to-face, mail, or phone communications; case presentations or publications that do not adequately disguise identifying client information; media coverage of an agency or a public event in which images of clients are published; and lack of restricted access to client files. Clinicians and agencies must regularly evaluate their practice and the environment of their offices to avoid negligent breaches of confidentiality. When staff are focused on how clients are experiencing the services, and are sensitive to the stigma that often accompanies mental health treatment, the danger of accidental breaches can be minimized.

SUMMARY

The concept of privilege provides mental health professionals and clients with a degree of confidence that the information uncovered in the course of treatment will be protected from unauthorized disclosure. The confidentiality of records, however, is becoming more illusion than reality. The legal system maintains a strong bias toward including all relevant information in any court proceeding. This professional value is as strong as the value of confidentiality is to psychotherapists. Because the case law has established a duty on psychotherapists to prevent harm, and privilege statutes have been written to give judges wide discretion to compel the production of records and testimony, therapists and clients are left with uncertainty. A review of the cases indicates that the decision about whether to uphold a privilege depends on a couple of factors, extraneous to the original treatment. First, the nature of the legal action is relevant to the decision of the judge. In criminal cases, there is much more incentive to order the production of records because the rights of individuals are constitutionally based and often a defendant's freedom is at stake. Second, it seems clear that a therapist who is being charged with misconduct will not be allowed to hide behind the mantle of privilege to escape liability. Finally, the concept of psychotherapist-client privilege seems to be so antithetical to the values of some judges that they will create ways to override the privilege.

As society becomes more vigilant about assigning responsibility to individuals and institutions when someone has suffered an injury, the standards for mental health professionals will continue to reflect hindsight bias. The privilege statutes demonstrate the need to balance the privacy interests of clients against societal interest in obtaining the particular information (*United States v. Layton,* 1981). The psychotherapy profession must be able to actively support the protection of the privilege against the creeping threat of the legal system undervaluing the importance of confidentiality to the effective practice of psychotherapy. There is virtually no quality research that investigates the premise of confidentiality on therapeutic effectiveness or on clients' willingness to fully use the opportunities to get help in therapy for those issues that may result in liability or embarrassment if made public. The mental health profession must use the research to advocate for universality and uniformity of state and federal rules protecting client confidentiality and privilege (Polowy & Gorenberg, 1995). Through a proactive approach, the field of psychotherapy can substantiate the importance of confidentiality to the effectiveness of practice and can determine the situations under which the protection should yield. The standard of care that would result will enable practitioners to understand where the balance lies between the needs of society and the rights of clients.

Chapter 4

THE STANDARD OF CARE
AND PRACTICE ISSUES

WHAT CONSTITUTES
REASONABLE PRACTICE?

While on a 12-hour pass from the hospital's chemical dependency unit, the client shot and killed himself. The second-guessing about the diagnosis and treatment plan began right away and escalated with the filing of the lawsuit by the man's estate. Were the actions of the mental health team within the standard of care? Was the hospital staff liable for malpractice in its handling of this case?

The client had symptoms suggesting recurrent major depression but also was consuming dangerous levels of halcion and alcohol prior to his hospital intake. Following evaluations and interviews with several staff members, the treatment team decided to treat the substance abuse as the primary need. The client was transferred to the chemical dependency unit. There were no available beds in a dual diagnosis facility.

At trial, experts disagreed about whether it was appropriate to transfer the client prior to treatment for stabilizing the depression. Some experts felt depression should have been the primary diagnosis with the treatment protocol of psychotropic medications and psychotherapy indicated. Others supported the assessment that the client's symptoms were consistent with chemical withdrawal. After hearing the evidence, the jury found that the diagnosis and subsequent actions of the treatment team were reasonable, given the situation. There was not sufficient evidence to find a violation of the standard of care, even though the outcome indicated that the professionals' judgment was wrong (*Cox v. Willis-Knighton Medical Center,* 1996).

Human service professionals have faced increasing numbers of lawsuits related to their practice, particularly in clinical settings. As discussed in Chapter 1, the influence of the legal system on psychotherapy has been both positive and negative. It has resulted in the improvement of practice by holding therapists to higher standards, yet the legal involvement has also intruded on the autonomy and creativity of the profession. Unfortunately, many therapists feel the legal system is ill-suited to deal with the complexities of mental and emotional health because there are so many variables in the control of the client, and treatment outcomes often do not correspond to the knowledge or skill of the professional. Despite the legitimacy of these concerns, it is important for psychotherapists to respond in a reasonable way to the possibility of being sued and to support the goal of eliminating bad practice. If the actions of a therapist are not within the standard of care, there *should be* a cause of action available to clients to receive compensation for the damages they suffer.

Civil suits may be based on a number of legal theories. Most of the actions against mental health workers involve a claim of negligence in the performance of professional duties. The complaint may be a result of either an action or an omission on the part of the worker. Therapists are also vulnerable to suits for intentional acts that include breach of confidentiality, libel, slander, and intentional infliction of emotional distress. In addition to negligence and intentional harm claims, most suits include breach of contract claims for failure to perform the agreed-upon service adequately. When a lawyer is preparing a suit against a mental health worker on behalf of a client, every applicable theory for recovery will be used in the initial stages. Usually, the specific facts of the case will determine which legal theory eventually is litigated.

A tort claim is the primary legal theory relied upon by those bringing suit against therapists engaged in clinical practice. A tort is a private or civil wrong for which the court provides a remedy in the form of an action for damages. This differs from a criminal case in several ways. First, a crime is considered a public wrong, violating a standard that is specifically articulated in a statute. Because a crime is a public offense, the state is responsible for prosecuting the case, as contrasted with a civil tort action, where the victim must hire an attorney to initiate a lawsuit. The penalties for violating a criminal statute are usually imprisonment, a related sanction such as probation, or a fine paid to the state. In a civil case, the victim is seeking monetary damages to compensate for the harm caused by the tortious act.

The conduct that is the subject of a tort is not necessarily in violation of a law but is alleged to be a breach of a "reasonable" standard of behavior. In some cases, both a criminal and a civil trial may be held. In these instances, the harmful act is alleged to be in violation of the law and is prosecuted by the state. The victim can still bring a tort claim to recover damages, regardless of the outcome of the criminal trial. The standards for the jury deliberation differ in the two types of trials. In a criminal case, the value of individual freedom requires a jury to find guilt "beyond a reasonable doubt" to convict an accused person. In a civil case, a jury only has to be convinced by a "preponderance" of the evidence to award damages to a plaintiff.

The four elements of every tort are (a) the existence of a duty between two parties; (b) an act or omission that constitutes a breach of that duty; (c) a measurable harm, loss, or damage suffered by one of the parties; and (d) damages that occurred as a direct result of the breach of duty (*Black's*, 1983). *Negligence* is the concept that describes those actions or omissions that constitute the breach of duty, while *malpractice* is a specific term for the negligence of a professional. In the same way that doctors and other professionals are held to certain standards for treatment, mental health workers are evaluated by the courts to determine if the worker practiced in accordance with generally accepted professional norms. A clinician will be found liable for malpractice only when all four elements of the case are proven.

Duty. The existence of a legal duty of care is established when a client-therapist relationship is formed. The question of whether a duty extends to a particular situation is not always clear. In many cases, a therapist may see an individual in connection with another person's treatment. For example, in the treatment of children, it is common to interview a parent or sibling periodically. Clinicians frequently conduct an intake session to determine the client's needs and to determine the appropriate services. If the worker refers the case to another provider rather than agreeing to accept the person as a client, has any duty been created? In other cases, a worker may intervene in a crisis situation such as when a school social worker is called in to interview an adolescent who is talking about suicide. Courts must determine when this type of "relationship" reaches the level of triggering a duty of care.

Breach. Psychotherapists must demonstrate that they exercised the degree of skill and learning commonly applied under like circumstances by the "average, prudent, reputable" member of the profession (*Black's,* 1983). If the therapist deviates from what is considered "reasonable" for the professional in a similar circumstance, it results in a breach of duty. This breach may lead to the responsibility to compensate the individual for damages flowing from the worker's actions. There are a wide range of treatment approaches in psychotherapy. A therapist is not required to choose any particular method of treatment or even to be correct about a diagnosis. The standard only requires the worker to have acted reasonably (Conte & Karasu, 1990). For this type of malpractice claim, an expert is generally required to testify. The role of the expert witnesses in malpractice cases is both to establish the relevant standard of care for the practice area in question and to evaluate the conduct of the professional against the standard (*Pisel v. Stamford Hospital,* 1980). In this way, a jury is not left to its own to decide on the merits of a clinical assessment or the appropriateness of a particular treatment.

Harm, loss, or damage. In a tort action, a person is entitled to recover compensation for all of the consequences of the defendant's harmful act. In malpractice suits against psychotherapists, the client generally must show an impairment in employment or employability including past and future lost earnings or some other direct injury for which an actual loss can be calculated. The client may seek to be reimbursed for the medical costs of the pain and suffering caused by the action, such as ongoing psychotherapy or medical treatment, or may seek general damages for emotional distress, pain and suffering, mental anguish, or loss of reputation as a result of the malpractice (Mackie, 1994). Punitive damages may be available in cases where the behavior of the therapist was malicious or reckless. In these situations, the damage award is meant to punish the defendant beyond the damages directly caused by the harmful act. In psychotherapy malpractice cases, ordinary negligence will not trigger these types of damages but extreme behavior, such as sexual exploitation of a client, may lead a court to apply punitive damages.

Causality. A major problem in cases alleging malpractice in psychotherapy is the difficulty of showing causation of injuries. Where the primary activity of therapy has been talking, it is difficult to prove how a worker caused damage to the client. Moreover, in therapeutic cases, as in other medical malpractice suits, the practitioner may raise the doctrine of informed consent as an affirmative defense. Thus a therapist should be immune from liability if the client has been informed of the risks of a particular type of therapy and has specifically consented to it (Bowman & Mertz, 1996). In many cases, the client may not recognize the treatment as deficient and thus not make the connection between the malpractice and the cause of subsequent injuries.

In one case, a client was being treated for bulimia (*Lujan v. Mansmann, Neuhausel & Genesis Associates,* 1997). The therapists believed her symptoms were consistent with a sexual abuse history. Their treatment included her cutting ties with her family, moving out of state, and hiding from those who may have been responsible for the abuse. The woman later returned to the area and, as a result of a lawsuit her parents had filed against the therapists, she claimed to have learned that the source of her psychological problems was the treatment she had received. The court found that understanding the causal link between negligent treatment and injuries is difficult in this context. The dynamics of the psychiatrist-patient relationship contribute to this finding. Clients do not immediately assume their treating therapists are perpetrating tortious acts through harmful and psychologically damaging treatment. Instead, clients are reluctant either to impute ulterior motives to the advice of their therapist or to automatically question the propriety of the treatment. The appropriate standard of care expected of a therapist is usually established by expert testimony. The client may have had no idea, as a layperson, what "proper" and "improper" treatment was. The client, quite typically, may have assumed her therapist was providing proper treatment and may not have become suspicious. Because of this, most courts give wide latitude to clients in their proof of causation, allowing a case to proceed to trial or to survive a dismissal action until the plaintiff can assemble all of the facts.

Malpractice

An Illinois case, *Horak v. Biris* (1985), examined the elements of malpractice by social workers. The defendant social worker was seeing a married couple in therapy. He was sued by the husband after it was disclosed that the worker was having sexual relations with the wife. The court found that the very nature of the therapist-client relationship gives rise to a clear duty to engage only in activity or conduct that is calculated to improve the client's mental or emotional well-being, and to refrain from any activity or conduct that carries with it a foreseeable and unreasonable risk of harm (*Horak,* 1985, p. 17). When a court finds an injury and legitimate questions about a worker's diagnosis or treatment, the case is likely to proceed to a trial because the assessment of whether the social worker acted reasonably is generally a question for a jury to determine.

Clinicians have been slow to address the issue of malpractice risk reduction, in large part due to the history and values of mental health practice. For example, Jones and Alcabes (1989) postulate that social workers have historically used a "service ideal" model characterized by dedication and concern for the person. Clients are socialized into this idea that the relationship is personal and committed, which reduces the chance of a lawsuit when goals are not met. The combination of the client's positive relationship with and feelings toward the therapist and the stigma of exposing one's own mental health history in court, has made malpractice suits against psychotherapists rare occurrences (Bowman & Mertz, 1996). However, with the increase in the fee-for-service model of practice (private practice as well as agency based), the risk of malpractice has increased. The experience of the helping relationship has become more businesslike, that is, a client hires a professional to perform a service. In the past, most psychotherapy was practiced in agency settings with limited direct costs to clients. Currently, the involvement of insurance payments and costly private practice fee scales have resulted in clients and society having higher expectations for therapy (Conte & Karasu, 1990). This has led to an inevitable increase in litigation when the sometimes unrealistic expectations are not realized.

Mental health malpractice is usually more difficult to prove than medical malpractice. First, there is often physical evidence in medical cases such as an X ray or other visual symptom that attests to the damages suffered by the patient. In therapy, the client's wounds primarily are psychic and difficult to measure or observe precisely, except in cases of egregious professional behavior followed by the onset or worsening of client symptoms or in cases of the sexual exploitation of a client, where malpractice is virtually ensured. The relevant standards of care in medicine are much more specific and defined than in psychotherapy due to the nature of the work. If a patient presents with severe abdominal pain, there are certain tests to be ordered and questions the doctor must ask to diagnose the underlying illness appropriately. Treatment options are limited and prescribed, and breaches of the standard of care are more obvious.

Although there is evidence concerning the rise in malpractice cases against psychotherapists, the absolute numbers remain low. However, a single lawsuit against a professional can jeopardize his or her livelihood, reputation, and career, which makes the statistics irrelevant. There are several reasons that the filing of this type of suit is still a rare occurrence. Conte and Karasu (1990) describe the nature of the work as being significant. In psychotherapy and counseling, the injuries that can be caused by negligent practice are seldom physical ones. The tort law system historically has not been supportive of claims for emotional injury. Usually a physical manifestation such as chronic sleeplessness, weight loss, stress disorders, and the like needs to be shown for a person to recover for these damages. Courts have been skeptical of legal claims for injuries that *could be* fabricated.

Another important reason for the small number of malpractice cases discussed by Conte and Karasu is the uncertainty of clients concerning the nature of mental health treatment. If clients are not sure of the elements of psychotherapy practice and the role of the therapist, they may not know when they have been treated in a substandard manner. The problems that bring people to counseling are highly personal. If someone is suffering emotionally, there is a sense of ownership and responsibility for the problem and the solution. A physical illness is experienced as an intrusion of the body by an organism or a malfunction of a body part. It is much easier for a medical professional to develop a treatment plan because a patient's expectation is to receive a diagnosis of the condition, provision of treatment, medication or medical procedure as suggested by the diagnosis, and a resulting cure or at least a reduction of symptoms and/or pain. The medical professional is expected to fix the physical problem. The onus of the responsibility for fixing emotional problems, by contrast, remains with the client. When there is a bad result in medicine, the blame is placed on the health care provider. When the bad result occurs in counseling, it is likely that the client will look inward.

Standard of Care

Washington interrupted the discussion with an expression of opinion that established his position beyond all question: "It is too probable that no plan we propose will be adopted. Perhaps another dreadful conflict is to be sustained. If to please the people, we offer what we ourselves disapprove, how can we afterwards defend our work? Let us raise a standard to which the wise and the honest can repair. The event is in the hand of God."

Farrand (1923, *The Framing
of the Constitution*, p. 66)

In the mental health arena, the development of a standard of care that can be accepted by the entire field seems as daunting as the tasks facing the framers of the Constitution. There are some characteristics of psychotherapy that complicate efforts to increase the specificity of practice standards. Despite recent gains in understanding biochemical processes, the pain and suffering of a client cannot be isolated to a part of the body, and there are few tests to be ordered that provide truly objective diagnostic information. Many schools of psychotherapy exist, each with its own set of treatment interventions. In many cases, therapists may select interventions from different schools of practice to treat a single client. Being able to match the treatment method to the needs and cultural style of the client is part of the "art" of practice. The difficulty with the eclecticism of the field is translating this desirable flexibility into a standard of care that can be used to set expectations for psychotherapy and for society. Further, one cannot always see the effects, negative or positive, of "talking cures" or other nonphysical interventions. Although startling advances are rare, new developments in research and treatment methods occur continuously. The standard of care thus becomes a moving target (Houston-Vega et al., 1997).

Each of the major professions that provide psychotherapy and counseling services has its own particular standards for practice. Counselors, social workers, psychologists, and other clinicians work with varying styles and orientations. However, there is much more commonality than difference in their work. The standards for practice, or what is reasonable behavior for each profession, can be established by expert testimony from leaders in that profession and by published standards of each of the professional organizations. In one recent case, the Ethical Principles and Code of Conduct of the American Psychological Association were accepted by a Georgia court as evidence of a breach of a standard of care (*Bala v. Powers Ferry Psychological Association,* 1997). The standard of care in psychotherapy is reviewed below without separate analysis of each profession because the general concepts of the duty to care, as well as most of the specific standards governing practice, are the same for each profession. At its roots, the duty involves the ability to make the correct assessment/diagnosis and to implement the proper treatment within a professionally appropriate relationship (Hirsh, 1995).

There is an ongoing and unsolvable debate in the legal community regarding the appropriate standard to use in setting expectations for professionals. Wiener (1992) analyzed this issue as it relates to the standard of care in medical and mental health practice. The issue involves the "technology-forcing" role of the judiciary discussed in Chapter 1. Wiener compared the customary standard with the accepted practice standard. The customary practice standard compares the actions of the professional with the normative practices customarily used by other professionals. The normative or accepted practice standard is based on the practices approved by the profession, not necessarily those customarily followed by its members (pp. 407-409). If the purpose of the tort system is to continually raise the bar for evaluating the performance of professionals, the normative standard accomplishes this goal. The problem is that it may result in "unfair" findings of liability against an individual practitioner as the price of holding the profession to a new standard.

An example of setting a standard of care is needed to clarify this process. The most well-known medical malpractice suit that considered standard of care issues is *Helling v. Carey* (1974). In this case, a woman consulted with two ophthalmologists in 1959. They prescribed contact lenses for her nearsightedness. In 1968, one of the eye doctors gave her a glaucoma test and found that the woman suffered from the disease and had experienced loss of some vision as a result. The woman sued the doctors for failure to conduct a glaucoma screening test at the time of her initial prescription. Expert testimony for the doctors established that due to the low incidence of glaucoma in her age group, it was not customary practice to administer the test routinely. The court found that because the test was harmless and inexpensive, there should have been a duty to perform it on all patients. When a court acts to set a standard outside of customary practice, it does so as a result of a lack of published standards by the profession. As treatment issues arise in psychotherapy, clear responses by professional organizations are the most important protection for practitioners.

As a result, the psychotherapist has to be committed to professional development, through regular supervision/consultation, journal reading, and continuing education opportunities, to stay current with changes in the field. But there are serious questions to be faced concerning the effect of a standard of care on counseling and psychotherapy practice. Any standard, by definition, is inherently conservative. By the time a standard is accepted by the professional community, it has gone through stages including research, peer review, publication, dissemination of the knowledge through professional workshops and the curriculum of professional schools, and, finally, a formal acceptance by professional organizations and publication of the standard to their membership. This process may take several years, by which time research may suggest a new standard. At times, the process is accelerated by a high-profile court case out of which the law determines what the standard of care "ought to be." When a therapist is found liable for having violated a standard developed ex post facto during a trial, professionals quickly respond by shaping their practice to avoid liability. This process, while quicker than the first route, results in standards that are rule-bound. The facts of the case being litigated tend to get diminished, and the "standard" is broadened to similar situations.

The duty to warn has become a well-known standard of care for counselors and psychotherapists. It evolved from the influential *Tarasoff* decision in which the therapist was required to use reasonable care to protect the potential victims of harm threatened by a client. The California Supreme Court determined that the protection could take several forms, including a direct warning to the victim. The reasonableness of the intervention can be determined only from the facts of a particular situation. Out of this holding, the professional community has latched onto the duty to warn as *the* professional standard (Slovenko, 1989). As a result, the clinical judgment of the professional in responding to a potentially violent client is unduly restricted by adherence to what is misconstrued as a legal requirement. The formality of such a rule may be comforting for practitioners but is not necessarily in the best interests of the client. While a duty to warn is one intervention, a therapist could alternatively or additionally seek commitment, evaluate for psychotropic medication, or inform the family so that they can initiate protective actions. A warning may be too strong of a response in some cases, while being insufficient in other cases. When standards for professional behavior are developed in legal cases, they seldom are the type of standards that prescribe a broad course of conduct for the professional community. Such standards of care must be developed by the mental health professions as a result of research and dialogue.

Malpractice law has developed different standards of care for psychotherapists and other mental health professionals by defining the duty of care as the ordinary care that would be taken, under the particular circumstances, by a practitioner trained and experienced in the particular school of therapy being practiced, as long as the approach is recognized by a "respectable minority" within the profession. The respectable minority rule allows for some flexibility and creativity within the profession but clearly supports the mainstream schools of practice. The respectable minority rule is one of those legal concepts that appears good on paper but, in practice, is a disincentive to creativity and progress. The dilemma about how to maintain standards while promoting growth and development in a field is a universal challenge. In many accreditation organizations, the standards for the institutions they regulate include language that allows for the development of alternative programs and various ways to meet standards. However, an agency, hospital, or school usually has strong reservations about attempting anything alternative or new, out of fear that it will result in a loss of accreditation. This is true even when the accrediting agency attempts to encourage innovation. The costs of being different are high. For mental health practitioners, the liability concerns arising out of the limited holdings of high-profile cases act in similar fashion to stifle creativity and research in developing new approaches to practice.

Schopp and Wexler (1989) warn that although published guidelines can go a long way toward insulating professionals from liability, they can serve as a double-edged sword. Courts may examine these standards literally so that a clinician who veers from the protocol because of an unusual confluence of facts or individual characteristics presumably might be found to be outside of the standard of care. Although some standards are crystallized in well-articulated guidelines, most standards leave extensive room for professional judgment. Schopp and Wexler identify problems with explicit standards. Essentially, they argue that the standards create an interest of the worker not to be sued. This interest, at times, can compete with the fiduciary duty of the worker to the client and may result in promoting undesirable conduct by the worker that is not in the interest of the client or society.

These arguments and the case scenarios that are presented as evidence by Schopp and Wexler fail to consider professionally developed standards. Rather, the authors focus on narrow legal rules such as the prohibition of certain historically abusive interventions with mentally challenged clients. The resulting analysis of the duty of the worker thus has limited application. The broader issue of whether the professional organizations should develop clear practice standards for specific practice settings or situations requires separate analysis. Close examination of professional standards, such as those governing the treatment of depression, recovered memories of child sexual abuse, suicide risk assessment, and many others, reveals that professional judgment is an important component of the standards. They are not so prescriptive as to remove all decision making from a professional. Rather, they provide general guidelines that can be used by clinicians to structure their practice and can be used by courts to assess the appropriateness of clinical behavior. In professionally generated standards, the interests of the client are best protected by adherence to the norm, but reasonable practice demands that these standards not be considered dogma. If challenged in a malpractice case, evidence of the standard of care would be presented by an expert witness who would also be questioned about how the defendant clinician's treatment departed from the standard of care. The clinician would then have the opportunity to present competing testimony as to why this action was reasonable, given the circumstances.

In practice, there are relatively few issues that benefit from formal treatment standards. Some of the expectations are commonsense, ordinary professional behavior. Among the basic expectations, therapists should keep adequate records; maintain client confidentiality; conduct thorough assessments; obtain informed consent for treatment interventions; arrange for coverage of client emergencies when absent from practice; refrain from dual relationships with clients, specifically including any sexual relationships with current or former clients; remain honest in all matters related to the business of practice; recognize when unqualified to treat a client and refer the case to a specialist; and receive clinical supervision/consultation and professional development on a regular basis. The overriding duty is to act so as not to cause harm to the client.

The correct assessment and diagnosis of a client is the threshold task of the mental health professional. In the preliminary sessions, the duty of the worker is to recognize emotional or psychological conditions that are reasonably evident from a clinical or intake interview. A diagnosis does not have to be correct. As long as the worker possesses the degree of learning, skill, and experience expected of someone in that profession, and the worker exercises reasonable and ordinary care in the assessment process, no liability will attach. Part of the expected standard in the assessment process is to refer the client for evaluations by other professionals when the worker is unqualified to make the diagnosis. For example, in seeing a child who was referred for counseling due to nightly bed-wetting, the psychotherapist would be expected to make a referral to a pediatrician or urologist for a physical examination to rule out medical causes. Failure to use due care in conducting assessments is a relatively soft standard that provides little guidance for professionals other than a general message to be careful and act professionally. For this reason, regular supervision is critically important because there is a greater opportunity to catch mistakes in the assessment and diagnosis of a client when the evaluations are being reviewed by a senior colleague.

Similarly, in the treatment process, the standard of due care is not well defined in most areas. Therapists must be aware of the basic duties arising out of the treatment phase. If the treatment is not resulting in client improvement or if the client is decompensating, the therapist should discuss this with the client and arrange for alternative treatment, or at least additional supervision and consultation (Mackie, 1994). As has been previously discussed, bad results do not support a malpractice action without evidence of negligence or malfeasance by the worker. But bad results without some reasonable professional response by the worker may justify a malpractice action.

A more specific standard of care is required in those areas of practice that could be considered specializations. These include such practice situations as evaluating the need to commit a client with psychiatric problems, including suicide assessment and case management of clients who may be dangerous to others; treating various types of disorders such as post-traumatic stress disorder, schizophrenia, and depression; or the use of diagnostic testing. The protocols that have been developed in the research and literature must be familiar to the worker and should be followed in practice unless a specific client situation suggests otherwise. In these situations, supervision provides the worker with a second set of eyes to view the clinical facts, and should the case proceed to a legal complaint, the supervision is evidence of reasonable professional behavior.

Clinicians who represent themselves as experts or specialists in an area of practice are held to a higher standard of care than an ordinary clinician. A client seeking help from a specialist would reasonably expect that person to have an advanced level of knowledge or skill. As a result, the expert testimony establishing the standard of care would have to distinguish the standard for someone who specializes in the area of practice. For example, clinicians who advertise or otherwise represent themselves as experts in eating disorders would be judged against the standard of care for an expert in this field. Although a "general practitioner" therapist working with an adolescent might not be aware of the need for a medical hospitalization for a client as a result of weight loss, the specialist would be expected to be knowledgeable concerning the extent and risks of physical symptoms.

Some commentators have criticized malpractice law for falling short as a vehicle for setting standards for practice (Wiener, 1992). If the standard is not explicit, the cases turn on the testimony of one or two expert witnesses rather than the voice of the professional community. If all expert witnesses spoke with a clear commitment to the current practices of the profession, or if the experts could articulate an evolving treatment standard that all practitioners should be held to, the court process would result in evolving and improving standards. Wiener argues for the need to make the standard of care in mental health practice as explicit as possible, even if it is temporary until newer, more effective procedures become accepted (p. 421). He recommends that the best way to develop professional standards is to create a pool of practitioners, representative of the professional community, to review the assessment and treatment plan of the defendant psychotherapist to determine whether they find the conduct outside of practice norms. Although impractical, the concept of encouraging the standard to emerge from the professional community rather than the adversarial court process is laudable.

One way the professional community may be able to influence the law so as to create a more reasonable legal process is to work for legislative reform of the malpractice system. In Illinois, for example, the legislature has enacted statutory language that requires supporting documentation in order to file a lawsuit. In "healing art" malpractice cases (this language is used by the statute), where the client seeks damages for injuries caused by the actions of the clinician, the client must provide an affidavit from a mental health professional from the same class of license as the defendant clinician, who is knowledgeable in the relevant issues involved in the suit. This consulting clinician, on the basis of reviewing the claims, must submit a written report verifying that there is a reasonable and meritorious cause of action (*Manning v. Crockett,* 1996). Processes, such as those outlined in the Illinois statute, serve a gatekeeping purpose that prevents spurious claims from reaching the court system where a sympathetic jury could award damages and set an unwarranted practice standard. This is another example of the effectiveness of professional self-advocacy that proactively influences the way the courts deal with cases involving mental health clinicians.

The most important agenda for the mental health professions must be to further define the standard of care for practice. The standards for professional behavior and ethical conduct provide guidance as to how the professional should act while clinical standards of care help to define the essential elements of competent practice. Absent the standards from the professional organizations, the courts will use the reasonableness standard, which gives them the discretion necessary to achieve situational justice. However, this often results in new standards that are antitherapeutic for clients (Wexler, 1996) and inappropriate for clinicians. The presence of professional standards permits neither the judge nor the jury to determine the appropriate standard of care. Rather, the professions set the standards and the courts merely enforce them.

MANAGING A TREATMENT RELATIONSHIP

Canst thou not minister to a mind diseased,
Pluck from the memory a rooted sorrow,
Raze out the written troubles of the brain,
And with some sweet oblivious antidote
Cleanse the fraught bosom of that perilous stuff
Which weighs upon the heart?

William Shakespeare
(*Macbeth,* act 5, sc. 3)

The management of the treatment relationship is complex and challenging. Each client brings a unique set of concerns and requires the clinician to enter into a relationship. Practice seldom provides opportunities for the kind of cure requested by Macbeth. Without a potion or magic wand, success in counseling/therapy requires a partnership characterized by trust, honesty, and integrity. At times, all clinicians experience the conflicts of personal needs, feelings, and desires leaking into the professional relationship. Many of these issues are quickly recognized and resolved by clinicians or processed and discussed in supervision. The treatment relationship requires professionals to act in the interests of clients at all times. It is the failure of this basic duty that can lead to legal consequences for practitioners.

Conte and Karasu (1990) identify Furrow's four general obligations owed to clients as a basis for the legal duty not to misuse the therapeutic relationship. These obligations are all related to the effective management of a professional relationship:

- The clinical duty of neutrality, which involves the proper handling of transference issues
- The obligation to obtain regular supervision, particularly when managing a difficult transference issue
- The duty of nonabandonment
- The duty to stop treatment when it appears to be ineffective or harmful to the client

Taken together, these obligations to clients arise out of the unique relationship in counseling/ psychotherapy. The fiduciary character of the relationship has been discussed previously. The therapist must act in the interests of the client at all times. There is a unilateral quality to the expectations in that it is the therapist who is obliged to keep personal feelings and personal interests under control to be fully available to the client. The therapeutic process rests on this important element because the client must be able to trust in the motives of the worker to let down defenses sufficiently to deal with difficult emotions. Clients often become vulnerable in this state of reduced defenses and trust. When the therapist has acted so that self-interests are implicated, the boundaries of the professional relationship are crossed and the therapist has violated the standard of care. This violation may include such self-interests as using the client to fulfill needs for friendship, sexual partnering, monetary gain, or power/control.

Informed Consent

Ray had an unhappy childhood. His father had been abusive to his mother and once tried to commit suicide. His paternal grandmother was domineering and controlling, constantly criticizing Ray's mother. His unhappiness continued through the death of his father, the remarriage and quick divorce of his mother, and his own brief marriage that ended while he was in medical school. A second marriage produced two children but his second wife left him. A third marriage began well but deteriorated into tension and conflict. Although his business thrived, it was a source of great stress. His second wife sued for custody of his two children who had lived with him since she had left the home. He began to drink too much and misused valium. Ray became suicidal but would not consistently take the antidepressant medication prescribed by several psychiatrists. Finally, he admitted himself into Chestnut Lodge, a well-known private psychiatric facility. He was diagnosed with narcissistic personality disorder and was treated with long-term psychoanalysis. The staff decided not to give him antidepressive medication as an ancillary treatment.

Ray did not improve noticeably in the seven months spent in residence at Chestnut Lodge. In fact, his mental health regressed; he paced the floor endlessly and was occasionally assaultive. Finally, his mother convinced him that he should transfer to the Silver Hill Foundation Hospital. There he was diagnosed as suffering from a psychotic depressive reaction, agitated type, and was placed on psychotropic medication with supportive therapy. Within two weeks, his agitation decreased and he began to participate in group sessions in a meaningful way. After three months, Ray was discharged.

In addition to a claim for failure to diagnose and treat his condition, Ray also sued Chestnut Lodge for failure to obtain his informed consent by failing to disclose to and discuss with him the alternative therapies (including drug treatment) and the costs/benefits of each of these alternatives (*Osheroff v. Chestnut Lodge,* based on case history summarized in Malcolm, 1986).

The professional duty to obtain informed consent prior to the provision of mental health treatment is based on the values of society and the helping professions. American society values freedom from government intrusion and is committed to guaranteeing core civil rights. The helping professions generally support the value of client self-determination and individual dignity. Taken together, there is a strong basis for ensuring that all clients understand the services that are available, the risks of the interventions, the alternative treatments, and the right to refuse treatment or to withdraw consent at any time. References to the importance of obtaining informed consent for medical treatment date at least as far back as Plato (Reamer, 1990), and contemporary professional ethical codes support informed consent. Despite this, the history of respecting clients' autonomy in decision making has been inconsistent. In many cases, clients have been marginalized and professionals have neglected to disclose completely the nature of the treatment. The reasons for the reticence of some professionals to include clients in decision making are complex. The effects of paternalism, racism, classism, and elitism may contribute to the problem. Some clinicians may feel that

    they know the best course of treatment as a result of their expertise;

    the client would not be able to fully understand or appreciate the nature of the treatment;

    a full disclosure of the goals of a particular treatment might skew the client's reported progress; or

    the client may make a poor choice and refuse the "best" treatment, thus interfering with the professional's ability to help the client regain optimal health and functioning.

The issue of informed consent has received the most attention in the mental health field. Most clinicians do involve clients in shared decision making but accept the reality that there are some circumstances in which a client is unable to consent to needed treatment. The current view of informed consent strikes a balance between the promotion of client autonomy and the promotion of health (Appelbaum, Lidz, & Meisel, 1987). In many states, the requirements of informed consent are detailed in statutes. The remaining states have no specific law but rely on the case law to set the requirements for effective consent (Simon, 1992, p. 129).

The legal bases for the duty of informed consent arise from two distinct theories. A *tort* previously has been defined as a private wrong done by one person or entity to another. The failure by a mental health professional to obtain valid consent prior to treatment may be challenged as either professional negligence or an intentional act, both of which are tort claims. The standard of care in counseling and psychotherapy includes the requirement that, where reasonable, a clinician must receive the consent of the client or authorized representative to begin treatment. A therapist who neglects this duty is at risk of being sued by a client. Clients may be surprised by an outcome occurring as a direct result of a treatment intervention. Some situations may involve a deliberate concealment of facts from a client. In one case, an agency that made use of rage therapy was sued by a client when she lapsed into a catatonic state following one of these sessions. Among other things, the suit claimed that the therapists intentionally failed to inform her of this risk, however slight, when she agreed to participate in the therapy (*Lujan v. Mansmann,* 1997).

In cases where there was no consent at all and the therapy involved physical touching, the client may have an action for assault. *Assault and battery* is defined as "any unlawful touching of another which is without justification or excuse" (*Black's,* 1983). The landmark case *Schloendorff v. Society of New York Hospital* (1914) established that a doctor who "performs an operation without his patient's consent commits an assault, for which he is liable in damages" (p. 93). In a Rhode Island case, a client confided in a psychiatric clinical nurse specialist that she had been sexually abused. The nurse, a holistic practitioner, treated the client using therapeutic massage, which triggered a reexperiencing of the abuse trauma. The client claimed that the therapist had not educated her about the procedures or the risks ("Woman Testifies," 1994). Although this case was not brought as an assault complaint, the client seemed to have a strong case to do so.

The second legal concept on which the duty of informed consent is based is the constitutional principle of *personal liberty,* which limits the states' power to deprive any person of life, liberty, or property without due process, unless there is a compelling justification. An informed consent has two main elements. The first is the opportunity to be informed, and the second is the opportunity to reject treatment. It is the latter element that is the true threat to personal liberty. If it is a state agency or a court that initiates the treatment of a client, the case takes on significance beyond the tort-based duties described above.

Treatment without consent, such as forced medication, participation in therapy, or involuntary commitment, triggers constitutional protections against governmental imposition in private lives. The government may still be allowed to require interventions for the protection of the individual or society, but this may be done only following timely notice to the client, a legitimate hearing, evidence demonstrating a compelling need, and an opportunity for the client and his or her representative to refute the evidence. The burden is on the government to demonstrate the need and to require that the client be treated in the least restrictive environment. The state has an interest sufficiently compelling to support treatment against the wishes of the client. When individuals are unable to care for themselves or determine their own best interests, the state assumes its *parens patriae* power to make decisions for the individual (Winick, 1986). When a client is dangerous to others, the state asserts its police power to control behavior. When the government demonstrates either of these conditions and provides due process hearings, mandated treatment can be constitutionally acceptable.

Informed consent involves two levels of agreement. For every client who enters treatment, the clinician should have a standard form for apprising the individual of the basic policies and procedures of the agency or practice. This includes such issues as payment for services, cancellations, confidentiality, interactions with third-party payers, and other similar matters. This information enables the client to be informed about the basic elements of the contract for services so as to make an educated decision about whether to participate. Although the literature has not tended to view the initial contracting issues as informed consent, it is important to do so. Beginning with the first telephone contact through the beginning stages of evaluation and treatment, clients need to be partners in the therapeutic process. Several authors have identified the efficacy of a consultant model during this stage, stressing clear communication with clients *about* the treatment experience itself as a means of handling clients' negative feelings as they arise and to clarify expectations about the treatment (Korner, 1995; Packman, Cabot, & Bongar, 1994).

A second level of consent is required after the initial assessment process is complete. The client must understand and consent to the specific intervention strategies that will be used in the treatment. The elements of an effective consent to treatment have been addressed by a number of authors (Appelbaum et al., 1987; Reamer, 1994; Regehr & Antle, 1997). Their recommendations for topics to be addressed with clients include the goals of treatment and the relationship of the interventions to the goals;

the advantages or disadvantages of the intervention;

the potential risks of the intervention, including effects on health, emotions, and relationships;

alternatives to the proposed treatment strategy;

the risks of refusing treatment; and

the anticipated duration and costs of the treatment.

It is important to consider how to make the process of informed consent a part of the therapeutic experience for the client and how the client's involvement in the decision making can be an intervention by itself. Because it is difficult to anticipate in advance the full extent of the risks of treatment, a standard form such as the model in Houston-Vega et al. (1997) anticipates many problems. It is imperative, however, that clinicians not rely on preprinted forms signed by clients to accomplish the goals of informed consent. In one study done in Colorado after that state passed a disclosure requirement covering all therapists, researchers found that therapists were obeying the letter of the law but were using forms that had a high readability grade level. The authors of the study questioned whether clients were truly being informed of relevant information in an accessible manner (Handelsmen, Martinez, & Geisendorfer, 1995). The law, from statutes and cases, requires clinicians to obtain informed consent. It is up to practitioners to discover how to integrate it into practice in a meaningful way.

For a consent to be valid, the law requires that it be effectuated by a competent party; the client consent must be voluntary; and the consent must be based on sufficient and accurate information. These requirements ensure the legitimacy of the process.

Capacity to consent. This baseline consideration is the most obvious but also the most complex. There are a number of conditions under which a client would be unable to give informed consent to treatment. First, minor children, in most situations, must receive the approval of a parent or legal guardian to participate in counseling or psychotherapy. There are several statutory exceptions to this general rule that vary by state. Some of these statutory exceptions are in cases where the minor child is emancipated, or where the legislature has determined that a youth would not seek treatment for certain conditions if parental consent was required (Saltzman & Proch, 1990). These services include abortion/birth control, suicide, and substance abuse counseling. The exceptions are designed to encourage minors to access needed help. Even when a child requires parental consent to receive treatment, practitioners should strongly consider seeking parallel consent directly from the child. Although there is not a legal requirement, the same principles that support the active collaboration with clients as being advantageous to the goals of treatment apply to work with minors.

The competence of a person with mental illness to consent to or refuse mental health treatment has been broadly debated for years. On one side of the debate are those who advocate for the rights of persons with mental illness to be able to make the same decisions about treatment as anyone else. Opposing them are advocates who argue that it is inappropriate to let incompetent individuals "rot with their rights on" (Gutheil, 1980). Grisso and Appelbaum (1995) identify three legal standards for determining competence to consent to treatment: understanding, reasoning, and appreciation. The authors are among a group of researchers currently developing instruments to measure a client's competence to consent. The current state of the law is in flux. Until recently, the controversy concerning informed consent has largely ignored the question of the benefits and detriments to the client (Wexler & Winick, 1992).

Counselors, social workers, and other mental health workers do not conduct many of the competency evaluations required for voluntary admissions (*Zinermon v. Burch,* 1990) or involuntary placements, because most states require these to be done by physicians. However, it is important that clinicians understand the basic concepts and support continued research to provide better guidance as to what constitutes competency. There are clinical and legal ramifications to this issue. For the practitioner, the issue is not just whether a client can refuse needed treatment. If a clinician receives a consent to treat from an individual who is not cognitively able to understand or appreciate what it is that is being agreed to, there may be liability for failure to obtain informed consent. Most mental health professionals desire to support the self-determination and active involvement of their clients. The presence of a mental illness or cognitive disability does not automatically strip a person of his or her ability to give informed consent to mental health treatment; rather, it places an added duty on the clinician to obtain meaningful informed consent.

Sufficiency of information. How much information does a client need to have to give valid consent to a treatment? The basic concept involved in this question is whether the client had sufficient understanding of risks, benefits, duration of treatment, and alternatives to make an actual choice about participation. In the *Osheroff* case that began this section, the client was not consulted about the decision to proceed with psychotherapy without an adjunct treatment regimen of psychotropic medication. Further, the client did not understand that the treatment plan called for inpatient services to last for an extended period of time. The courts are particularly concerned about the quality of the consent when the clinician has a monetary interest in the treatment. In *Osheroff*, the private hospital certainly derived economic benefits from the long-term inpatient treatment.

In another frequently cited case, *Moore v. Regents of University of California* (1990), a physician strongly recommended to his patient that he have surgery to remove his spleen. The California Supreme Court chastised the physician for failing to inform the patient that the physician had an economic interest in extracting body tissues for the purposes of creating a cell line. The court said that a physician who is seeking a patient's consent for a medical procedure must, to satisfy his fiduciary duty and to obtain a patient's informed consent, disclose personal interests unrelated to the patient's health, whether research or economic, that may affect his medical judgment (p. 485).

The standard for determining whether a client has been adequately informed has changed during the past 40 years. Originally, the reasonable *professional* standard was used to evaluate whether a client had been adequately informed prior to treatment (Regehr & Antle, 1997). Under this analysis, the court would question whether the level of information given to the client was what an average professional would judge to be adequate and appropriate for the client to make an informed decision (*Salgo v. Stanford University,* 1957). In recent cases, courts have changed to the reasonable *patient* standard (*Canterbury v. Spence,* 1972). The rule that has emerged is that the clinician is required to disclose all information that a reasonable person, in that client's circumstances, would find material to a decision either to undergo or to forgo treatment (Appelbaum et al., 1987, p. 45).

Coercion, undue influence. Sometimes it is obvious and intentional, while other times it is subtle and subconscious. But the effects of the differential power in the relationship between the client and the professional may lead to undue influence in decision making by clients. There are many times in practice when professionals want clients to enter a program, agree to take medication, or follow through on a particular course of therapy. Some clients are particularly susceptible to influence and thus jeopardize the validity of their consent (Reamer, 1990). Coercive power comes into play if the clients sense that they will be adversely affected by failure to conform to expectations (Epstein, 1985). The fiduciary relationship requires that the professional act in the best interests of the client. Although most practitioners do so, there may not be adequate consideration of the ability of some clients to decide on treatment options. The information about treatments may be highly technical. Clients may be unable to adequately consent unless the practitioner has taken the time to fully explain the options using understandable terms. Because clients trust the professionals to act in their interests, there may be a tendency for both workers and clients to "leave it to the professional" to determine the choice of intervention. Practitioners need to be aware of the doctrine of informed consent and to initiate procedures in which clients are partners in the process of change and are in control of their health care decisions.

The question of informed consent in human services becomes more complex when the court or other agency with authority has ordered the client to participate (Regehr & Antle, 1997). There is a fundamental conflict between the statutes and case law on informed consent that stress self-determination and the role that many clinicians play in educational, mental health, corrections, and child welfare settings. This question may be more of an ethical dilemma than a legal one. It is likely that courts will recognize evaluation and mandated treatment situations as excluded from the requirements of informed consent, but it is important for each agency and clinician to determine the extent of consent that can be obtained from clients, regardless of their status.

Exceptions. Rozovsky (1984) summarizes the major categories of exceptions to the requirement for informed consent. The most commonly cited exception is for emergencies. If an adolescent stops in to see a school counselor and is in crisis, the counselor is not necessarily required to obtain parental consent prior to providing counseling services. If a client has ingested dangerous amounts of alcohol or drugs, a worker may initiate an intervention for medical attention or a detoxification program for the client. However, there are limitations to the emergency exception. First, the client must be in some physical or emotional jeopardy to justify the immediate need for treatment. Otherwise, if the client could consent to the intervention in the future without suffering harm due to the delay, the rationale for supporting the exception would be eliminated. Similarly, when an emergency treatment is undertaken, the clinician needs to obtain an informed consent as soon as practicable, once the crisis has abated or once the client is capable of consenting.

The requirement that a clinician disclose information to the client concerning the intended treatment is not absolute. If giving certain information to a client would create a substantial risk of seriously upsetting the client, and affect the client's ability to "dispassionately weigh the risks of refusing treatment," the clinician has discretion not to inform the client fully (*Cobbs v. Grant,* 1972). These situations, called *therapeutic privilege* in the literature (Reamer, 1994), are classic second-guessing opportunities. The clinician who is considering withholding some information about the treatment due to concerns that the client would be unduly influenced by the risks, should seek out supervision to obtain a second opinion before proceeding with the intended course of treatment. This will provide evidence as to the reasonableness of the professional judgment and behavior, and will protect clients from overly patriarchal clinicians.

Clients may waive the requirement for informed consent by asking professionals not to tell them about the risks of treatment. In these cases, clients may feel more comfortable not knowing, implicitly trusting the judgment and motives of the clinician. The worker should document the decision of the client and require a signature attesting to the client's wishes. The issue of client waivers is complex because the motives and capacity of a client may be difficult to determine. If a client is unable to comprehend the content of the choices described by the professional, the overwhelmed client's response might be to waive the right to know. Questions about the legitimacy of a client waiver are difficult to determine, and clinicians should attempt to explore the motivation of a request for a waiver with the client (Meisel, 1979).

The rise in managed care involvement in the provision of mental health services has precipitated a serious problem in the area of informed consent. Many providers have contracts with managed care companies that include nondisclosure clauses (gag rules). These clauses prohibit a clinician from discussing with a client any limitations imposed by the managed care organization (Corcoran & Vandiver, 1996). For example, if a worker felt a particular therapy would be helpful to a client, but the managed care company did not cover that type of intervention, the provider would be prohibited from discussing that option with the client. On its face, a nondisclosure clause violates the standard of care for informed consent. The withholding of information from a client concerning an alternative treatment compromises the historic fiduciary nature of the client-worker relationship and eviscerates the validity of a consent. Clinicians should be cautious when entering into contracts with managed care providers and must work on a policy level using administrative and legislative advocacy to ban the use of nondisclosure clauses.

Summary. The relationship between individuals and professionals in society is experiencing a shift from an expert model to a partnership model. The ramifications of this consumerism-influenced development are significant for the human services. The use of informed consent is an important component of the effective treatment of clients and can be used as a therapeutic intervention that gives clients a sense of control over their treatment and a validation of their competency to improve their life situation (Jensen, Josephson, & Frey, 1989). When courts have examined informed consent in mental health and counseling relationships, the analysis has focused on the genuineness of the process. Clinicians need to be aware of the expectation that, in most cases, clients can and should make legitimate choices about treatment. An uninformed or invalid consent is tantamount to no consent at all.

Dual Relationships

"Well, I appreciate what you're doing for Savannah. I really do," I said, feeling dreadfully uncomfortable.
"Have you been lonely?"
"Lowenstein, you are speaking to the prince of solitude . . ."
"Loneliness is killing me lately," she said, and I could feel her eyes upon me.
"I don't know what to say."
"I'm very attracted to you, Tom. No, don't leave just yet. Please listen to me."
"Don't tell me, Doctor," I said, rising to go. "I can't even think about this now. I've considered myself incapable of love for so long that the mere thought of it terrifies me. Let's be friends. Good friends . . . I can't even consider falling in love with someone as beautiful as you are and as different from me. It's too dangerous." (Pat Conroy, 1986, *The Prince of Tides,* p. 344)

In the novel *The Prince of Tides,* Tom, an unemployed football coach, went to New York to help his twin sister, Savannah, who was being treated in an inpatient psychiatric hospital. Dr. Lowenstein, Savannah's psychiatrist, began to see Tom to gather information relevant to her treatment of his sister. Soon the sessions became therapeutic for Tom. Dr. Lowenstein engaged Tom to coach her son in football. She socialized with him at parties, met with him at her home, and, eventually, they developed a sexual relationship. Although the interaction between the two is not the main focus of the book, the gradual slide into different roles by the psychiatrist clearly illustrates how dual relationships develop. One can question whether Tom was a "client," triggering the duty not to participate in dual relationships, but he was a family member of a client who was participating in her treatment. The problems associated with this type of entanglement can have negative implications for the therapeutic relationship and expose the clinician to legal and professional sanctions.

Dual relationships are defined as occurring when a therapist engages in another significantly different relationship with the client. The two relationships may run concurrently or sequentially (Pope, 1991). If this definition seems less than definitive, it is because there is not clear agreement as to what constitutes a dual relationship and when assumption of a different role by the therapist results in harm to the client. The different roles may include social, business/financial, religious, or romantic relationships. There is near-universal agreement that sexual intimacy with a current client is harmful and always prohibited but less certainty exists for other roles.

Some authors argue that breaks in and disruptions of professional boundaries are unavoidable, and the focus of inquiry should be on *exploitation,* not *duality* in the relationship (Bader, 1994; Clarkson, 1994). One example of the difficulty with strict enforcement of a ban on dual relationships is pastoral counseling, where the use of spiritual interventions may appropriately mix with more traditional interventions (Richards & Potts, 1995). The dual relationship has been explored in situations where multiple roles are common such as working in a small town where ongoing extratherapeutic relationships with clients are common and sometimes unavoidable (Sobel, 1992) and also in work with isolated men with AIDS who need friendship as well as therapy from their clinicians (Madden, 1995). Further, Rinella and Gerstein (1994) argue that contemporary psychotherapy models are very different from the psychoanalytic models under which the strict prohibition of dual relationships was established. Therefore, the professional community needs to rethink the underlying moral and ethical rationale for the rules in this area.

There are ethical and legal components to the issue of dual relationships. The question of liability for a clinician arises when there is client harm, exploitation, or a destructive impact on treatment resulting from the boundary violation. Despite agreement about these dynamics, there are no clear guidelines for practice except in the area of sexual relationships (Youngren & Skorka, 1992). A prohibition of dual relationships in professional standards provides evidence to the legal system of a breach of a duty of care. For example, the American Psychological Association ethics code (1992) contains a significant statement guiding the behavior of its members. Rule 6(a) provides as follows: Psychologists are continually cognizant of their own needs and of their potentially influential position vis-à-vis persons such as clients, students, and subordinates. They avoid exploiting the trust and dependency of such persons. Psychologists make every effort to avoid dual relationships that could impair their professional judgment or increase the risk of exploitation. Examples of such dual relationships include, but are not limited to, research and treatment of employees, students, supervisees, close friends, or relatives.

The most important factor in determining whether a dual relationship is inappropriate is the degree to which the nontherapy role affects the decision making of the clinician. If the role elevates the interests of the clinician in the interaction, the client's needs may be subjugated. When initially considering a secondary role with a client, the risk of injury to the client may seem low. However, when examined retrospectively, the conduct may be judged differently. Some of the dynamics of dual relationships change with the role of the worker. If the professional is acting in a clinical role, the degree of trust and dependence and the level of intimacy increase the potential for dual relationships to be exploitive and end badly. A worker in a case management or advocacy role is not dealing with the transference issues and may have more flexibility in assuming roles.

In one case, a counselor who ran a homelessness prevention program allowed her clients, a young parent and her child, to rent a room in her family's house. The family had rented the room in the past to persons in the community who needed temporary, cheap living space. The difference, in this case, was that the tenant was being referred through the counselor's agency. Because the professional relationship was nonclinical, and the rent was nominal and below market rates, there was no strong rationale for prohibiting the dual relationship. However, this type of situation poses risks to the professional should there be a negative outcome of the case. The clients could claim that the worker had an economic interest in fostering their dependency.

Transference/Sexual Relationships

The most exploitive and damaging of the dual relationships a clinician can engage in is a sexual relationship with a client. The prohibition is clearly and consistently enforced by the courts. In some states, legislatures have passed statutes that criminalize this activity. In Wisconsin (1984), it is a felony for a therapist to engage in intentional sexual contact with a client during an ongoing professional relationship. The crime is treated much like a statutory rape against a minor child in that consent is not a defense. The rationale is that the dynamics of the therapeutic relationship make it impossible for there to be actual consent, especially to a behavior that has such a clear history of leaving a client with psychological injuries. Several other states, including Minnesota, Maine, Michigan, and Colorado, have similar *criminal patient sexual abuse* statutes while many other states have specific administrative regulations prohibiting the behavior (Levin & Hill, 1992). Some statutes use language that prohibits intimate contact during *medical treatment,* a term that includes counseling and psychotherapy services. The clear purpose of these statutes is to "protect patients from abuse by professionals who, under the guise of treatment, take advantage of the patient's vulnerabilities to achieve a sexual purpose" (*Michigan v. Regts,* 1996, p. 898).

The therapeutic relationship is frequently intense and emotionally close. Clients may become confused about their feelings in the intimate environment of the clinician's office. They may fantasize that the unconditional acceptance, support, and caring of the professional could be an ongoing part of their lives. *Transference* is the term used to denote a client's emotional reaction to a therapist. It is generally applied to the projection of feelings, thoughts, and wishes onto the clinician, who has come to represent some person from the client's past (*Steadman's,* 1982). Inappropriate emotions, both hostile and loving, directed toward the therapist must be dealt with appropriately. The crucial factor in the therapist-client relationship that leads to the imposition of legal liability is that the course of treatment and counseling is predicated upon handling the transference phenomenon. In the past, some courts have not understood the concept of transference and have decided cases on the basis of consent. The professional community must continue to educate legal professionals concerning the dynamics of transference and the centrality of the process to clinical practice. In *Simmons v. United States* (1986), a federal appeals court concluded that the clinician had failed to handle the romantic feelings of his client, thereby breaching his duty of care.

> After consideration of all the testimony, the court found: The impacts of sexual involvement with one's counselor are more severe than the impacts of merely "having an affair" for two major reasons: First, because the client's attraction is based on transference, the sexual contact is ordinarily akin to engaging in sexual activity with a parent, and carries with it the feelings of shame, guilt and anxiety experienced by incest victims. Second, the client is usually suffering from all or some of the psychological problems that brought him or her into therapy to begin with. As a result, the client is especially vulnerable to the added stress created by the feelings of shame, guilt and anxiety produced by the incestuous nature of the relationship, and by the sense of betrayal that is felt when the client eventually learns that she is not "special" as she had been led to believe, and that her trust has been violated. (*Simmons v. United States,* 1986, p. 1367)

When a clinician experiences a romantic attraction to a client or when the client gives evidence of having strong feelings toward the clinician in the course of treatment, supervision is critically important to manage the clinical issues. It would seem to be obvious that clinicians would recognize the impropriety of acting on these feelings but, unfortunately, there are many cases in which that did not occur. The justifications made during trials include statements such as "this was a mutual attraction in which nobody forced anything . . . it just happened"; "the treatment had already ended before the romantic relationship began"; or "the person wasn't directly my client, I only saw her in connection with the treatment of her family member." These rationalizations are disturbing to read but the responses of supervisors are equally troubling. In *Masterson v. Board of Examiners* (1995), a clinical supervisor failed to recognize the seriousness of a dual relationship and provided minimal guidance (the client names have been changed).

Dr. Masterson began treatment with Ferne around issues relating to her relationship with Claudia. What had begun as a friendship between the two women had gotten more intimate and romantic but, as time went on, the relationship deteriorated. During this time, Dr. Masterson held some sessions with both Ferne and Claudia. Soon after, it is alleged that the doctor negligently ended treatment with Ferne, referring her to an inpatient facility, even though her insurance would not cover the costs of the treatment. Dr. Masterson began seeing Claudia socially at this time and, within a couple of months, the doctor and Claudia were living together as a couple.

As this scenario was unfolding, Dr. Masterson discussed this relationship with her clinical supervisor, Dr. Smith, informing him that she wanted a relationship with Claudia and inquired if such an association would pose ethical problems. He advised her to seek guidance in this regard from the American Psychological Association. In September and October 1992, Dr. Masterson reaffirmed her desire to establish a relationship with Claudia to Dr. Smith. On October 12, Dr. Masterson informed Dr. Smith of the possibility that she and Claudia might live together. Dr. Smith advised her to wait six months, or at least until after the upcoming holidays to avoid the appearance of acting in dual roles, that is, therapeutic, as her counselor, and nontherapeutic, within the social relationship. He was also concerned that Ferne would feel abandoned by her transfer to another therapist and become angry as a result of any relationship between Dr. Masterson and Claudia.

As a result of the actions of Dr. Masterson, the Delaware Board of Examiners in Psychology revoked her license to practice and the appeals court upheld their determination. The actions ascribed to Dr. Masterson are an excellent example of the conflict of interests that arises when a clinician becomes involved in a dual relationship. Clinical judgment may be affected by self-interests rather than the standard of care, which is to act in the client's interests. The courts have been clear in their decisions by awarding clients damages in virtually all cases.

Although the increased vigilance of the professional organizations and the legal system in enforcing the prohibition against sexual contact between therapists and clients has resulted in higher rates of imposition of sanctions, there has been one negative development. A breach of practice in this area is considered *negligence per se,* which means that it is so clearly a breach of conduct that no experts are required to testify as to the impropriety. The cost of this clarity has been an attempt by malpractice insurance carriers to exclude claims, or cap the amount of money that will be paid out for claims, involving sexual misconduct. In a similar vein, agencies have attempted to distance themselves from these claims by arguing that the sexual activity was outside of the scope of the professional's duties, and therefore they should not be held liable.

The issue for courts in these cases is whether the sexual interactions were severable from the overall professional services rendered by the clinician. Some courts have held that policy limits for sexual misconduct apply when allegations of sexual exploitation are mixed with allegations of other wrongdoing by the therapist (Slovenko, 1993). Courts that have dealt with therapists' mishandling of the transference phenomenon and the concomitant therapist-patient sexual relationship have recognized that the sexual relationship simply cannot be viewed separately from other aspects of the therapist's malpractice or the therapeutic relationship developed between the therapist and the patient (*St. Paul Fire & Marine Ins. Co. v. Love,* 1990, p. 701). Other courts have rejected the claim that sexual acts were only one factor, not an "essential element" in the therapist's malpractice, and have upheld the application of the insurance policy provision that excludes claims arising out of any sexual acts allegedly performed by the insured (*American Home Assurance Co. v. Stephens,* 1996).

This question is unsettled in the courts but professional organizations need to advocate for the legislative banning of these exclusionary clauses. The public policy concern is for the appropriate reimbursement to clients when they have been injured as a result of sexual exploitation by clinicians. Also, innocent agencies and partners in group practices may be exposed to collection on judgments against a clinician whose insurance failed to cover the damage award. In the appeal of *American Home Assurance v. Stone* (1994), this question was addressed by the federal district court. The client had been awarded nearly $3 million in damages by an arbitrator but the insurance company refused to pay beyond the $25,000 limit for cases involving sexual impropriety. In an ironic necessity, the malpracticing clinician and the injured client joined in suing the insurance company, seeking to invalidate the exclusionary clause and indemnify the client from the $3 million limit in the general policy. The court was not convinced of the merits of their argument, concluding that "no matter how sympathetic we might be with the client's position as a victim of Stone's alleged misconduct, the public policy argument is nothing more than an attempt to rewrite a private agreement which the tortfeasor, Stone, had entered into with his insurer, American Home" (p. 1321).

The rules regarding romantic relationships with former clients are more vague than the prohibition of sexual contact with current clients. But even in the absence of an express statutory imposition of criminal or civil liability, there is persuasive authority for the proposition that sexual contact between a psychotherapist and a former client is a harmful act. In *Noto v. St. Vincent's Hospital and Medical Center of New York* (1988), a New York trial court considered whether sexual relations with a patient after termination of a professional psychiatric relationship could give rise to a medical malpractice action. The patient had been under the care of the psychiatrist while receiving inpatient treatment for depression, drug and alcohol dependency, and "seductive behavior." The psychiatrist then rotated to another unit in the hospital. After the patient's discharge, the psychiatrist entered into a personal relationship with the plaintiff in which they drank alcohol, smoked marijuana, and had several sexual encounters.

The posttherapy sexual relationship violates the standard of care in most instances because the parameters of the professional relationship continue to influence the interactions of the parties, which creates a strong risk of inequality in power and decision making. In *Clausen v. New York State Department of Health* (1996), a psychiatrist challenged the actions of the state administrative board that had suspended his license for three years. Clausen argued that the relationship had occurred after the treatment had ended. The board, supported by the appellate court, found that the doctor's actions confused the patient and contributed to her inability to separate from the doctor. He continued to visit the client, accompanied her to sessions with her new therapist, asked her out socially, and professed his love for her. Professional services are goal directed and time limited. Ongoing relationships with clients, particularly romantic ones, create enormous risk of harm to the client, with the attendant legal liability.

There are other dual relationships such as becoming a client's friend following the end of the treatment relationship, entering into business deals, bartering goods or services, exchanging gifts, or seeing a client's former spouse in therapy (Houston-Vega et al., 1997). Clinicians need to consider the ramifications of such relationships prior to the situation arising in practice. Those practitioners who are clear and consistent with practice policies and who share these policies with clients at the beginning of treatment can reduce the risks of sliding into a dual relationship that can lead to harm for the client and liability for the worker.

Ending Treatment/Abandonment

When a mental health professional agrees to accept a client for services, a number of duties attach to the decision including the duty to see the case through to a satisfactory conclusion. Premature or erroneous termination of services may result in liability for the practitioner. The formal definition of *medical abandonment* is "a failure to continue to provide service to the patient when it is still needed in a case for which the professional has assumed responsibility and from which he has not been properly relieved" (*Brandt v. Grubin,* 1974, p. 84). Actions for abandonment arise out of various situations. The cause of action is essentially a negligence claim, stating that the clinician ended treatment without adequately providing for the client's needs. There are few cases that have reached the courts on the question of abandonment. The ones that have raised this claim fall into three main categories: negligent care, termination by clinicians based on self-interest, and terminations of clients due to necessity or life events.

Abandonment can occur as a result of negligence by a clinician. The most common examples are when the clinician has failed to give notice to clients of absences, moves, or the closing of a practice. The standard of care for every practitioner is to have a plan for coverage of the practice should injury or illness prevent the worker from meeting with clients. It is important for a clinician in a private practice to have instructions in a will or related document that specifies how to handle the practice should death or incapacity occur. An important element in this area is for the clinician to provide adequate notice to clients when unavailable for sessions. Without such notice, clients may have no opportunity to arrange for alternative services. If the client suffers damages as a result of this lack of availability, the proper claim is abandonment.

In cases of sexual misconduct by the clinician, the malpractice action often must raise alternative issues to attempt to circumvent the exclusionary clauses prohibiting or limiting coverage for these transgressions (*American Home Assurance v. Stone,* 1994). When a clinician begins a sexual relationship with a client, the treatment relationship is considered to be ended because it can no longer be effective. In many cases, the clinician may also stop seeing the client when the sexual relationship becomes known. In a California case, two insurance carriers were in litigation to determine which should defend a malpractice action against a psychiatrist. The doctor formally terminated treatment in his office following a sexual encounter with a client. An expert witness, testifying in the case, found the psychiatrist's termination to be below the standard of care. The doctor provided the client with the name of another therapist but did not actually set up an appointment or take any further steps to ensure that his client received continued treatment. The expert testified that this constituted abandonment and resulted in an increase in the client's psychiatric symptoms (*Cranford Insurance Co. v. Allwest Insurance Co.,* 1986). When terminating a client who continues to need treatment, the professional has an obligation to take reasonable steps to ensure that the client receives the necessary treatment.

Another type of case in which therapists have been accused of abandonment occurs when a client learns that his or her spouse is having a sexual relationship with the couple's clinician. In *Masterson v. Board of Examiners* (1995), the therapist was accused of ending treatment with her client by improperly referring her to an inpatient hospital program so that the therapist could further a romantic relationship with the client's partner. These cases are clear examples of abandonment of a client for the self-interests of the clinician, and the facts generally support a large award when the client can show a relationship between the abandonment and subsequent damages.

Other premature terminations based on a self-interest of the clinician include ending treatment with a client whose insurance benefits have run out. The provider's duty is to give all of the care that is necessary to the client, regardless of the decision of the managed care company to authorize payment for the services. Although this may seem unduly burdensome on clinicians, particularly those in a private practice setting, these are important legal guidelines that protect clients while not causing undue financial hardship to the clinician. The decision to terminate treatment must be based on clinical evidence, not managed care authorization (Corcoran & Vandiver, 1996). The duty of the clinician is to seek approval, through any and all appeals processes, if continued treatment is indicated. Further, the clinician should try to make arrangements with the client for payment including such options as reduced fee/sliding scale options. Alternatively, the clinician may refer the client to an agency that provides reduced fee or free services. As noted above, the referral process should be carefully attended to so as to ensure that the client actually receives the services. This issue comes down to a decision by the mental health care provider to decide whether to run the risk of a malpractice suit by not providing treatment that is judged to be necessary by the clinician but not by the managed care company.

A promising development in denial of treatment cases is the possibility of opening up courts to hear suits against the managed care companies. Essentially, the issue is one of abandonment because, without the payment, many clients cannot access appropriate services. This area of the law is extremely complex and involves issues of federal statutes such as the Employee Retirement Income Security Act (ERISA, 1974), which have generally prohibited malpractice claims against managed care companies (Reuben, 1996). It is likely that the Supreme Court will rule on the issues related to direct suits against managed care companies for injuries suffered by clients as a result of denial of services (Sculnick, 1996). The most likely situation for finding liability is when the client is denied benefits in a prospective review, that is, prior to beginning treatment. If this denial of benefits results in a client not accessing services, there would seem to be a strong rationale for finding that the managed care company was negligent and directly responsible for the client's injury. In cases where treatment has been proceeding with a clinician and the managed care company refuses to authorize any more sessions, the clinician has established the treatment relationship and continues to owe a duty to see the process through. If denial of treatment cases against managed care companies begins to succeed, there may be some return to reliance on the judgment of the clinician concerning the need for treatment. The change would carry increased control over treatment decisions along with the associated increased risks of liability for the clinician.

There are several other situations in which the termination of a client from counseling is indicated. These terminations need to be handled as treatment interventions and require a level of due care to avoid liability for abandonment. When the termination is being recommended by a clinician because the client's problems are beyond worker's expertise

(*Brandt v. Grubin,* 1974) or because of a lack of progress, the worker has a duty to provide an appropriate referral to the client and to act as necessary to ensure that the client has the opportunity to connect with the resource. If a client is depressed or has difficulty with initiative, providing a name and phone number would not be sufficient because it may not result in a completed referral (*Cranford Insurance v. Allwest Insurance,* 1986). Instead, each case should be handled with planning, in consideration of the client's needs including ability to pay, transportation, ability to follow through to make appointments, and the degree of dependency the client may have had with the referring practitioner, as well as the appropriateness of the referral agency's ability to serve the client. Interventions to address these needs may include having a joint session with the new clinician, eliciting the help of family members or other support systems to assist the client in making the transition, and taking the time in concluding sessions to deal with termination reactions.

The same duty theoretically applies to situations in which the therapist is afraid of the client due to direct threats against the clinician or a generalized fear of a client who is angry and potentially assaultive. Although it is inappropriate for a worker to end treatment unilaterally, the worker is not obligated to put him- or herself at risk of harm (Leong, Spencer, & Silva, 1994). Instead, the duty of the worker would be to consider options that would effect the transfer of services including pursuing commitment proceedings if the client is mentally ill or eliciting the help of supervisors or consultants.

SUPERVISION AND CONSULTATION ISSUES

There is a growing trend in mental health law to hold supervisors legally liable for the practice of those they supervise (Reamer, 1994). Supervisor liability is essentially a negligence claim in which the actions of the clinician that cause damages to a client are not the direct subject of the lawsuit. Instead, the argument is advanced that the supervisor assumed a duty of care to the clients of the worker to adequately monitor and evaluate the performance of the worker. Most of the claims involve incorrect diagnoses, confidentiality violations, misguided interventions, and other clinical issues such as mishandling of the transference phenomenon. As a result of inadequate performance of the supervision role, the supervisor breached the standard of care; the practitioner's actions were not corrected; and an injury to the client occurred as a result.

A second legal theory relied on for supervisor liability is *respondeat superior* (let the master respond) (*Black's,* 1983). This contract-based theory is relevant in agency settings and holds supervisors and agencies responsible for the actions of workers that occur within the scope of their job responsibilities. The rationale is to ensure that the legal entity not be able to avoid responsibility for actions carried out by employees by claiming that it was the individual who was at fault. An important aspect of respondeat superior is the effort by courts to compensate plaintiffs to the full extent of their damages. Usually the individual clinician has limitations on the amount of assets or insurance coverage in a policy. The naming of the supervisor and/or the agency allows a plaintiff to hold a second party partly responsible for the injury suffered as a result of the poor practice. Not only does this approach help to satisfy the judgment, it provides an incentive for improved practice in the form of an expectation that supervision is important and failure to fulfill this role adequately can result in liability.

Cases in which a supervisor has been found to be vicariously liable for the actions of a supervisee, although quite common, are rarely analyzed in the literature. Supervisor liability is generally a secondary claim, attached to the primary complaint against the clinician. However, the areas of supervisor duty can be delineated. As a preliminary matter, it is important to establish the role of the clinical supervisor. In many agencies, the clinician's primary supervisor handles both administrative issues and clinical issues. This is a practice that should be avoided given that the roles are very different and are not complementary. In clinical supervision, the clinician should be encouraged to explore questions, to acknowledge mistakes, to freely discuss transference dynamics and other clinical processes. When the supervisor is also in the role of evaluating the worker's job performance, the clinician may hold back some of the issues from supervision. If a clinician is reticent to take such risks with his or her job supervisor, important practice issues may not be dealt with, and problems may not be corrected. Should the clinician subsequently commit malpractice, the supervision arguably could be found to have been insufficient.

The duty of care for clinical supervisors has its roots in the elements of the legal doctrine of respondeat superior. An obligation to the supervisee and his or her clients is established when the supervisor agrees to, or is assigned to, provide clinical supervision services. Similar to a malpractice action that requires the establishment of a treatment relationship, the duty of care is established when this relationship is formalized. The supervisor becomes responsible for scheduling regular sessions with the worker. Regular meetings, however, are insufficient to fulfill the duty of adequate supervision in all cases (Reamer, 1994). When a clinician is a student who is still in training, a new worker, or a practitioner who is impaired in some way, the duty of the supervisor must adjust to meet the need. The supervisor has a duty to provide the information required by the worker to diagnose and treat clients, to determine when a referral to a specialist or a more experienced clinician is indicated, to monitor progress toward treatment goals, to examine the records and reports prepared by clinicians, and to provide regular feedback to clinicians, including identification of those areas of practice in need of professional development. Given that the records and verbal reports of workers may be limited and distorted, the supervisor should engage in some direct observation or review tapes of sessions. Further, many supervisors arrange to meet with the clients so that clients are fully informed about the supervision process. Also, should the clinician be incapacitated or absent, or in the event of an emergency, the supervisor is known to clients.

Some of the supervisor liability cases that reach the appellate courts involve the question of whether the worker was acting within the scope of professional duties that would trigger the responsibility of the supervisor. The main area of litigation occurs in cases of sexual impropriety because the clinician's malpractice insurance may exclude coverage for this type of claim. In these cases, the supervisor and/or agency are named as parties to allow the plaintiff to recover damages beyond what is available from the individual clinician. The cases analyze whether the supervisor can deny responsibility for the actions of the clinician who had engaged in a sexual relationship with a client. The argument is that the therapist's actions fell outside the scope of employment and therefore it would be unreasonable to expect supervision to control that behavior. In some cases, the argument that the sexual relationship was outside of the scope of professional duties has found favor with the court, and suits against supervisors and agencies have been blocked

(*Cosgrove v. Lawrence,* 1986). In other cases, the argument of the injured client is that the sexual relationship represented the clinician's failure to handle the transference phenomenon appropriately, and thus was inseparable from the treatment. When courts have accepted this argument, vicarious liability has been applied to supervisors and agencies (*St. Paul Fire & Marine Ins. Co. v. Love,* 1990).

Chapter 5

LEGAL AND CLINICAL STANDARDS
Determining "Reasonable Care"

Mr. Cobo had sought the help of a local psychotherapist upon moving to a new area to accept a position as a researcher. He had previously been diagnosed and treated for depression while in graduate school. The doctor who saw him at that time prescribed an antidepressant drug that produced adverse side effects. When he began treatment with the new psychotherapist, he shared this information and indicated that he would not consider medication. The therapist diagnosed Mr. Cobo as suffering from chronic depression and began to see him four times a week in psychotherapy. Because Mr. Cobo was concerned with protecting his identity and keeping the treatment secret, he requested that the therapist not keep any notes.

During the course of treatment, the depression worsened and Mr. Cobo experienced negative effects on his family life, marriage,

AUTHOR'S NOTE: Information in the section on the standard of care in recovered memory cases is adapted from Madden and Parody (1997) and is used with permission.

and work performance. He began to increase his use of alcohol and drugs, and also he began having homosexual encounters, including the use of male prostitutes. Some time later, Mr. Cobo was diagnosed as being HIV positive. Finally, after several years of treatment with the psychotherapist, Mr. Cobo terminated the sessions and consulted a psychiatrist. This doctor diagnosed Mr. Cobo as having a major depression that was characterized by chemical imbalances in the brain. The new doctor prescribed antidepressant medication and soon Mr. Cobo's depression improved markedly. In court, he testified, "There was a sense of happiness that I was connected to my kid, to my wife, and that there was a reason to live, not just to suffer."

Mr. Cobo and his wife filed a complaint against the first therapist, seeking damages and alleging misdiagnosis for incorrectly diagnosing Mr. Cobo as suffering from chronic depression. The expert for the plaintiffs testified as to the types of depression and the standard of care for treating each type. He testified that chronic depression usually results from an event or occurrence in a person's life and is thus effectively helped with analytic psychotherapy. Major depression, by contrast, represents a biological disregulation that is treatable and responds well to medication. The jury agreed that the therapist had violated the standard of care and awarded the plaintiff $850,000 in damages. The case subsequently was appealed by the therapist and a new trial was ordered. The appeals court found that the jury had to consider whether the client, Mr. Cobo, was partly at fault (contributory negligence) because he had refused to be evaluated for medication at the start of the treatment. The trial court had only instructed the jury to decide whether the clinician had been negligent by incorrectly diagnosing Mr. Cobo (*Cobo v. Raba,* 1997).

Although a clinician has a duty to diagnose a condition correctly, this does not mean that the professional must always be accurate (Mackie, 1994). It is only when the misdiagnosis is the result of negligence that liability may be found. The most common misdiagnosis cases are those in which the clinician failed to seek expert help or supervision with a difficult case, or when referrals for diagnostic and medical evaluations were not made. In most cases, as a result of the negligent assessment, the treatment plan failed to help the client or may even have harmed the individual. In *Cobo,* the trial court analyzed the question of liability for incorrect diagnosis as involving the *initial* assessment of the client: chronic depression. Regardless of the decision by the client not to accept the treatment option of medication, the therapist had the duty to diagnose correctly. The lack of progress after several years of very costly psychotherapy treatment was more than sufficient evidence for the clinician to recognize the correct diagnosis and to stop ineffective treatment while advocating for the client to pursue a trial of medication.

For a client to be successful in a suit for improper diagnosis, there must be evidence that the clinician either did not possess the degree of learning, skill, and experience required or did not exercise reasonable and ordinary care in their application. Further, this failure must be the proximate cause of the damages suffered by the client (Mackie, 1994, p. 138). A misdiagnosis case usually comes down to a battle of the experts in court. The plaintiff expert testifies as to the standard of care elements in the diagnosis of the disorder in question while the defense expert would attempt to balance the information available to the jury by either providing a contrary view of the standard or by identifying the particular aspects of the particular case that required deviation from the usual standard.

The diagnosis and assessment of mental health conditions has become more standardized with the publication of the *Diagnostic and Statistical Manual of Mental Disorders* (hereinafter *DSM-IV*) (American Psychiatric Association, 1994). Clinicians who use the manual and base their diagnoses on the standards articulated in this volume can demonstrate an objective basis and reasonable belief for their judgments. Many clinicians, however, are uncomfortable with the labeling and rigidity of the diagnostic categories, which often do not reflect the clients they know. The choice concerning the use of *DSM-IV* is dependent on the setting and funding source of the worker, but the manual provides comforting support if questions arise as to the proper diagnosis of a client.

The question of whether a therapist has provided correct treatment to a client is clearly related to the issue of correct diagnosis/assessment. Because there are so many schools of psychotherapy, determining the best treatment approach for a client has always been a challenge to mental health professionals. The task is part of the art of therapy in which the clinician seeks to identify the approach that will be most effective with a given client. Recently, discretion has yielded to standardization due to the increased presence of managed care. The managed care companies have sought to identify treatment interventions that are effective and efficient, although their profit motive lends skepticism to their recommendations. The standards represent an attempt to "define the parameters within which appropriate clinical care may take place" (Appelbaum, 1992). Corcoran and Vandiver (1996) analyze components of what are called *preferred practice approaches* required for authorization in managed care reviews. Using Eddy's structured policy categories, they contrast the following:

• *Treatment standards* are the essential elements of treatment that most practitioners feel should be followed in every case and that have been validated by extensive research.
• *Practice guidelines* are more flexible than standards and allow for more clinical judgment. Guidelines should be followed in most cases and, as with standards, are based on empirical evidence of effectiveness.
• *Options* are neutral in terms of recommendations for practice and may be chosen by a clinician based on professional training, orientation, or experience. There is little, if any, research to assess the efficacy of these treatment interventions.

The preferred practice approaches are predominately short term, goal oriented, and characterized by clear delineation as to what will occur in treatment. Clinicians must be vigilant in using treatment protocols as outlines within which to fit the idiosyncratic elements of a client's culture, background, gender, and life situation.

RECOVERED MEMORY/
FALSE MEMORY CASES

The area of recovered memory/false memory of childhood sexual abuse provides a useful set of cases and principles to understand the general duty of reasonable care owed by mental health professionals to clients and others. This practice area has generated much controversy as there is no universal agreement among clinicians and researchers concerning the processes of repression and dissociative amnesia. Although there are many ways in which a worker can be brought into a legal proceeding in a recovered memory case (e.g., witness, expert, consultant, or defendant), this section will focus on the malpractice issues, such as when and to whom a duty of care is owed; what the evolving standard of care in trauma treatment is; what clinical behaviors and interventions put practitioners at risk of breaching the duty of care; how a clinician should practice so as to provide effective therapy that is ethically delivered and within accepted practice parameters; and in what ways the legal system can be shaped to create more therapeutic outcomes from cases involving recovered memories.

The following sections will explore each of the elements of psychotherapist malpractice using the example of recovered memory/false memory cases.

Negligence/Malpractice

The controversy concerning recovered memories/false memories of child sexual abuse has split the professional community and confused the public. It is not surprising that the practice area has generated an increasing number of lawsuits and made many therapists wary of taking on clients with symptoms consistent with an abuse history. There is clearly a greater likelihood for questions to arise out of the treatment process as a result of the theoretical uncertainty, the severity of client symptoms, the potential damage to reputations and family relationships, and the cultural history of denial and subterfuge about child sexual abuse. The intense emotions in these cases increase the likelihood that some individuals will feel sufficiently victimized and damaged to seek legal redress (Madden & Parody, 1997). The harm that can result from negligent treatment of a client whose symptoms suggest a trauma history can be just as severe as those arising from negligent or intentional "planting" of memories. These damages include direct emotional and physical harm to the client, a deterioration of functioning, and damage to reputations, as well as the disruption of family relationships arising from the therapist's instructions to "break all ties."

Some therapists have responded to the confusion by not accepting cases where child sexual abuse is suspected (which may be appropriate where a worker has not received training or experience in the field). However, in addition to being ethically troublesome, this is unlikely to be an effective strategy given that memories may emerge only in the course of treatment. Instead, all clinicians should become well versed on memory, trauma treatment, the standard of care, and the risks of certain interventions. Given the controversy about repressed memory and the diversity of opinion on the use of memory recovery techniques, there is usually enough of a question of fact that a lawsuit against a therapist probably would survive efforts to get it dismissed. As a result, repressed memory cases charging clinicians with malpractice are very serious and have a strong potential to proceed until a settlement is reached or until the case gets a full hearing in court.

Standard of Care

Therapists who specialize in working with trauma have developed a standard of care for responding to cases in which a symptom profile suggests possible sexual abuse. The standard has begun to be refined during the past couple of years, primarily in response to a large number of legal challenges and debate in the media. The recovered memory controversy thus provides a unique opportunity to examine the phenomena of a clinical practice standard of care being developed in a dynamic, interactive environment featuring the following:

- Courts creating a new duty for clinicians to nonclient third-party family members
- High-profile cases in which the theoretical debate about a clinical issue was played out in the spotlight of adversarial litigation
- Professional organizations being pressured by membership to develop position statements and practice guidelines for working with clients presenting a symptom profile consistent with sexual abuse history
- State legislatures, responding to constituent pressure on both sides of the recovered memory debate, passing legislation that in some states makes it easier, while in other states makes it more difficult, to file lawsuits in recovered memory cases

Because this controversy has emerged so quickly and because it has engendered strong emotions and a concentration of resources, it has resulted in a magnified image of the reciprocal relationship between the law and mental health.

The standard of care in recovered memory work is not universally accepted because the underlying concepts of repression, dissociation, and traumatic amnesia remain unproved by scientific studies and are rejected by some clinicians and researchers. However, for clinicians who work with trauma survivors, some practice standards have emerged. Many clients present with a variety of diagnoses before the underlying history of trauma emerges. Clients often present with burdensome symptoms that are consistent with a sexual trauma history including low self-esteem, sexual problems, difficulties in relationships, and various types of self-abuse including eating disorders, increased depression, anxiety, and fear. Once the memories begin to emerge, clients may experience post-traumatic stress symptoms characterized by repeated reexperiencing of the trauma through vivid memories, night terrors, dissociative episodes, and somatic complaints, among other symptoms.

Herman (1992), Brown (1995), and Whitfield (1995) assert that a phase- (or stage-) oriented approach is necessary when working with survivors of childhood sexual abuse. The first stage, *establishment of safety* (Herman, 1992), *stabilization* (Brown, 1995), and *beginning recovery* (Whitfield, 1995), consists of symptom management and stabilization through enhancement of coping skills. Therapists can assist in normalizing clients' symptoms and experiences combined with developing new coping skills to help clients to gain mastery and a sense of control over symptoms. A therapeutic error during this stage is the premature engagement in exploration of traumatic material, prior to the establishment of safety and the development of a trusting therapeutic alliance. Another danger of this stage is the interpretation of symptoms by the therapist. It is important that therapists continue to explore the history of the client's symptoms without interjecting any bias toward suggesting an abuse history. This is a difficult task for the therapist. Patience and a slow pace are very important and allow the clients' stories to unfold gradually and with their own interpretations.

Whitfield (1995) describes the first stage (Stage Zero) as manifested by the presence of an active illness or disorder, such as an addiction, compulsion, or other disorder. Without recovery, it may continue indefinitely. At Stage Zero, recovery has not yet started (Whitfield, 1995, p. 254). The disorder is the central feature of the client's concern and may serve to propel the client to seek therapy. Memory retrieval and recovery is further inhibited by the client's perceived lack of safety. The healing of Stage Zero disorders cannot begin until safety is established during this first stage of treatment.

The second stage involves *systematic uncovering*—a graduated process of integrating memories and associated affect about the trauma into consciousness (Brown, 1995). Herman (1992) refers to this stage as *remembrance and mourning,* where survivors tell the story of the trauma, which allows for healing to occur. Creation of the therapeutic "holding environment" (Winnicott, 1965) allows clients to feel safe and to internalize the therapist's calming, predictable presence. During this phase of treatment, intensification of symptoms is to be expected. The internal structures for containment that were mastered during the first phase of treatment (safety) are of paramount importance. The third stage of therapy allows for incorporation of the trauma into daily life (Whitfield, 1995). This stage of therapy often includes an exploration of spirituality and launches clients on the road of healing toward self-actualization. Armed with skills and insight acquired in therapy, clients embark upon life with the ability to analyze and confront old patterns of behavior. Within the supportive context of the therapeutic relationship, clients can explore their patterns of behavior and examine them to gain insight into and understanding of the past to avoid replication of abusive situations in the present. As clients become empowered, the decision to disclose their traumatic histories to others may surface. The role of the therapist is to rehearse with clients all possible outcomes and reactions to the disclosure as well as explore the underlying fantasies regarding the disclosing.

The client should be allowed to set the pace for therapy and to explore issues and symptoms without coming to premature conclusions. The role of the therapist is to serve as a guide, assisting clients in monitoring their reactions, modulating disclosure, and revisiting the stage of safety and containment as needed throughout the course of therapy. Some clients may immediately wish to spill details of their trauma without having the necessary skills to cope with the affective aftermath of disclosure. Other clients will do anything possible to avoid remembering. Anxious to ascribe meaning to symptoms, clients and/or therapist may express an interest in using techniques specifically designed for memory retrieval.

The stage-oriented models all share a basic approach to the treatment of clients in recovered memory cases. These models contain the primary elements that constitute the *standard of care* for practice. The critical practice skills include maintaining an empathic, nonjudgmental, neutral stance so as not to inappropriately influence the client (American Psychiatric Association, 1993). Although these models instruct affirmatively, the use of some specific techniques has been identified as putting clients and therapists at risk and thus may violate the *standard of care.*

Brown (1995) cites four primary interacting risk factors in the creation of false memories in psychotherapy: (a) high hypnotizability; (b) uncertainty about past events; (c) clear evidence of interrogatory suggestive influence; and (d) extratherapeutic influences, for example, peer and familial influence, especially self-help group experiences and literature on recovered memories. Other risk factors for the creation of false memories include therapists who have an expectation of abuse because of a personal agenda or practice specialization as well as clients who seek approval or who are easily influenced. The temptation to offer an interpretation prematurely (such as a history of childhood abuse) to explain the client's symptoms and suffering can have long-term negative consequences for both client and therapist. Moving at a slower pace may be difficult for the client who seeks rapid relief and affirmation of suffering. The slower pace is also difficult for the therapist who is limited by the ever-changing restrictions of insurance companies and managed care. Moreover, it is difficult to sit with the suffering of clients.

Techniques Commonly Used to Facilitate Memory Retrieval

It is clear from a review of case law and relevant literature that some memory retrieval techniques put therapists at greater risk of inappropriately influencing clients. The scope of this chapter does not allow for a thorough examination of each technique but therapists employing techniques such as guided imagery, age regression, journaling, dream work and interpretation, body work, eye movement desensitization and reprocessing (EMDR), art therapy, feelings/emotional release work, group therapy, and even bibliotherapy may wish to examine use of these techniques in their practice with the awareness that such techniques have been targeted as instruments in false memory creation. Therapists must caution clients about using the methods for memory retrieval described in the self-help literature. Some self-help literature encourages the use of techniques that should not be undertaken without professional supervision.

Legal Issues in Recovered Memory Cases

In recent years, the number of lawsuits involving recovered memories of child sexual abuse has grown dramatically. It is an area of practice that many clinicians have become wary of due to the risks and uncertainties. There are some important reasons that recovered memory cases have generated many lawsuits that involve clinicians. Child sexual abuse has been a taboo subject, denied by society and hidden by families. As a result, cases that include accusations of sexual abuse against an individual are defended vigorously. Zoltek-Jick (in press) has argued that new abuse defense strategies that have emerged over the past 10 years focused not only on denying the abuse but also on advancing a political motive. Clinicians have been accused of being culpable in the creation of trauma, an astounding twist for individuals who perceive their role as advocates for the resumption of health. The legal strategies of those accused of the abuse are designed to make the point that all claims of abuse without corroborating evidence are unreliable, regardless of the specific facts of a case. Zoltek-Jick identifies three related abuse defense strategies, each of which has implications for therapists.

The first strategy employed by those defending persons accused of child sexual abuse is to attack the trustworthiness of the complaint due to the possibility of implantation of memories by a therapist. It is often argued that the therapist negligently or intentionally influenced the client by prematurely or inaccurately labeling a client as having been sexually abused. This strategy can be summarized as "blaming the therapist" because it seeks to portray the professional as the party responsible for creating a false memory in the vulnerable client. The legal approach is to characterize inappropriate techniques used by the therapist as poisoning the client's ability to provide evidence. It relies on the rules that apply to testimony by witnesses who have been hypnotized. The law of many states recognizes that a person who is in a hypnotic state may be vulnerable to suggestions that would affect the accuracy and validity of his or her memory of an event. The argument is extended to claim that therapists who use techniques that assist a client in recovering a repressed memory may irreparably distort that memory. In the preliminary stages of a lawsuit, the defense would attempt to have the testimony of the client excluded on the basis of this contamination.

For therapists, the first strategy means that during the discovery phase of the lawsuit when information is collected by each side, there will be extensive questioning as to the specific techniques used in therapy. Lawyers will seek to determine the sequence of the techniques in relation to the unaided recovery of the memory. The aim is to find information supporting the theory that the therapist used interventions that had the potential for suggesting sexual abuse to explain the client's symptoms. Hypnosis, premature referral to a survivors' group, and providing access to literature on childhood sexual abuse are interventions that defense lawyers will examine.

The second defense strategy that directly affects clinicians is the claim that the memories retrieved in therapy are nonfactual and narrative in character (Zoltek-Jick, in press, p. 41). The purpose of treatment is not to uncover historical truth but to help the client to regain social and emotional health. The defense argues that when the memories that were recovered in therapy form the basis for a legal action, they cannot be relied on as proof of what actually happened. The therapist has been less prone to direct attack in these cases, although the case records and notes are likely to be reviewed closely to uncover inconsistencies in the client's memories reported in therapy.

Finally, the third new defense strategy is to attack the scientific validity of repressed memory (Zoltek-Jick, in press, pp. 46-49). The law requires that evidence must meet a threshold standard of acceptance by the scientific community before it can be introduced into a trial (*Daubert v. Dow Chemical,* 1993, hereinafter *Daubert* test). The reason for this is to preclude the use of dubious or unproved theories from being offered as scientific testimony, which could inappropriately influence a jury. The defense strategy is to argue that because of the controversy in the professional community as to the validity of repression and dissociative amnesia, the theory does not reach the level of scientific validity to allow any evidence about recovered memories to be introduced. The evidence that would be excluded includes both the testimony of the therapist and the testimony of the client concerning any memories recovered as a result of therapeutic interventions. Zoltek-Jick argues that the third strategy is attractive to accused perpetrators because it seeks to refute the legitimacy of the claim by dismissing it as meritless fiction. If a case is dismissed because the statute of limitations has run out, the merits of the case never get resolved. The defendant may not be liable but neither has he or she been absolved.

Although some clinicians do not accept the notion of recovered memories, the professional organizations and the *DSM-IV* cautiously support the existence of dissociative symptoms in the wake of sexual abuse trauma in some clients. The professional community has been lax in not demanding an equal amount of proof from the research for the existence of the false memory syndrome as has been called for to support the existence of recovered memories. Pope (1996) articulately challenges the claims of those who assert that therapists create false memory syndrome as an iatrogenic disorder by examining the scientific credibility of the theory. Few cases to date have used the *Daubert* test to exclude attempts by defendants to have their theory of the case introduced as evidence. In one case that did turn on this issue, the court found insufficient basis in the evidence presented to determine that such a syndrome existed.

The area of recovered memories/false memories is very unsettled in the professional literature. The resulting legal cases provide excellent examples of how the courts will fashion outcomes based on the quality of the experts, the skill of the attorney, the particular facts of the case, the sympathetic qualities of each party in the suit, and the politics and inclinations of the judge. The following two cases were both decided in 1996, one in Massachusetts and the other in Maryland. Each case dealt with the question of whether there was sufficient scientific validity in the theory of repressed memories to allow the case to proceed. The divergent results demonstrate the vagaries of the legal system when it is left on its own to decide on clinical issues due to a lack of clear direction from the research literature, the mental health community, or the professional organizations.

Shahzade v. Gregory (1996, opinion of the court). The plaintiff in this case alleges repeated episodes of nonconsensual sexual touching of her by the defendant from 1940 to 1945, more than 47 years prior to her filing a complaint. The plaintiff was between the ages of approximately 12 and 17 at this time; the defendant is approximately five years her senior. The plaintiff claims that these episodes had been completely blocked out and that she had no memory of them until she recovered so-called "repressed memories" of these touchings during psychotherapy in November 1990. The defendant admits to some degree of sexual activity between himself and the plaintiff, but there is a dispute with regard to the nature and extent of such activity. The plaintiff now wants to introduce evidence relating to these alleged repressed memories. When a proffered scientific theory is beyond the general understanding of a jury, in order to introduce evidence relating to this theory, an individual must rely on expert testimony as to the validity of the theory. The proposed expert must qualify as an expert and must offer testimony relating to reliable scientific knowledge. The Court acknowledges the appropriateness of an expert in this type of case and concludes that the plaintiff's expert, Dr. Bessel van der Kolk, is not only qualified as an expert in the field of memory but that he is one of the country's most renowned psychiatrists in this specialty. For the following reasons, the Court finds the subject matter, repressed memory syndrome, to be reliable and therefore admissible.

For evidence to be admissible, the trial court must conclude that "any and all scientific testimony . . . is not only relevant, but reliable." The reliability standard is grounded in Federal Procedure Rule 702's requirement that an expert's testimony relate to "scientific knowledge." To qualify as "scientific," the theory must be grounded in the methods and procedures of science. To qualify as "knowledge," the testimony must be more than subjective belief or unsupported speculation. In addition, to qualify as scientific knowledge, an inference or assertion must be derived by the scientific method. In cases dealing with scientific evidence, reliability is based upon scientific validity. The Supreme Court in *Daubert* set forth several criteria that should be considered when determining whether the reasoning or methodology underlying the testimony is scientifically valid. The factors to be considered when deciding if proffered testimony is valid "scientific knowledge," and therefore reliable, are (a) whether the theory has been tested, (b) whether the theory has been subjected to peer review and publication, (c) the theory's known or potential rate of error, and (d) whether the theory has attained general acceptance within the relevant scientific community. After considering these factors, this Court finds that the reliability of the phenomenon of repressed memory has been established, and therefore will permit the plaintiff to introduce evidence that relates to the plaintiff's recovered memories.

In a case raising the same issue, *Isely v. Capuchin Province* (1995), the court stated that in order to introduce repressed memory evidence, a witness must "testify as to whether that theory can be, or has been, tested or corroborated, and, if so, by whom and under what circumstances; whether the theory has been proven or not proven under clinical tests or some other accepted procedure for bearing it out; and whether the theory has been subjected to other types of peer review." . . . Obviously, this part of this foundational element will include testimony as to whether or not the theory of repressed memory is widely accepted in the field of psychology.

Dr. van der Kolk's testimony sufficiently satisfies these foundational factors. Dr. van der Kolk discussed in detail several studies
that focused on the concept of repressed memories and ultimately,
through their findings, serve to validate the theory.

In brief, Dr. van der Kolk testified that repressed memories are not
a scientific controversy, merely a political and forensic one. Dr.
van der Kolk stated that currently the major detractors of the theory are so-called outsiders, "psychologists who do not treat trau-
matized patients." Although the defendant's expert, Dr. Bodkin,
was a clinical psychiatrist, he does not specialize in the field of
memory. Nor do his credentials and expertise in the area of
memory compare with those of Dr. van der Kolk. Furthermore, Dr.
Bodkin did not claim that the theory of repressed memory was
invalid, he merely stated that, in his opinion, the 52 studies
relating to repressed memories that he critiqued contained meth-
odological deficiencies and therefore could not serve to validate
the theory. According to the expert who testified in *Isely*, the only
controversy among the majority of clinical psychiatrists with
respect to the issue of repressed memory "is specifically in the
area of elicitation of repressed memories, not with the concept
itself."

Dr. van der Kolk expanded on this point in recognizing that some
memories may not be accurate. "I think there has always been
controversies about whether people can trust a patient still. So at
the end, just like every other story you hear, you take your
subjective self and eventually you decide what you believe—
whether you believe what people tell you is true or not, it's how
we all make up our minds. So at the end, there really is no
scientific proof whether something is true or not unless there is
independent corroboration, unless there was somebody there taking a movie."

The American Psychiatric Association, which is the major professional association for psychiatrists in America, recognizes the
theory of repressed memories and believes it to be very common
among people who have experienced severe trauma. . . . The
Diagnostic and Statistical Manual of Mental Disorders, which is
a widely used manual by psychiatrists to define mental diagnostic

categories and is published by the American Psychiatric Association, also recognizes the concept of repressed memories.

Based on the evidence and testimony of Dr. van der Kolk, the Court finds that the plaintiff has satisfied the four foundational factors that are to be considered, although not independently determinative, in order to introduce evidence relating to repressed memories. The plaintiff has presented sufficient evidence through both Dr. van der Kolk's testimony and various submissions to the Court that (a) the theory has been the subject of various tests; (b) the theory has been subjected to peer review and publication; (c) repressed memory, as is true with ordinary memories, "cannot be tested empirically," and may not always be accurate; however, the theory itself has been established to be valid through various studies; and (d) the theory has attained general acceptance within the relevant scientific community, namely, that of clinical psychiatrists. It is important to stress that, in considering the admissibility of repressed memory evidence, it is not the role of the Court to rule on the credibility of this individual plaintiff's memories but on the validity of the theory itself.

For the foregoing reasons, the Court hereby denies the Defendant's Motion to Exclude Repressed Memory Evidence. For the law to reject a diagnostic category generally accepted by those who practice the art and science of psychiatry would be folly. Rules of law are not petrified in the past but flow with the current of expanding knowledge. [Citations omitted; text edited for style and readability.]

Doe v. Maskell (1996, opinion of the court). Jane Doe and Jane Roe were students at Seton Keough High School, a parochial school in Baltimore City. During their tenure at Keough, both girls, individually, were referred for counseling to the school chaplain, Father A. Joseph Maskell. According to the complaints filed in the cases, Maskell subjected the girls to repeated sexual, physical, and psychological abuse, hypnosis, threats of physical violence, coerced prostitution, and other lewd acts, and forced the students to perform sexual acts. Both girls were allegedly threatened with extreme punishments if they informed anyone of the abuse, which continued until the girls graduated and left Keough in 1971 and 1972, respectively. At some point, both plaintiffs claim that they ceased to recall the abuse suffered at the hands of Father Maskell, due to a process they term "repression." Both plaintiffs began to "recover" memories of this abuse in 1992.

The statute of limitations for filing a complaint of this type is three years from the time the plaintiff reaches the age of majority. Therefore, if Doe or Roe had not yet repressed the memories of the sexual assault by the defendants by even the day after their attaining majority, the statute of limitations barred these claims three years after their eighteenth birthdays. At the hearing, both plaintiffs testified, as did expert witnesses offered by both plaintiffs and the defendants. At the conclusion of the hearing, Judge Caplan entered summary judgment for the defendant counselor and school. Doe and Roe appealed to the Court of Special Appeals.

This discovery rule initially arose in the context of medical malpractice but soon expanded to encompass other forms of professional malpractice. In order to activate the running of the statute of limitations, it must be proven that the plaintiff had actual knowledge of all facts. We find that the critical question to the determination of the applicability of the discovery rule to lost memory cases is whether there is a difference between forgetting and repression. It is crystal clear that in a suit in which a plaintiff "forgot" and later "remembered" the existence of a cause of action beyond the three-year limitations period, that suit would be time-barred. Dismissal of such a case reflects our judgment that the potential plaintiff had "slumbered on his rights," should have known of his cause of action, and was blameworthy. To permit a forgetful plaintiff to maintain an action would vitiate the statute of limitations and deny repose for all defendants.

Plaintiffs in this case, however, claim that in order to avoid the pain associated with recalling the abuse they suffered, their memories were "repressed," not merely "forgotten," and later "recovered" rather than "remembered." They argue that this difference renders them "blamelessly ignorant" and excuses their failure to file suit in a timely manner. I can opine that there is no consensus within the medical community that such a phenomenon can occur.

Finally, critics of repression theory argue that the "refreshing" or "recovery" of "repressed" memories is more complicated than repression proponents would have us believe.

After reviewing the arguments on both sides of the issue, we are unconvinced that repression exists as a phenomenon separate and apart from the normal process of forgetting. Because we find these two processes to be indistinguishable scientifically, it follows that they should be treated the same legally. Therefore, we hold that the mental process of repression of memories of past sexual abuse does not activate the discovery rule. The plaintiffs' suits are thus barred by the statute of limitations. If the General Assembly should wish to rewrite the law, that is its prerogative and responsibility.

The trial judge found that "there is no question with the evidence that I have seen in this case that both Doe and Roe were very competent during the period of time, during the period of time from the years of their alleged abuse until the present time. They managed their affairs. One, raising four children in the process, and one continuing business and doing fairly well from a practical point of view. So there is no issue of insanity in this case, from my finding of fact." As there is no contrary evidence in the record, we shall affirm the summary judgment in favor of the defendants on the ground that plaintiffs' claims were barred by the statute of limitations three years after they reached their eighteenth birthdays. [Citations omitted; text edited for style and readability.]

When two cases, occurring at the same time, dealing with similar clinical questions, result in completely opposite results, there is a problem with the legal system. One of the functions of tort law is to help define expectations for behavior so that professionals can have notice as to what constitutes a breach of duty. The current situation is akin to driving in a state that decided to remove all of its speed limit signs but continues to enforce the speeding regulations. Drivers would be unsure of their limits and anxious in their driving performance. The professional community can influence the law in the recovered memory area by continuing the task of conducting research as to the existence of both recovered memories and false memory syndrome. The courts seem to want a definitive answer based on scientific evidence. Unfortunately, human cognitions and emotions are difficult to isolate and study objectively.

Does repressed memory keep some people from remembering trauma until recovering it in adulthood? There is some research that supports this process (Whitfield, 1995; Williams, 1994) and many anecdotal examples from clinicians that enable the general professional community to accept the concept of repressed memory. On the basis of research studying normal memory, we know that memory is malleable and can be influenced by the suggestions of others (Loftus & Ketchum, 1994). There are also cases detailing dangerous practices used by clinicians that worsened the mental and emotional health of their clients (*Couch v. DeSilva,* 1991). As a result, it is also plausible to accept the concept of iatrogenic disorders being created by the negligent or intentional acts of therapists. To avoid the type of conflicting results as occurred in *Shahzade* and *Maskell,* the evidence as to the syndromes should be presented to the jury for a decision in light of the facts of the case and in the context of the behavior and techniques of the clinician.

THIRD-PARTY LIABILITY

A jury awarded $500,000 to Gary Ramona, a wine executive, who had sued two therapists for planting false memories of child sexual abuse in his adult daughter (*Ramona v. Isabella,* 1991, reported in Slind-Flor, 1994). Holly Ramona entered treatment for bulimia and several months later began to report memories of abuse. Holly informed her mother about the memories, and they planned to confront Mr. Ramona. The therapist and her consulting psychiatrist, seeking confirmation, conducted a sodium amytal interview. Following this interview, the therapist facilitated a family meeting where Holly confronted her father. He denied the charges but, thereafter, he was divorced, estranged from all three of his daughters, and lost his job (Butler, 1995).

It has always been assumed that clinicians owe a duty of care to clients. This duty is based on professional standards and an implied or express contract between the parties. Therapists also may be held liable to third parties for damages occurring to others if they are injured as a result of the treatment to a client. Traditionally, the common law did not recognize a duty of care to a person in the absence of a special or preexisting relationship, such as a contract, a treatment relationship, or other direct interaction. But, recently, parents and others, although not receiving direct services, have brought lawsuits against mental health clinicians in increasing numbers. They argue that the therapist acted negligently or intentionally, which resulted in injuries to them. They seek to recover damages from clinicians, even though they are "third parties" to the therapeutic process. Several recent court cases have explored the conditions under which third-party liability may be considered.

Legal Issues in Third-Party Liability

The main obstacle to filing suits of this type involves the legal issue of standing. The requirement of standing is satisfied if it can be said that the person seeking to file a suit has a legally protectable and tangible interest at stake in the litigation (*Black's,* 1983). Courts generally do not allow individuals to pursue legal actions against someone who is not a direct player in a transaction or interaction unless the injury to that person was foreseeable. Also, third-party liability is not favored in most legal contexts because it tends to be fraught with difficulties including causation problems and the question of how far the scope of duty extends.

Courts have been willing to allow suits by third parties when the actions of the clinician were directed at the individual. Although it has been applied inconsistently in recent decisions, the *direct victim standard* provides courts with the rationale for establishing a duty. When the clinician involves another individual in the treatment by directing an intervention at that person that causes damages, some courts have held this to be sufficient to allow a suit to proceed. The direct victim standard creates difficulties for clinicians who are involved in a client's environment or when the case supports the use of directive interventions. Would a client's spouse have a cause of action against a therapist who recommends a divorce? Could a corporation file suit against a therapist who directs a client to curtail involvement in an important deal to reduce stress? Does a clinician have a duty to an acting-out adolescent if it is recommended to parents that they not allow him to continue to live in the house?

Appelbaum and Zoltek-Jick (1996) argue convincingly that the direct victim standard leaves therapists unclear about the extent of their duties to third parties, which may lead to avoidance of certain types of cases or feelings of intimidation about using directive interventions. It is unlikely that the courts would be willing to return to the formerly explicit rule prohibiting all suits by third parties. However, the mental health professions need to clarify the type of damaging interventions that legitimately should be compensated and educate the courts about the antitherapeutic outcomes that arise from liberal criteria for finding a duty to third parties.

One of the major concerns about third-party suits is the effect on the nonparty client and the therapist. In most of the cases filed to date, the client has not identified the treatment as defective and has not partici-pated in the suit. This takes a case outside of the normal liability pattern where behavioral and performance expectations exist in the context of a treatment relationship. Some third-party suits have been filed for political or strategic purposes. There is the potential for third-party suits to operate similarly to a SLAP suit, which is a legal strategy of filing a counterclaim that serves to attack those who filed the original suit. For example, in a case in which a sexual abuse claim has been filed against a parent, a countersuit against a therapist may include a vindictive, reactionary attack that makes pursuing any further activity in this area too costly and painful for the client. It may also serve the purpose of seeking to eviscerate the charges so as to rehabilitate the parent's reputation. These lawsuits frequently violate the privacy of the client and may require the release of privileged communications because the evaluation of the duty owed to the third party must be based on what occurred during treatment.

At times, a third-party claim by a parent precedes the filing of a claim by the client. Recently, a client who was being treated for traumatic memories of child sexual abuse filed her own claim against her former therapists (*Lujan v. Mansmann, Neuhausel & Genesis Associates,* 1997). The impetus for the suit was the ongoing litigation between her parents and the therapists. When Lujan (the former client) returned to the area after being away, she learned about the lawsuit in which the parents sought to establish third-party liability (*Tuman v. Genesis Asso-ciates,* 1996). She allegedly developed an awareness of the harmful nature of the treatment she received. In her lawsuit, Lujan claimed that the therapists breached their duty to provide her with psychological counseling that was within the standard of care of licensed therapists practicing in the Philadelphia area. This breach occurred when therapists provided advice and counseling that was described as being "cult-like in nature." The counselors were accused of encouraging Lujan "to believe in certain memories, including memories of satanic abuse, satanic murders, and deviant sexual assaults." They convinced Lujan that her life was in danger, induced her to undergo plastic surgery to alter her features, informed Lujan that she would have to detach herself from her parents and eliminate all communication with them for approximately two years except concerning financial matters, and encouraged her to travel away from Pennsylvania (p. 3).

There are four areas in which the courts have struggled with the determination of whether to extend a duty to third parties to the clinical relationship. The duty-to-warn situations (discussed in Chapter 3 in the section "Dangerous Client Exceptions" to confidentiality) have been the most widely analyzed third-party liability cases. Courts have used a "social good" rationale to support the creation of a duty to an intended victim, prioritizing protection over confidentiality concerns. The mental health professions have, for the most part, agreed with this limited duty and have cooperated by integrating it into the standard of care. The other areas of potential third-party liability are more contentious and are not supported by the majority of professionals. These situations are discussed below.

Recovered Memory Cases

There have been a number of recent cases of third-party liability in the recovered memory context in which accused parents have sued the therapist. The important issues that give rise to third-party liability relate to the harm to accused perpetrators and family relationships as a result of claims made by clients in recovery therapy. In *Ramona,* the defense tried to have the case dismissed on issues of standing prior to trial. Citing a case where a husband was granted the right to sue a health maintenance organization for mistakenly diagnosing his wife as having a sexually transmitted disease (*Molien v. Kaiser Foundation Hospital,* 1980), the judge found a basis for potential liability. It was successfully argued that the therapist owed a legal duty of care to the father. The *Ramona* court found that the negligent practice of memory recovery therapy, like the misdiagnosis of a sexually transmitted disease, would foreseeably cause harm to the reputation of the third party and to his family relationships (Slind-Flor, 1994).

The second major case to allow a third-party suit against a therapist is *Sullivan v. Cheshier* (1994). A federal district court in Illinois denied a therapist's motion to have the case dismissed. A woman being treated by the therapist remembered being sexually abused by a sibling when she was a child. This memory was recovered during hypnosis; however, the client had no prior memories of the abuse. The therapist instructed his client to have no contact with her family unless they admitted that the memories were true. The court found that the therapist specifically directed his actions against the parents and thus allowed the suit to proceed to trial.

The courts in both *Ramona* and *Sullivan* sought to determine whether the interventions of the therapist were directed at the plaintiff parents. When the third parties are direct victims of the actions of the clinician, the connection is deemed sufficient to trigger a duty of care owed to the parents. These court decisions have been given extensive publicity, but the threat to the integrity of psychotherapy is not substantial. The cases of third-party liability in the recovered memory area have mostly been appellate decisions as to whether a suit should be allowed to be brought into court. The actual trials may or may not occur and, if they do, the jury would still need to determine the extent of the duty to third-party parents and whether that duty had been breached by the actions of the therapist. In recovered memory cases, third-party liability likely will be imposed if there was a treatment relationship with the plaintiff. When, as in *Ramona* and *Sullivan,* no treatment relationship existed, the court may still find third-party liability if it can be shown that the therapist's actions could reasonably be foreseen to cause harm to the plaintiff.

A more appropriate standard to review the actions of clinicians directed at third parties was articulated in a 1995 Illinois case, *Lindgren v. Moore.* A father and siblings of a recovered memory client brought suit against a therapist and her supervisor based on the treatment of a 28-year-old woman. The court rejected the attempt by the father and siblings to claim that the therapist's actions constituted negligence or malpractice as to the family members. A mental health professional should owe a duty to the client, and not to anyone else. Once a duty to a third party is established, treatment decisions may not be made based on a determination of what is best for the client. If the treatment is deficient, the party who should be allowed to file an action is the client.

The court in *Lindgren* did allow the family members to bring a tort action for intentional infliction of emotional distress. If the clinician's actions are meant to cause harm to a third party, the justification for carving out an exception to the traditional rule barring third-party suits is strong. Absent this intentionality, a potential duty to a third party for treatment decisions creates an inappropriate conflict of interest between the need to act in the client's interest and the need to protect oneself from potential lawsuits.

Alienation of Affection Cases

There have been a number of cases in which a third-party suit was brought against a therapist as a result of a sexual relationship with a client. In these cases, the spouse or partner of the client claims that the actions of the therapist resulted in interference with the family relationship. The archaic legal term for this is *alienation of affection.* Although this term is no longer legally recognized in most jurisdictions, it still stands for the concept that many people accept: No one should be allowed to interfere in another person's marriage. It is particularly attractive in situations where the intervening party has undue influence over the partner such as occurs in psychotherapy sexual abuse cases. As a result, where an appeals court finds some basis on which to premise a duty, such as some involvement in treatment, an average jury is likely to hold the offending clinician liable to the innocent spouse.

In a 1993 California case, *Smith v. Pust,* a husband sued a therapist who was treating his wife. The therapist had a sexual encounter with the wife. The court upheld the dismissal of the husband's third-party suit on the grounds that no duty of care was owed by the therapist to the husband (the wife maintained an independent cause of action against the therapist). The court examined similar cases and determined that there has to be a "specific professional relationship" and a "genuine connection between the conduct giving rise to the emotional distress and the purpose of that relationship" (p. 370). If the therapist was treating the couple, the duty to the spouse is likely to be assumed (*Horak v. Biris,* 1985). Although this result may seem unfair, it is consistent with the traditional rule that limits the duty of a clinician to the nonclient. These cases may have the most emotional response when the only party suing is the innocent spouse, sometimes because the relationship between the therapist and the client is ongoing. In these cases, the nonclient arguably has been harmed by the acts of the therapist but may have no legal recourse other than filing an administrative complaint to prohibit the professional from further practice.

Child Abuse Evaluation Cases

Sharon Zamstein filed for divorce from her husband in 1988. In the midst of a custody battle, she accused her husband of sexually abusing their two daughters. Mrs. Zamstein engaged the services of a child psychiatrist, Dr. Marvasti, to perform an abuse evaluation of the children. Marvasti videotaped the interviews during which he allegedly used inappropriate techniques such as asking leading or suggestive questions and offering candy as a reward. Later, Marvasti edited the videotape to remove some comments the children made that tended to exonerate their father. Another psychiatrist, evaluating for the court, found no evidence of sexual abuse and Mr. Zamstein was awarded joint custody. Dr. Marvasti then turned his videotape over to prosecutors, who used it as the basis of criminal charges against Mr. Zamstein. On cross-examination, Marvasti acknowledged that he had edited the tapes, and, as a result, the charges were dropped. Mr. Zamstein filed suit against Dr. Marvasti for negligence, arguing that Marvasti owed him a duty of care not to negligently evaluate abuse allegations resulting in false charges of sexual abuse to be filed (*Zamstein v. Marvasti,* 1997).

In child custody cases, accusations of abuse brought by one parent against the other frequently put the therapist in the middle of the fight (Bowman & Merz, 1996). When the evaluation of a child leads a clinician to file a child abuse report or to testify concerning an assessment that includes allegations of abuse, the parent against whom the report was made may attempt to file suit against the evaluator. The question in these cases is whether the clinician owed a duty of care to the parent in evaluating the suspected abuse. Mental health professionals retained to evaluate children for evidence of child abuse should be allowed to focus their complete attention on the child whom they are to evaluate. However, accused parents claim that a negligent assessment of a child results in damages to them in the form of investigation by child welfare workers and police, possible criminal prosecution, and loss of rights in custody decisions. The filing of a child abuse report and the in-court testimony detailing abuse allegations are both interventions that are arguably directed at the third-party parent and fulfill the direct victim standard. In child abuse evaluation cases, however, some competing interests and privileges militate against courts allowing third-party liability in almost all cases.

In *Zamstein v. Marvasti* (1997), the Connecticut Supreme Court rejected a duty of care to parents, focusing instead on the public policy reasons for not allowing alleged abusers to sue mental health professionals for negligence. The court reasoned that professionals should not be distracted from their duty by the specter of potential liability to the suspected abuser in the event their assessment of the child eventually turns out to be incorrect but honest. This rationale is consistent with the position that a potential for third-party liability creates a conflict of interest for the professional whose primary concern should be to the client, in this case the child being evaluated. The public policy argument is bolstered by several other legal principles that have led courts to reject third-party liability in all but the most egregious cases.

Schwarz v. Regents of the University of California (1990) upheld the dismissal of a father's negligence claim against his son's therapist. The therapist had helped the child's mother to remove the child from the country and conceal the child's whereabouts from the father. The court rejected a third-party liability claim on the grounds that the therapist had no duty of care to the father, even though he had agreed to pay for the therapy and to attend counseling sessions when requested. Here the element of privity was seemingly satisfied by the father's involvement in the counseling as a client. In the well-known California case *Marlene F. v. Affiliated Psychiatric Clinic* (1989), the court found that a mother's participation in the therapy of her children enabled her to file a malpractice suit against the therapist who abused the children. But unlike similar fact situations in the psychotherapist sexual abuse cases, the importance of encouraging unimpeded evaluation and reporting of child abuse sometimes outweighs the need to compensate the parent for any injury suffered as a result of being falsely accused.

The general trend has been consistent against allowing third-party suits in child abuse allegations. In addition to the public policy rationale articulated in the above cases, mental health workers have additional protections located in various state statutes. First, most states, in their mandatory reporting laws, include immunity from suit for "good faith" reporting of suspected child abuse. Courts have interpreted this to include those instances in which the clinician was wrong about the presence of abuse or about the identity of the abuser (*Bird v. W. C. W.,* 1994). A second source of statutory protection exists in the sovereign immunity laws in many states that severely limit the ability to sue state workers for activities related to their official functions. Finally, if the allegation of abuse is made attendant to a court proceeding, the testimonial privilege would apply, shielding a clinician from liability. In California, for example, the courts have found an expanded immunity for the activities of a clinician leading up to making the report of abuse including all professional services undertaken in the evaluation process (*Krikorian v. Barry,* 1987; *McMartin v. Children's Institute International,* 1989).

The behavior of a professional must reach an exceptional level of culpability to overcome the usual rule of no third-party liability. Such was the situation in *James W. v. Superior Court* (1993).

On the morning of May 9, 1989, 8-year-old Alicia complained of pain when she went to the bathroom. Her parents brought her to the hospital, where the staff determined Alicia had been raped and sodomized. Alicia stated that a man had come through the bedroom window and hurt her. After investigating, the hospital clinician and the police accused the father of the crime. He voluntarily submitted to polygraph, rape, and DNA tests to prove his innocence.

During the same month as the assault, a convicted sex offender had entered the bedroom window of the house across the street and abducted and attempted to rape a 4-year-old girl. The state child welfare agency seemed to dismiss the significance of this event and obtained an order of temporary custody of Alicia. They referred the family to a private counselor who strongly suspected the father and who worked with police and child welfare authorities in preparing the prosecution of the father.

Over the next two and a half years, the counselor, attorneys, police, and prosecutors allegedly misrepresented evidence and refused to consider any other suspects. The counselor aggressively attempted to get Alicia to name her father as the perpetrator, telling her that if she wanted to go home, she would have to say her father did it. The counselor saw the mother and sibling in conjoint sessions in which she instructed the mother to treat the father as if he were dead when Alicia was present, accused the mother of participating in the rape, and violated her confidentiality by sharing details of the mother's childhood with her children without consent.

The family eventually filed suit against several professionals including the counselor. They argued that the statutory protections for child abuse evaluators and reporters amounted to absolute immunity for those professionals who have any contact with abused children. The court agreed and refused to find the activities of the counselor and others to be protected by the child abuse statutes. They allowed the mother to file her negligence suit against the counselor because she was a participant in the treatment process.

Although the conduct alleged in *James W.* is more egregious than most situations, clinicians need to be aware of the multiple agendas and various strategies used in attempting to establish third-party liability. As this brief review has shown, the courts are hesitant to find liability owed to any individuals outside of the treatment relationship but will find a way to enforce liability when the conduct of the clinician is either extremely culpable or "directed at" the third party with malice. The mental health community can have an influence over the decisions of the legal system by working to pass legislation that limits the liability of practitioners to those who have engaged in treatment with the clinician. Including language to allow for a duty to refrain from "wanton or reckless" behavior directed at a third party would serve to address the exceptional situations in which a clinician should be responsible for damages caused to a third party. In this way, the sanctity of the treatment relationship can be secured, and conflicts of interest can be minimized.

DANGER TO SELF/SUICIDE
RISK ASSESSMENT CASES

A Vietnam veteran with a long history of psychiatric problems had been seeing a social worker and a psychiatrist through the Veteran's Administration Hospital. He also had the support of a lay counselor who, because of his status as a vet, was able to maintain a close relationship with many outpatient clients. During a session with the lay counselor, the client told him that he was planning to kill himself. The counselor attempted to get the client to see the social worker, without success. The counselor also testified that he warned the client's father, who had accompanied him to the session, of the threat. After leaving the counselor's office, the client jumped from a cliff, killing himself.

The Hawaii Supreme Court was asked to rule on the duty of a mental health worker to an outpatient client. The court found, in this case, no special relationship between the client and the worker that would trigger a duty to prevent the suicide. Without actual custody of an individual, the control over his actions is limited. The court opined that to rule otherwise could jeopardize the provision of outpatient services to persons with depression. When coupled with the importance of maintaining confidentiality in professional relationships, the court found a strong public policy rationale supporting its decision (*Lee v. Corregedore,* 1996).

When a loved one commits suicide, family and friends are left with emotional scars that include common feelings of grief mixed with guilt. "If only . . ." seems to be the expression that finds its way to the lips of those dealing with the suicide. Litigation against the mental health professionals involved with the deceased person may serve several functions for the family. First, it displaces some of the grief and helplessness onto the clinician, providing someone to blame, somewhere to put the anger. Second, the focus on the lawsuit may serve a grief-avoiding function (Sadoff & Gutheil, 1990). As a result, legal complaints against mental health workers arising out of a suicide have been among the most frequently litigated cases (Nurcombe & Partlett, 1994, p. 248). There are several key elements to suicide-related lawsuits. A clinician's liability for the death of a client by suicide depends on the existence of a special relationship, the forseeability that the client was actively suicidal, and the breach of a duty of care that could have prevented the client's act.

Special Relationship

There are several situations that may lead a court to find that a special relationship existed between the suicidal person and the professional to trigger the duty to care. First, when a client is in an institutional setting, the degree of control over the person is an important factor. There have been a number of cases examining the duty of a mental health facility to prevent a suicide. The cases have tended to find that a state or private facility does not have the duty to protect individuals from themselves. However, a mental health facility is required to provide conditions of reasonable care and safety to patients (*Estate of Cassara by Cassara v. Illinois,* 1994). When a client's suicidal ideations become known to staff, the "conditions of reasonable care and safety" would include appropriate monitoring and denial of access to potentially dangerous means and instruments.

Another situation that has been interpreted as creating a special relationship is when the client is a minor child. A majority of these cases have examined school-based incidents. In the lead case, a 13-year-old girl confided to friends her plans for a murder-suicide pact with another youth (*Eisel v. Board of Education,* 1991). The friends informed the school counselors, who interviewed the girl. She denied making the threats or harboring any suicidal intent. The counselors did not notify either parents or school administrators. Subsequently, the girl died in a double shooting. The court examined the facts and found a basis for the existence of a duty to use reasonable means to attempt to prevent the suicide. The school staff stands *in loco parentis* (in the place of the parents) when the child is at school. The notice to the counselors of the girl's intent was deemed sufficient to require the counselors to take more action than just interviewing the girl and accepting her denial of the threat, even though the murder-suicide occurred on a school holiday and not on school grounds. The court found that the school policy specifies the steps that must be followed in a case where a student has threatened suicide, including the involvement of school personnel and possible notification of parents.

Although the special relationship criteria have been applied in most cases, some courts have avoided that issue by focusing their view on the actions of the mental health worker earlier in the case. In one Connecticut case, for example, an appeals court allowed a case to proceed on a malpractice claim despite a client's discharge from a mental health facility several weeks prior to a suicide. The court rejected an attempt to have the case dismissed on the grounds that the facility no longer had the control over the client's actions. Instead, they allowed a claim that the discharge from the facility was premature. The focus was on the question of whether the actions of the mental health professionals proximately caused the injury, that is, the subsequent suicide (*Shelnitz v. Greenberg*, 1986).

Foreseeability

The mental health worker is considered to have a duty to prevent a harm only where suicide is reasonably anticipated from the facts of the case. Foreseeability is found when a client has a history of suicidal feelings and/or actions, is being treated for suicide prevention, or exhibits suicidal tendencies while being treated for something else, or when the therapist is negligent for not having assessed a client's suicidal tendencies (Bednar et al., 1991). Because most persons who commit suicide have given some notice or indication of intent, courts may be able to infer foreseeability retrospectively. However, in most cases, there has to be some evidence of the risk. In a New York case, during the intake of a man to a psychiatric facility, the patient's wife withheld information concerning his past suicide attempts. As a result, the staff could not be held to have violated a duty of care by failing to order more stringent monitoring of the patient prior to his suicide while on the unit because they had no knowledge of his history of suicide attempts or current risk (*Krapivka v. Maimonides Medical Center*, 1986).

Clinically, suicide is difficult to predict because there is a low percentage of completed suicides compared with the number of threats and attempts. For this reason, even with excellent skill, there are certain to be a high number of false positives (Bednar et al., 1991, pp. 104-105). Despite the presence of an established duty for a mental health professional to adequately assess suicide risk (*Meier v. Ross General Hospital*,

1968), defensive actions that overemphasize protection can result in unnecessary confinement and improper breaches of confidentiality in attempting to fulfill a duty to prevent harm. What is important for practitioners to remember is that the standard for judging foreseeability is whether the assessment was done within accepted professional norms and whether a reasonable practitioner would have foreseen the suicide risk. This is a different standard from the question of whether the prediction turned out to be correct. Knowledge of the elements of a suicide assessment, routine reevaluations of clients, and regular supervision to guard against missing obvious signs of suicide risk are necessary for every practitioner in every field of practice.

Breach of Duty

Once the precursor conditions of special relationship and foreseeability are established, the court will examine the actions of the mental health worker to determine whether there was a breach of duty. The standard of care will depend on the setting and the degree of control that is possible over the behavior of the client. Many cases have found a breach of duty when proper prevention interventions were not effectuated despite evidence that the worker knew or should have known about the risks. For example, in one case, a residential treatment facility was found liable for breaching its duty of care to an adolescent mental health client. The therapists knew of the boy's suicidal risk but failed to inform all of the residential care staff so as to effectively safeguard the client (*Psychiatric Institute of Washington v. Allen,* 1986). The primary issue in breach of duty is the professional's response to the threat of suicide. The action of the therapist should be consistent with the level of risk presented by the client, with the most aggressive interventions such as involuntary confinement and warning family members reserved for cases with serious risk factors.

One possible consequence of an aggressive response to a suicidal client is a suit for false imprisonment. In a recent Washington, D.C., case, a mental health worker in the Emergency Response Division was sued by a woman under this legal theory. Ms. M. had been talking to her friend about committing suicide. The friend was concerned and requested that the worker listen in to a telephone conversation during which Ms. M. made explicit suicide threats. The worker involuntarily detained Ms. M. and had her transported to a psychiatric hospital with the help of local police and hospital employees. The court found that the worker was not liable because he was empowered to detain her by statute and he reasonably believed she was mentally ill and was likely to injure herself based on the content of the phone conversation (*Magwood v. Giddings,* 1996).

A review of recent cases results in a relatively clear scope of duty for clinicians. The courts have been sensitive to the limits that workers have on controlling all of the actions of a client. When the client is confined or in the custody of an institution, a special relationship is inferred that requires a greater duty to protect the client from self-injury. Given that all litigation follows a suicide or suicide attempt, there is the danger of hindsight bias in evaluating what the clinician knew or should have known about the client's mental status. The best protection for workers, and the most important for client safety, is for the clinician to reassess clients on a regular basis, to receive professional clinical supervision, and to follow an accepted suicide assessment protocol when a client expresses suicidal ideation. (For a summary of clinical duties and assessment tools, see Bednar et al., 1991, pp. 104-132.) The primary elements of the standard of care are adequate diagnosis, or the identification of risk factors; the exercise of reasonable care to initiate preventive interventions; and the ability to provide effective treatment or referral for a suicidal client.

OTHER AREAS OF
PROFESSIONAL LIABILITY

Defamation

In 1989, Ms. Johnson began counseling with Dr. Adams. In April of that year, Ms. Johnson informed her mother about some statements that Dr. Adams had made to her during a treatment session. Dr. Adams was reported to have said the mother was mentally ill with a borderline personality and in need of extensive psychotherapy. Further, Dr. Adams recommended that Ms. Johnson sever all ties with her mother. The relationship between Ms. Johnson and her mother deteriorated during the time she was in counseling. In June 1989, Ms. Johnson told her mother that she was not to attempt to visit with her grandchild. Ms. Johnson threatened to kill her mother and rejected all efforts by her mother to continue a loving relationship, "justifying these actions with the diagnosis of Dr. Adams that the mother is a borderline personality who has abused her." The mother sued Dr. Adams, claiming that he had made slanderous statements that caused her to be ostracized from her daughter. The court rejected the malpractice action, upholding the rights of health care providers to express opinions, even if they have adverse effects on third parties (*Russell v. Adams,* 1997).

Defamation is the publishing of a statement about another person that is untrue, misleading, malicious, and damaging to the person being written about (Barker, 1995). A defamatory statement can take either a written form, called *libel,* or a spoken form, called *slander.* Truth is an absolute defense to defamation. Alternatively, someone accused of defamation might argue that the statement was made without malice or that it was not damaging to the complainant. In the context of mental health, the claim of defamation is frequently part of a malpractice or breach of contract claim. Clients and others who file a lawsuit for defamation usually target the unauthorized release of records that publish false statements. For example, a school social worker completed a referral form on a child who was transferring to a new school district. The referral included statements that named the child's father as being a drug addict. The worker had obtained this information from a teacher who had mistakenly assumed that the student and his older sibling had the same biological father. Although the social worker discovered the mistake, she did not correct the document, believing that the father probably was involved in some illegal activity. The father received a negative reception at the new school and could have had a cause of action for defamation.

An extremely contentious Pennsylvania case, *Tuman v. Genesis Associates* (1996), allowed the parents of a woman receiving treatment related to recovered memories of childhood sexual abuse to bring a civil suit for defamation. The court held that under Pennsylvania law, a therapist owed a duty of reasonable care to the parents of a client. The claim of defamation was based on statements made by the therapists in group therapy that the parents were sexually abusive to the client, thus "publishing" the statements to all the members of the group. This case is still being litigated as of this writing, but the claim for defamation has been allowed to stand. The potential chilling effect on the practice of group therapy is significant if this case establishes the claim of defamation in group communications. The judge in *Tuman* suggested that the defamation action was possible even if the therapists did not make the statements but the client spoke the words as their "mouth-piece" in naming her parents as her abusers (p. 189).

In the *Bird* case, discussed above in the context of a court's refusal to find a basis for third-party liability, the Texas court also rejected a claim of defamation. Although the court determined that the clinician owed no duty to the father for her improper diagnosis, it had serious questions about her contention that she was functioning within a "treatment and diagnosis" role when she communicated to the family court, via affidavit, her opinion that it was the father who had abused his son. This case provides a good example of some statutory protections for clinicians that can defeat a claim of defamation. The court found that because the Texas child protection law requires only the reporting of the suspected abuse, but does not specifically require the reporting of the actual perpetrator, the clinician's affidavit was not protected under the immunity clause of that statute. The court strangely reasoned that her conclusions concerning the identity of the suspected abuser were not based upon some special diagnostic skill or expertise but upon "the outcry of the child" (pp. 770-771). Therefore, she was not acting in a psychotherapy role with its protection of privilege. Like any other person, by naming the father as the abuser in her affidavit to the court, she subjected herself to liability for defamation. The clinician success-fully argued that because the statements were made in the context of a judicial proceeding, the privilege should apply in this case, and the father's defamation claim was dismissed.

Breach of Contract

A breach of contract claim against a clinician is based on either an express or an implied contract between the client and the professional. The express part of the contract is what is included in any forms or written service agreements entered into at the beginning of therapy or at any point thereafter. The contract states the expectations on each party in terms of obligations and responsibilities. The basis of an action for breach is the claim that the clinician fell short of fulfilling expectations, and the client suffered damages to the extent that the services were paid for but not adequately delivered. An implied contract is based on the standards of the profession. A client entering treatment has certain expectations based on these standards. If the clinician deviates from the standards, even if complying with them has not been written as part of a contract, the court can assume a breach of an implied contract. In those cases where an action for malpractice cannot be proven because of the amount of time that has passed since the therapy was concluded, the breach of contract claim is used. The statute of limitations in most states is longer for breach of contract claims (four to five years) than it is for negligence claims (two to three years).

The contracts that mental health professionals enter into with clients to provide counseling and psychotherapy services help to define the standard of care. The clarity of expectations that comes from careful use of procedures and documentation of services is important to clinicians to prove that they practiced in a reasonable manner. Although few cases are actually decided on the basis of a breach of contract, the adherence to contractual specifications can assist a clinician in justifying practice decisions.

Intentional Infliction of Emotional Distress

In many of the most emotional cases, the therapist is charged with the tort of intentionally inflicting emotional distress on the client or other party. The criteria for this cause of action is clearly described and difficult to reach. The laws in each state vary in language but are consistent in approach. In Connecticut, for example, four elements must be present for a jury to find that a clinician has committed an intentional infliction of emotional distress tort.

- The clinician intended to inflict emotional distress or should have known that emotional distress was a likely result of the conduct.
- The conduct was extreme and outrageous.
- The conduct was the cause of the plaintiff's distress.
- The emotional distress sustained by the plaintiff was severe (*Petyan v. Ellis*, 1986).

If a client is able to present facts that, if true, would satisfy each of these elements, a court usually allows the case to proceed to a trial. The questions in these cases are subjective in that they need to be evaluated by a jury to determine whether the behavior of the clinician was extreme and outrageous (see, e.g., *Lindgren v. Moore*, 1995; *Tuman v. Genesis*

Associates, 1996). The claim of intentional infliction of emotional distress has been used by third parties when there is no standing to file a claim for negligence or breach of contract. The duty not to intentionally cause harm to another person is not bound by the presence of a professional relationship but is the basic expectation of all members of society to each other.

SUMMARY

The standard of care for social workers, counselors, and other mental health professionals encompasses both commonsense practice guidelines and professionally accepted technical standards. Developing an understanding of the various legal theories on which clients base complaints against therapists helps clinicians to categorize the elements of the professional standard of care. The malpractice standards define reasonable professional behavior based on expert testimony. A general negligence standard asks the jury to determine whether a clinician's actions were reasonable, given the circumstances. Breach of contract actions hold the clinician accountable for following through with agreed-upon services in a professionally accepted manner. Intentional tort claims can be pursued when a clinician's actions are purposefully harmful to an individual. In some situations, such as sexual relations with clients, the standard of care is painted in a bright line. In other areas of practice, such as deciding between treatment options, the standard of care is fuzzy and sometimes unknown to the practitioner. Although court cases can help to define reasonable care, the mental health professions must be active players in the legal environment, shaping the thinking of the courts and using the legislature to promote therapeutic outcomes.

Chapter 6

INTERACTIONS WITH THE LEGAL SYSTEM

STYLE, FORM, AND FUNCTION
OF THE PROFESSIONS

Many species of high quality can inhabit the same world. Such multiplicity is indeed the highest promise of the modern age.
Vincent Scully (Introduction to R. Venturi,
Complexity and Contradiction in Architecture, 1966)

The study of architecture involves an analysis of styles, form, and function. The materials, designs, and breadth of a project are inseparable from the cultural tradition from which it springs and the purpose for which it is intended (Whitaker, 1996). The study of the legal and mental health professions has many similarities to the study of architecture. It should not be surprising that the styles and forms of practice can be so different, given the diverse functions of these professions.

Doesn't she understand that my time is important, too? She never returns my phone calls, reschedules my court appearances and expects me to change all of my client appointments. And furthermore, she doesn't seem to know anything about my work. (Anonymous clinical social worker commenting on her recent dealings with an attorney)

The function of the attorney is to represent the interests of the client by assuming roles such as advocate and counselor (the information-bearing, advice-giving variety). The function of lawyering is oriented toward results: preventing a client from activity that has negative legal implications, protecting a client who has been accused of violating some standard of behavior, or ensuring that a client is compensated for any injuries suffered as a result of the intentional or negligent act of another. The style of the attorney must suit the function. Most clients want the person in this role to be decisive, zealous, argumentative, intelligent, knowledgeable, and undeniably fighting for them. Attorneys are caricatured as people who dress well, carry themselves with a professional and confident style, and exhibit what has been called a bulldog mentality as they pursue the interests of their clients. Fernald (1989) notes that mental health clinicians "rely so heavily on the subjective that ambiguity is a natural by-product of their professional conclusions" (p. 193).

The mental health clinician, by contrast, assumes similar roles but with a different function. The roles of advocate and counselor are influenced by the values of self-determination and empowerment. The function of counseling is often as focused on the process as on the results: helping clients to get through difficult crisis situations and life transitions, supporting clients who have a mental illness or other disability to strengthen their ability to live life more fully and functionally, and linking clients with those resources that will strengthen their supportive network in their environment. The style of the mental health clinician must suit the function. Most clients want the person who is in this role to be warm, nonjudgmental, supportive, an effective listener, intelligent, knowledgeable, and undeniably on their side. Mental health clinicians are caricatured as people who dress comfortably and casually, carry themselves with a professional and caring style, and exhibit what could be called a puppy dog mentality as they support the interests of their clients.

Obviously, these caricatures reflect stereotyped images but they hold some level of truth at their basis. Style and form follow function. When a mental health professional comes into contact with an attorney, it is important to understand function so as to manage the interaction effectively. Too often, the lawyer is approached as the clinician would approach another mental health professional. The expectations regarding the attorney's motivation and goals are unrealistic given the function. The hope that the lawyer will appreciate the subtleties and nuances of mental and emotional health and the treatment process as they relate to the client is not in keeping with the orientation of the lawyer. A case is only as good as its facts. The lawyer expects the clinician to be definitive, precise, and objective, even when the client's mental and emotional state is variable and imprecise. Each professional needs to understand the role of the other. Clinicians must concentrate on effective education of the legal system so that lawyers and judges understand mental health treatment. The education process, however, must cut both ways. Clinicians need to develop an understanding of the purpose of a legal proceeding to know what the lawyer is trying to accomplish. It is only then that the clinician can start where the lawyer is (a fundamental counseling skill that is somehow neglected in these interactions) to improve the quality of the interactions.

Often the expectations of one profession are projected onto the other. By putting oneself in the client's shoes, it is possible to view the lawyer as operating in a desirable manner to accomplish the goals of effective legal advocacy. Zealots rarely make friends. An attorney seeking mental health counseling would want a clinician who is warm, empathic, and open minded. But when hiring an expert or deposing a clinician as a witness, the same attorney wants an unequivocal assessment from a credible and confident professional. Similarly, when a mental health clinician needs legal representation, the traits that are seen as negative in professional interactions might be comforting when being employed to protect the clinician's interests.

INVOLVEMENT IN A LEGAL PROCEEDING

Mental health clinicians are asked to participate in a wide variety of legal proceedings as witnesses, experts, or, at times, defendants. The invitation process can be stressful and foreign. The language and formality of the forms and procedures are intimidating and may prompt clinicians to respond in ways that place themselves and their practice or agency in jeopardy. It is important for clinicians to understand the processes and the purposes of the various stages of a legal proceeding so as to respond safely and effectively. In this section, a case is used to illustrate typical questions and challenges experienced by mental health clinicians. Following each section of the case vignette, the legal issues will be explored in detail and recommendations for action will be discussed. Most of the cases that have been reviewed in previous chapters have come from the appeals courts. These cases are the "precedent-makers" or those that spell out the law in a particular area. These cases, however, do not illustrate the usual experiences of clinicians who receive a subpoena in the mail and who are asked to appear in court to testify about some aspect of their treatment of a current or past client. The goal of this chapter is to walk through a more typical case so that the lessons of the precedent cases can be applied to the everyday experiences of clinicians.

The Subpoena, Depositions, and Pretrial Preparation

Mr. Scott was frustrated and upset as he talked to his legal consultant for the third time in four days. He was particularly annoyed by his inability to speak with the attorney representing his ex-client in a pending legal case. He had received a subpoena to testify but the date had been changed and Mr. Scott did not understand the nature of the case or what they wanted him to testify about. Despite numerous phone calls and conversations with a novice legal assistant in the lawyer's office, Mr. Scott had not been able to set an appointment with the attorney to go over the expectations for his testimony or even to find out when the trial might begin.

Mr. Scott worried about his personal liability and the security of his private practice. He was concerned with the prospect of having to cancel or reschedule many clients to accommodate the scheduling of the meetings, depositions, and testimony for this case. Mr. Scott also felt uneasy about the financial implications of his involvement. Would he be reimbursed for the preparation of records and for his time?

It had been almost two years since Mr. Scott last saw Charlene for counseling. When she began therapy, Mr. Scott assessed her as suffering from post-traumatic stress disorder resulting from several abusive relationships and a sexual assault. Her symptoms included severe dissociation and flashbacks. Mr. Scott referred her for an inpatient evaluation, which confirmed the diagnosis. The hospital psychiatrist prescribed medication and ongoing psychotherapy.

Charlene's mental health difficulties were putting a tremendous strain on her marital relationship. Jed, her husband, was a high-profile town manager. They had four children, all of whom were then living on their own. The psychiatrist referred the case back to Mr. Scott for supportive counseling for Charlene and marital counseling for the couple. Mr. Scott saw Charlene weekly and had numerous conjoint sessions. On three occasions, he saw Jed in individual counseling sessions. Charlene exhibited ongoing dissociative symptoms and Mr. Scott documented the presence of multiple personalities, a diagnosis supported by the psychiatrist who continued to see Charlene monthly to monitor her medication.

After about two years, Jed filed for divorce and refused to continue counseling. Soon after, Charlene was rehospitalized and, upon release, began psychotherapy with Dr. Hearns, a clinical psychologist from the hospital who specialized in dissociative identity disorders. Mr. Scott had no further contact with Charlene until he had received a phone call from her two months ago. In this call, Charlene indicated she was involved in a lawsuit with her husband related to their divorce. She said she had filled out a release form to allow her attorney to speak with Mr. Scott and receive a copy of her records. Charlene indicated that the attorney would be in touch to discuss the case and Mr. Scott's testimony prior to a trial.

Following that phone call, Mr. Scott received the proper release forms to share his records and to speak with Charlene's attorney, Ms. Hall. Mr. Scott had few written notes beyond session dates and periodic treatment summaries. He did have extensive audiotapes covering individual and marital sessions throughout the two years of treatment. Mr. Scott tried unsuccessfully to reach Ms. Hall by phone to express his concerns about releasing these tapes, out of concern for both the privacy of the clients and the mental health of Charlene. Mr. Scott felt that it would be inappropriate for Charlene to hear tapes of her alter egos and of sessions that dealt with her trauma history without proper psychiatric consultation.

Several days after the release form arrived, Mr. Scott received a subpoena in the mail asking him to appear in court in three weeks with Charlene's case records. Once again, his phone calls to the attorney were not returned. The legal assistant explained that Ms. Hall was litigating another case and was in court all week. At this point it was just one week before the scheduled date of his testimony. Mr. Scott was unclear about what to do and consulted

his legal consultant. He requested assistance from his consultant
on the following issues:

Although the subpoena indicated he was to bring all records, Mr.
Scott wanted to know how to protect information about Jed, who had
not provided a release, and how to handle the audiotapes and limited
written records.

He needed guidance about how to answer pretrial questions in trial
preparation sessions and depositions. What were the issues he would be
asked about? How should he respond if asked for information or opinions about Jed?

Finally, Mr. Scott needed to vent his anger at the lack of response he
has gotten from Ms. Hall and to strategize about how to help her
understand the counseling process, the risks to Charlene of indiscrimi-
nate use of the clinical information in the case record, and concerns
about violating Jed's statutory privilege.

Responding to Subpoenas

It is important to understand what a subpoena is to know how to
respond properly. It can be an intimidating experience when a subpoena
arrives in the mail or is delivered by a court officer or sheriff. Subpoenas
appear to be and, in fact, are very official and carry the force of law.
They often include arcane language such as "commanded to bring with
you and produce . . . here under penalty of the law in that case provided." A subpoena may also include the Latin term *duces tecum,* which
means that the clinician must bring certain records to court at the
scheduled appearance time. Receiving a subpoena, however, is not the
same as being compelled to testify. It only compels the mental health
professional to appear, not to testify (Simon, 1992). In most states,
subpoenas are prepared by the attorney of one of the parties in a legal
action. They are signed by a court clerk but there is usually no legal
ruling that has determined that the testimony of the clinician is admissible, and there is no official decision as to whether the subpoena is
valid. In some states, a judge must sign off on subpoenas that request
mental health or substance abuse records. In these cases, and in cases
where a judge makes a ruling on the admissibility of the testimony and

records of the clinician, the official request to appear is in the form of a court order.

Regardless of the form of the subpoena, it is important that clinicians respond promptly and with an understanding of their rights and obligations. Mr. Scott was anxious about his subpoena because of the uncertainty regarding the nature of the case and the expectations for his testimony. His response in this case was to consult with an attorney who specializes in mental health law. At this stage, it was not necessary for the attorney to be retained to represent him. Mr. Scott needed guidance and support for his response to the subpoena. The first question upon receiving a subpoena is to determine who has issued it and what jurisdiction will hear the case. If the subpoena is issued in a state other than the one the worker lives or works in, it may not be enforceable. Also, each state has specific requirements about how a witness is to be notified, such as how a subpoena must be delivered (by registered mail, by hand, or other means) and how much notice (number of days) must be provided to the witness. For questions of this nature, an attorney would be required to interpret the status of the subpoena and to challenge its validity.

More common than problems with validity are questions concerning whether the testimony of the mental health clinician would be admissible and whether a privilege protects client information. Once clinicians determine who issued the subpoena, when and how the worker is to respond, and the identity of the client, the next step is to contact the client directly. Mr. Scott had been notified by Charlene that she supported his involvement in the case and she had supplied copies of release forms. However, Jed had not been consulted and retained his right to keep his information confidential. In cases where there is a question as to whether confidential information may be compromised by complying with a subpoena, the clinician has several options.

The first option is for the clinician to discuss the confidentiality concerns with the attorney who has issued the subpoena. To do this, the client must sign a release allowing the clinician to talk to the attorney. Mr. Scott, on the advice of his legal consultant, asked for and received a written release to speak with Charlene's attorney. He sought to explain the facts of the treatment, particularly the issues related to the privilege rights of Jed. Ms. Hall accepted the limitations and indicated that the scope of her questions would be limited. She affirmed that she would ask no questions regarding Jed. In many cases, negotiation can lead to positive outcomes for court testimony (APA, Committee on Legal Issues, 1996). Because evidence introduced in a court case must pass the test of being relevant to the issues being litigated, attorneys often want to have a mental health professional testify about a specific issue. In the example case, Ms. Hall was trying to show that Charlene had long-standing and chronic mental health needs and would require extensive treatment, perhaps throughout her lifetime. The issue was relevant to the divorce action because the medical expenses she is likely to incur would need to be provided for. The judge was presiding over the disbursement of the marital property and Jed was not willing to pay for her future mental health treatment.

The responsibility to maintain confidential records in the face of the demands of the legal system can be a challenge to mental health professionals. A subpoena is not the same as a court order. If the subpoena seeks testimony or records that are confidential, and the client has not consented to a release, the clinician must act to object to the disclosure. The following case illustrates the ramifications of not under-standing the process of responding to a subpoena.

Rost v. State Board of Psychology (1995, opinion of the court). Polly Rost, a clinical psychologist licensed to practice in the Commonwealth of Pennsylvania, brought this appeal from an order of the State Board of Psychology, which reprimanded her for having violated the Professional Psychologists Practice Act. An unlicensed supervisee of Rost began giving psychological treatment to Sarah, a female juvenile. Sarah was treated in Rost's practice for recurring headaches that allegedly were caused when Sarah fell and struck her head at the York Jewish Community Center (YJCC). In March of 1988, Sarah's mother filed suit against the YJCC on Sarah's behalf, alleging that YJCC's negligence had caused her daughter physical and emotional harm.

In December 1989, YJCC's attorney mailed Rost a subpoena requesting the treatment records for Sarah. Rost subsequently provided YJCC with these treatment records. Although Sarah's mother had previously signed a release allowing Rost to turn over the records to Sarah's own attorney, Rost had not obtained permission to release the records to YJCC. Furthermore, Rost did not attempt to contact Sarah's mother, or Sarah's attorney, to obtain permission to release the records or to advise them of her intention to release the records prior to doing so. Rost did not attempt to gain permission because she believed she was already authorized to release records to YJCC based upon the release that had previously been given to Sarah's attorney.

On January 25, 1993, the Commonwealth of Pennsylvania, Bureau of Professional and Occupational Affairs (BPOA), charged Rost with having violated three sections of the Act. The hearing examiner issued a decision in which he concluded that Rost was not subject to disciplinary action because Sarah had waived the client-psychologist privilege by asserting a claim for emotional damages in her lawsuit against YJCC. In response, the BPOA filed an appeal. The Board disagreed with the hearing examiner's recommendation and, by an amended order, officially reprimanded the psychologist . Rost's appeal to this Court followed.

Rost's first argument is that she did not violate Sections 8(a), (9), and (11) of the Act because she released the records pursuant to a subpoena and Sarah waived her right to confidentiality by initiating a lawsuit in which her psychological condition was at issue. However, we must agree with the Board that Rost's argument is misplaced. We are not faced with the question of whether YJCC should have been barred from introducing Sarah's records at trial based on the psychologist-client privilege. That is a determination properly made by a judge and not by a psychologist lacking formal legal training. Rost is also mistaken when she attempts to equate the psychologist-client privilege with the rule of confidentiality found in the Code of Ethics for psychologists. Although the two are similar, the privilege is limited in scope to the question of admissibility of evidence in a civil or criminal trial.

In interpreting the psychologist-client privilege, we are guided by the same rules that apply to the attorney-client privilege. The duty of confidentiality is absolute and cannot be waived except after full disclosure and written authorization by the client. Unlike the privilege, it continues even when the information has been previously disclosed to third parties or is material to litigation initiated by the client. Whenever a professional in possession of confidential information is served with a subpoena, a conflict naturally arises between one's duty to the courts and one's duty of confidentiality toward one's client. In this respect, Rost is no different from the numerous other psychologists, doctors, lawyers, and clergymen who receive subpoenas in this Commonwealth each year. The value of a psychologist's, or other professional's, duty of confidentiality would be illusory if it could be overridden anytime a conflicting duty arose that was thought to be more important. Although Rost may have been placed in an unfavorable position, she is not excused from following the ethical guidelines of her profession, which plainly forbid her from disclosing a client's records without consent.

Rost argues that it is unreasonable to expect a psychologist, lacking formal legal training, to know the proper procedure to follow after receiving a subpoena. Rost apparently believes that she was in an untenable position in which she would have had either to violate the rules of professional conduct or to disregard a subpoena. However, this argument is flawed. Rost could have challenged the subpoena in court or obtained permission from her client before releasing the information. If Rost was uncertain about her legal rights and responsibilities, she should have at least obtained advice from an attorney instead of unilaterally releasing her client's records. Even if the attorneys acted unprofessionally, this would not excuse Rost's own unprofessional conduct. Accordingly, we affirm the order of the Board that reprimanded Rost for having violated Sections 8(a), (9), and (11) of the Act. [Citations omitted; text edited for style and readability.]

Contesting subpoenas. There are several strategies available to a mental health professional who seeks to contest a subpoena. First, the clinician or legal representative can write to the court specifying the legal and ethical basis of the objection. For example, in the case involving Mr. Scott, if Ms. Hall had indicated that she needed him to testify about the marital relationship at the time the couple was in therapy, there would be a serious risk of improperly releasing privileged information about Jed. Mr. Scott would need to articulate these concerns to the judge in the letter with a copy sent to each attorney. A more formal procedure would be to file a motion to quash the subpoena (void the order to appear to testify) or a motion requesting a protective order.

In many states, the privilege statute specifies a process for judicial review of potentially privileged communications. The judge may request the opportunity to review the counseling records privately, a process known as *in camera* review (see the Chapter 3 section on privilege). The in camera review process allows a judge to determine relevancy, materiality, and whether the information can be adequately proven without overriding the privilege. Based on the in camera review, the court may consider several options.

The judge has the option of finding the subpoena valid and the information from the clinician to be relevant. The clinician would then be ordered to comply with the subpoena. A judge can rule that there is no privilege or that the privilege has been waived. The clinician would be required to testify as to all aspects of treatment. Once the order comes from the court, it is unlikely that any action could be brought against the clinician for violation of confidentiality. At times, the evidence of the clinician is relevant, but the judge limits the scope of the questions that can be asked and the issues that will be addressed in court. This is done to protect clients to the extent possible while still allowing crucial evidence to be heard by the court. Finally, a judge can rule either that the information to be given by the mental health professional is not relevant or can be demonstrated by other witnesses, or that the privilege makes the client-worker communications protected from disclosure.

In most cases, the attorney for the client will be invested in supporting the client's right to have the counseling information kept private. When negotiating with the client and his or her legal representative, the clinician's interests are usually consistent with the client's interests. The motion to quash a subpoena would be filed by the client's attorney. This saves the clinician from the expense of hiring an attorney to intervene in the case. However, it is important for the mental health professional to fully understand the nature of the legal system's requests and to seek competent consultation and/or representation by an attorney who specializes in mental health law prior to releasing records or testifying in court.

The American Psychological Association Committee on Legal Issues (1996) has developed a list of possible grounds for opposing or limiting production of client records. The arguments include the following:

- The court does not have jurisdiction over the professional, or insufficient notice was given.
- The professional does not have care and custody of the requested records; they belong to the agency.
- The therapist-client privilege protects the records.

- The information sought is not relevant to the issues before the court.
- The information sought is overly broad and beyond the scope of the issues before the court.

If a clinician continues to object to the production of certain records and testimony after receiving a valid subpoena or court order, legal representation is strongly advised. In depositions, the clinician can rely on the advice of counsel as to how to respond to questions that jeopardize someone's confidential information. The clinician must go to court on the scheduled day and state objections to the testimony in court. Refusal to answer questions can lead to a contempt of court citation or other sanctions imposed by the judge. This is why all objections need to be made within a legal venue with articulated legal grounds supporting the objections. An appeal of the judge's order to produce records or to testify is available in these cases, particularly when the failure of an appeals court to intervene would result in irreparable harm to the client.

It is important for a mental health worker to document all activities involved in responding to a subpoena. If a client subsequently sues for violation of confidentiality, the case records can demonstrate a pattern of behavior that is reasonable and professional. When possible, the objections to a subpoena should be made in court so that a judge can rule on the question of compelled testimony. In this way, clinicians can ensure a full hearing with the possibility of appeal on the issue and in the process can protect themselves from future lawsuits related to the testimony.

Testifying as a Witness

Mr. Scott nervously scraped the toe of his shoe against the uneven marble floor of the old courthouse. Despite attempts to convince Ms. Hall that he really had nothing important to add to the testimony to be provided by Charlene's psychiatrist and her current therapist, Mr. Scott found himself impatiently awaiting his moment on the witness stand. Ms. Hall had finally met with him over the holiday weekend when both were available. He had been scheduled to testify the previous week and had canceled a full day of client appointments at a mental health clinic where he does per diem work. Then, the day before the appearance date, the judge decided to attend a workshop and pushed the trial back one week.

Mr. Scott was angry about the time and money he was losing in this case, especially considering that his contribution to proving the case seemed trivial. The one redeeming aspect of his involvement was his hope that Charlene would be awarded sufficient resources to be cared for in a decent fashion. He felt angry that Jed would abandon her and deny the seriousness of her ongoing mental and emotional problems, especially because he had played a part in exacerbating her condition over the years.

Litigation is a unique and complicated method for resolving disputes among people. The process can be analogized to a game or, in some cases, to a dance. The rules of procedure and the rules of evidence are the framework within which the facts and laws are analyzed and argued. The actual controversy in legal cases becomes well defined as the case gets closer to trial. The essence of the art of lawyering in a trial is asking the right questions of the right people. In Mr. Scott's case, the issue was whether Charlene should be awarded a larger share of the marital property so that she could use it to pay for ongoing mental health treatment because the mental illness will affect her ability to maintain employment. The issues to be litigated are determined by the lawyers and the judge prior to the actual trial. Based on the information uncovered in the discovery process, the sides may agree to stipulate some issues as true, eliminating the need to present evidence about these facts. The issues to be litigated in the example case are as follows:

- Clarification of Charlene's mental health diagnosis including whether her symptoms are evidence of a psychiatric disorder or merely evidence of malingering
- Assessment of Charlene's prognosis
- Valuation of the costs of ongoing treatment
- Application of the laws of the state governing divorce and the dissolution of marital property

Ms. Hall had prepared Mr. Scott for his appearance in court by reviewing the history of his involvement with Charlene. She took copious notes on the dates of service, the original diagnosis, the referral for inpatient evaluation, and the actual treatment goals. Ms. Hall reviewed the "foundation" questions that she would ask regarding Mr.

Scott's identity, qualifications such as education and experience, and the capacity in which he knew Charlene. Ms. Hall reassured Mr. Scott that she would not ask him to violate Jed's privilege. She also explained it was likely that Jed's attorney would question Mr. Scott's credibility and expertise. She asked Mr. Scott if he had any personal or professional issues that might be used by Jed's attorney to discredit him such as a disciplinary complaint, malpractice suit, suspension of his professional license, dismissal from an agency, substance abuse history, mental health treatment, or any other relevant issues.

Mental health professionals must be prepared to deal with the schedule changes and uncertainties involved in testifying in court. More often than not, the scheduled date and time for a court appearance will be changed. Postponements in a trial, called *continuances,* are granted by a judge for a variety of reasons. Once the trial begins, however, there is increased pressure to conform to the identified dates. In many cases, the mental health professional is called to testify early in the morning and then must sit and wait all day before taking the stand. It is important to communicate with the attorney to determine how the case is proceeding and to receive guidance as to the actual time of testimony. However, unless there is direct word from the attorney, the clinician should follow the instructions on the subpoena because a witness can be held in contempt for failure to appear at the designated time. Attorneys who are made aware of the scheduling needs of the professional can sometimes arrange to have the testimony begin the day or initiate the afternoon session to make the clinician's scheduling of clients more reasonable. Finally, clinicians should be aware that many cases reach a settlement at the eleventh hour. Hours of work preparing for testimony and a great deal of anxiety developed in anticipation of the court appearance may seem wasted. However, it may be that the opposing counsel, upon reviewing a clinician's report and deposition, might agree to settle a case rather than leaving it to a judge or jury to decide.

In the example case, Mr. Scott never had to testify. On the opening morning of the trial, Dr. Hearns was the first witness. He was scheduled to resume testimony in the afternoon, to be followed by Mr. Scott. During the lunch break, the attorney who represented Jed met with Charlene's attorney, at the urging of the judge, to reach an agreement concerning the distribution of the marital property and assets. Mr. Scott had mixed feelings. He was angry at the wasted time, the financial losses, and the disruption to his life. He had conflicting feelings about not getting to testify. On one hand, he believed that his testimony could have had a role in assuring that Charlene was treated fairly and would be cared for. Not giving the testimony left him feeling that he had nothing to show for all of his work, worry, and expense. On the other hand, Mr. Scott was relieved that he did not have to go through the actual testimony. He was not cross-examined on his assessment and diagnosis, and he did not have to risk divulging privileged information.

Guidelines for testifying. Being called as a witness in a court proceeding produces anxiety and fear in the most experienced clinicians. Prior to testifying, there are several guidelines that should be reviewed. First, in cases where a client has requested the testimony to support an issue in the litigation, it is important to review testimony with the client's attorney prior to the court appearance. This allows the clinician to be prepared for the type of questions that will be asked. If a clinician is required to give a deposition prior to trial with the opposing counsel, it is important to remember that statements made in depositions may be used in cross-examination to point out inconsistencies or to attack specific conclusions. The primary consideration for all testimony in depositions and in the courtroom is to be completely truthful. The main reason is that one can be subject to criminal penalties for perjury, but, also, if a false statement is uncovered, the credibility of the witness is destroyed, and the professional's reputation can be damaged.

The court testimony begins with direct examination by the attorney who called the witness. This questioning is usually comfortable because it has been reviewed prior to trial and the questions are designed to allow the clinician to provide supportive information to the judge and jury. The cross-examination follows and is characterized by attempts to discredit the clinician's qualifications, methods, and conclusions. In all stages of testimony, mental health clinicians should attempt to respond narrowly to the question that has been asked. The clinician witness should ask for a restatement of the question if it is ambiguous or confusing. It is a good strategy for the clinician to pause prior to answering each question to consider what is being asked. In responding, clinicians should direct their comments to the jury, or to the judge if it is a bench trial without a jury. Frequently, opposing attorneys will object to a question that has been asked. If this occurs, the clinician should not answer until directed to by the judge. If the intervening discussion has been distracting or protracted, the witness should ask to have the question repeated. Clinicians should avoid the use of professional jargon that the jury will not fully understand. Jargon is useful as shorthand communication between professionals, but it can lead juries to tune out the witness or discount the significance of the testimony. The most effective witness is one who is trusted and liked by the jury. Although preparation is essential to delivering effective testimony, if a witness sounds too rehearsed, the opposing attorney is likely to ask questions intended to make the jury believe that the content of the testimony was coached and biased toward the other party. Clinicians who are overly cautious or defensive may increase the intensity of the cross-examination. The opposing attorney, sensing an opportunity to discredit the clinician in front of the jury, may be more aggressive. A confident, professional witness who does not personalize attacks made in cross-examination is more dangerous to the opposing attorney's case the longer the questioning continues.

Testifying as an Expert

There are some generally accepted standards for the admissibility of expert opinions that can help mental health professionals to understand the court's expectations when they are asked to testify in this role. The purpose of an expert witness is to provide scientific, technical, or other specialized knowledge that will assist the judge and jury to understand the evidence or decide on a factual question (Melton, 1994). There are two important elements to this standard. First, the expert must be able to provide relevant testimony as to a material issue that is contested in the case. Under the rules of evidence in most jurisdictions, ordinary witnesses are able to give opinions when they are "within the rational perception" (Federal Rules of Evidence, 701) of that individual, even if he or she is not an expert. The opinion testimony is carefully limited by the rational perception rule. The rule is a commonsense approach that allows a witness to give "experiential" opinions that are obvious from an interaction or situation. For example, even if he was not certified as an expert, Mr. Scott would be allowed to testify as to whether Charlene's emotional difficulties interfered with her ability to sustain regular employment. He had treated her for an extended period and observed her functioning during that time. He probably would be allowed to give his opinion on the effect of the mental and emotional problems on her employment, even though he did not directly observe the relationship.

The decision about whether an expert witness is required is based on the type of testimony that is required to support the version of the case advanced by each party. If a point of fact in dispute requires specialized knowledge to understand, an expert may be needed to offer an opinion to the judge and jury to help them decide on the issue. An attorney must demonstrate that a proposed expert has the skills, education, and experience to qualify as an expert. The main purpose of the expert is to provide assistance to the trier of fact (judge or jury). To do this effectively, the expert's status must convince the judge that the individual's testimony is necessary and he or she is qualified to help to clarify the issues in controversy.

There are several roles that an expert may assume in a case. First, it is common for attorneys to seek to qualify the treating professional as an expert (Dombroff, 1987). If successful, the witness may be allowed to testify about the facts he or she witnessed as well as offering expert opinions to the court. Dr. Hearns, the psychotherapist who is treating Charlene currently, is an expert on dissociative identity disorder. He has written two articles and given numerous presentations about this topic. Ms. Hall would not need to hire an additional expert to testify as to the extent of the symptoms, the accuracy of the diagnosis, and the prognosis for future adaptive functioning and treatment needs because this clinician probably would be acceptable to the judge as an expert in this subject area.

Following the court's acceptance of his expert status, Charlene's current therapist, Dr. Hearns, was asked to explain the dynamics of how individuals respond to the trauma of a rape and involvement in a series of abusive relationships. The therapist provided an overview of the clinical symptoms that follow these experiences. He cited some recent research on the duration of mental health treatment that is required by clients who have gone through similar circumstances. Finally, the therapist was asked to give his opinion as to Charlene's diagnosis, current mental health status, and need for ongoing treatment.

At times, an expert may be retained by a lawyer as a consultant who may not be asked to testify at trial (Dombroff, 1987). The expert might be used to prepare for depositions, to formulate questions for witnesses, or to prepare materials for cross-examination of opposing expert witnesses. Many attorneys will engage a mental health expert to evaluate a client prior to filing a case to determine the issues that may suggest alternative legal strategies to pursue (Vandenberg, 1993), especially given that a large percentage of cases get settled prior to trial. If an expert is involved throughout the process of the case, it may affect the objective, unbiased testimony that juries will expect. For this reason, the expert is usually retained to fulfill only one role in a case.

The third major role of an expert is to testify as to the standard of care applicable to a particular case or to give an opinion as to the ultimate issue in the case (Dombroff, 1987). In the case example, the current therapist was asked to give his opinion as to the accuracy of the diagnosis and whether Charlene was likely to require lifelong treatment. This is the ultimate issue in the controversy because the judge's decision about how to divide marital property depends on her judgment of whether Charlene has special needs that militate against an even splitting of assets.

One of the ways the legal system operates to influence mental health practice is to create rules out of contested cases that are eventually appealed to higher courts. At the trial level, the basic facts of a case are litigated, which makes the issue on appeal rather narrow and limited. For this reason, the ethics of expert testimony are particularly important to consider. If a case is decided on evidence from an expert that is biased, not based on legitimate research, or otherwise tainted, the foundation of the decision may be illegitimate. Each successive appellate court decision, based on the initial ruling, becomes similarly poisoned. Because the court system is constructed on the legal principle of *stare decisis* (the policy of courts to stand by the precedents set in prior cases in the higher courts of a jurisdiction), a single, convincing expert witness could have enormous influence, well beyond the scope of the particular case.

> The time has come to stop pandering to zealots who misuse social science to serve their own personal likes and dislikes. They must be exposed for the dangerous charlatans they are.
> Allen Dershowitz (*The Abuse Excuse, 1994, p. 119*)

Cross-examination, impeaching the expert. The adversary system is designed to arrive at the truth by vigorous debate, out of which the judge or jury can decide upon an equitable result. Lawyers may portray supportive facts as infallible, and opposing facts as ludicrous, in a zealous effort to represent their clients. Expert witnesses can be seduced by this process but also can fall victim to its venom. Attorneys hire expert witnesses because they hope the testimony will support the client and help to prove the case. A mental health professional, however, cannot succumb to the lure of glamour, prestige, adventure, or hefty fees that can be offered to be a "hired gun" (Vandenberg, 1993). Melton (1994) cogently suggests that expert witnesses have to maintain the orientation of being "of assistance to the trier of fact." Rather than seeing their role as an agent of the party who has retained them, expert witnesses must testify honestly and within their zone of expertise. This role of assisting the court triggers a duty to experts to be forthcoming about any uncertainty or conflicting evidence regarding their testimony.

In some cases, the adversarial system creates tremendous discomfort for the expert witness. Because the cross-examining lawyer can use leading questions, jurors can be influenced through the tactical use of questions that are designed either to elicit misleading information from the witness or to impart misleading information to the jury (Kassin, Williams, & Saunders, 1994, p. 514). For the lawyer, the process of proving one's point includes the task of attacking opposing evidence. In the case of expert witnesses, the strategies of cross-examination are used to shoot at both the messenger and the message.

The "bible" used by attorneys in preparing to cross-examine mental health clinicians is Ziskin's two-volume work, *Coping With Psychiatric and Psychological Testimony* (1981). The character of the adversarial system is in evidence with the first sentence of the chapter on strategies and tactics. Ziskin writes, "The basic approach of this book is oriented to accomplishing disbelief and rejection of the testimony of psychiatrists and clinical psychologists by demonstrating serious doubts that they possess the knowledge or expertise that they profess" (p. 32). What is most interesting about this quote is its tacit acknowledgment that the process may not be as much about finding the truth as it is about playing the game to win the case. Mental health clinicians who testify as experts must understand the legal process and be prepared for an attack on their credentials, conclusions, motives, and professional knowledge base.

In one recent case, a well-known national expert in trauma work was preparing to serve as an expert witness in a personal injury case. The attorney for the defendant unsuccessfully tried to subpoena the expert's personal divorce records. Most of the time, the attacks do not get this personal but potential expert witnesses can always expect attacks on their clinical findings. Slovenko (1996) offers a condensed sampling of a number of ways Ziskin instructs defense attorneys to challenge a mental health clinician's report (p. 50):

- Is the expertise shown by psychologists or psychiatrists in the court any better than the judgment of the ordinary man or woman?
- Isn't there considerable controversy about the usefulness of psychological evidence in legal matters?

- Are you aware of the great number of studies that show that more experienced psychiatrists are no more accurate in their assessments than inexperienced ones or even laypeople?
- Can you demonstrate a clear relationship between diagnosis and alleged consequences?
- Can you offer any scientific evidence that the psychiatric theories upon which you base your conclusions have some basis in fact?
- Has there ever been a scientific study of the accuracy of your professional judgment?
- Have you ever gathered evidence that indicates that the conclusions you offer in the courtroom are usually correct?
- So you haven't any idea if the diagnostic opinions you have been offering year after year are actually correct?

It is evident from these questions that cross-examination of expert witnesses requires clinicians to be well prepared in a number of areas. First, it is useful for the witness to provide to the attorney a bibliography of articles, research, and texts that form the theoretical basis for the testimony. This will allow the attorney to ask questions that highlight the professional acceptance of the theoretical approach. It also is useful to prepare for court by reviewing any opposing literature in the substantive area to be ready to address the questions likely to be posed in cross-examination. Not knowing about an opposing viewpoint leaves the witness looking unprepared.

The role of the expert in a case is to provide objective information to assist the trier of fact. This maxim helps clinicians to ensure that their testimony remains nonpartisan. Once the expert witness sounds like an advocate for one side, the credibility of the testimony is suspect. If asked, it is important to be honest about having reviewed testimony with the attorney who retained the expert and to acknowledge the fee to be received for work done in the case. A competent attorney usually will ask these questions on direct examination to remove the power of the hostile queries by the cross-examining attorney. The suggestions for testifying that were discussed earlier in this chapter also are relevant for the expert witness. The intensity of the cross-examination is likely to be greater in the case of an expert witness due to the weight that many juries place on the testimony of a competent and credible expert.

Expert witnesses often face a challenge to their status as an expert. If the individual has an outstanding reputation with an impressive résumé, the opposing counsel may offer to stipulate that the witness be accepted as an expert. This is a tactical maneuver designed to limit the review of the witness's impressive background because it might be influential with the jury. In addition to the challenges concerning the expert's credentials, there may be a challenge to the scientific validity of the theories on which the testimony is based (Dickson, 1995). As discussed in Chapter 5, courts may hold an initial hearing on the validity of scientific theories prior to allowing testimony that relies on them. For example, there have been infamous cases in which "scientific" evidence was used to argue that a defendant should not be held liable for his actions because he ate too much junk food (the twinkie defense) or watched too many violent television shows. An expert who offered to testify as to the effects of junk food consumption or television viewing on violent behavior might face a hearing in which the theory would be evaluated for its validity and acceptance in the professional community. Depending on the jurisdiction, courts vary as to whether they favor admitting nearly all testimony, leaving it to the adversarial process and the intelligence of the jury to give it proper consideration; in some courts, the lack of widespread support for the theory might lead a judge to rule against the admission of testimony about the theory, thereby excluding the expert witness.

CONSULTING AND
RETAINING AN ATTORNEY

Choosing an attorney is a process that should not be undertaken without careful preparation. The educational process for lawyers is similar to the training of mental health clinicians. Everyone studies the basic principles, but, once in practice, the professional determines an area of specialization. Some lawyers are general practitioners. They usually handle cases such as real estate transactions, probate matters, wills and estates, and other similar cases. For a clinician who needs guidance or representation, it is important to find an attorney who has specialized knowledge and experience in the area of law involved in the matter. This is similar to the process that most people go through when choosing a physician. There are so many areas of the law, an attorney cannot be an expert in every subject. A general practicing attorney can often identify the type of expert needed for a given set of facts, so this is often a good place to begin. If a clinician is seeking consultation regarding how to handle a legal issue such as a confidentiality question or is in need of guidance about how to respond to a subpoena, a professional who speaks two languages is needed. Local professional organizations such as the state chapters of the American Psychological Association, the American Counseling Association, or the National Association of Social Workers maintain lists of attorneys who specialize in mental health law, including some who hold both legal and clinical credentials.

The fee arrangements vary with the type of case and the type of services required. For a consultation, an attorney should charge a fee to create an attorney-client relationship to which a privilege would attach. Otherwise, a conversation between a clinician and a lawyer could be subject to discovery, and the attorney could be required to divulge the contents of the discussion in a subsequent trial. Many lawyers require a retainer fee to be paid when they accept a case, which covers the costs up to a certain point in the case (Barker & Branson, 1993). If the clinician is suing for tort damages, the attorney may be willing to accept the case on a contingency fee basis. In this arrangement, the lawyer charges nothing up front, but if the case is won and payment for damages is received, the attorney will get a percentage of the award, usually about one-third of the total. The other possible fee arrangements are a straight hourly rate or a flat rate for a particular service such as filing incorporation or partnership papers for a practice group. In any case, the clinician needs to be clear about the agreement and monitor the charges throughout the case. Unlike mental health practice, every phone call or other contact is charged on the hourly rate. Clinicians need to be aware of this, to be well prepared for meetings, to avoid unnecessary telephone calls, and to provide clearly identified documents and materials that are well organized.

Responding to malpractice complaints. At times, the notice comes as a complete surprise, while in other cases, the threat had been recognizable since the start of the treatment relationship. But the telephone call, office visit, or legal document that confirms the filing of a malpractice action against a mental health clinician is always a paralyzing shock. Clinical training may make the professional inclined to seek out the client to work through the "obvious" displacement or to problem-solve to make the client satisfied. There is a protocol for clinicians to follow when faced with a malpractice claim. It is important to follow the guidelines to protect oneself and one's practice or agency.

Upon notification that a malpractice suit is to be filed, the clinician should cease all contact with the client as well as the family and other representatives of the client. The worker should immediately notify the insurance company that has written the malpractice coverage. Generally, the procedures for this are included in the insurance policy documents. The insurance company will assign a claims adjuster to the case who determines the particular policy's coverage and the obligations of the insurer. The adjuster usually will assign a local attorney to the case (Houston-Vega et al., 1997). It is important to review the policy to determine if the coverage extends to the type of claim being made against the clinician. Some policies exclude coverage for intentional acts of wrongdoing such as sexual relations with clients. Other policies limit the amount of damages for these acts. If the alleged harm occurred outside of the usual treatment setting, the insurer may refuse to cover the case. This denial of coverage also means that the company will not agree to hire a lawyer to defend the case.

When the insurance company assigns an attorney to a case, the lawyer is representing the interests of the company, not necessarily the interests of the clinician. Usually, these interests coincide in the effort to have the malpractice suit dismissed or to win in court. However, the main interest of the insurance company is to limit the amount of damages paid out in any case. If a lawsuit has a chance of succeeding because of the facts or the presence of a sympathetic plaintiff, the attorney may recommend settling the case. This usually involves a payment to the person making the complaint. The clinician may be victimized in this process when the payment of damages appears to be an admission of wrongdoing, when it is actually the decision of the lawyers to minimize the exposure of the insurer to potential damages. Active involvement in the case, including regular consultation with the attorneys, can keep the clinician informed and help to minimize undesirable results.

Mental health clinicians may need to be represented at various stages of a malpractice suit to ensure that their personal interests are being protected in the process. In some cases, an agency might try to distance itself from the actions of the clinician to avoid liability. This usually occurs when the alleged breach is for an activity arguably beyond the scope of the duties the clinician was hired to perform. For example, in one case, a therapist was hired by an agency to provide mental health counseling to children. The therapist read about holding therapy with children who had attachment disorders and decided to integrate it into his work with a very aggressive child. He arranged to do the session at the child's foster home to involve the foster family. The child's mental health functioning deteriorated following the treatment and eventually a malpractice suit was threatened. The agency disciplined the worker and argued that the treatment was beyond the scope of what he was hired to do. Therefore, the agency sought to avoid being named in a suit should one have been filed in the future.

Mental health clinicians who are asked to give depositions or to testify concerning a client should carefully consider the ramifications of the testimony. Barker and Branson (1993) describe a case illustration in which a worker was asked to testify in front of a grand jury that was trying to determine if a father and mother should be tried in relation to the death of their 8-year-old daughter. The worker answered a series of questions about the circumstances of the family but, eventually, the questions became directed at her actions in reporting the case and safeguarding the child. The worker was later charged and convicted of failing to protect the child. Her answers, given under oath, without legal representation present, were significant evidence in the case against her. Consultation with an attorney knowledgeable about mental health law can provide a clinician with guidance prior to testimony to protect personal interests and prevent unintentional breaches of professional duty.

When a complaint is lodged with the state administrative agency or a professional organization, mental health clinicians should consider hiring an attorney to represent their interests throughout the process. A negative result in these procedures can result in sanctions or loss of license. A regulatory agency must have procedures for reviewing complaints. An attorney can help the clinician to determine whether due process procedures are being followed; whether the testimony in the disciplinary procedures could be used to help prove a lawsuit against the clinician; and, if the outcome of the complaint is a sanction against the worker, whether the action was within the power of the regulatory agency.

Chapter 7

KNOWLEDGE FOR PRACTICE
Common Legal Problems for Clients

Mental health professionals frequently work with clients who are involved in the legal system. Parents and children going through changes in family composition such as divorce, shared custody, and adoption need the help of counselors and psychotherapists to adjust to the losses and life transitions. Clients with mental illness may experience times during which they are not competent to make decisions or live safely in the community. Workers need to understand the commitment process and the legal rights of persons with mental illness. Elderly clients and those persons with terminal illness need help making decisions concerning financial matters and planning for end-of-life medical interventions. Families that are marked by ongoing violence regularly consult mental health professionals for both treatment and advice. At times, the mental health professional is required to report incidents of abuse that occur against children, persons who are elderly, or individuals who have disabilities.

In all of these situations, the mental health practitioner should be prepared to assist clients to navigate and survive the legal system. This help includes providing information as to the legal process and the basic tenets of family and mental health law. Clients may be unaware of the legal resources available to protect their rights and interests. They may need help understanding the operation of the law and the unintelligible documents produced by attorneys for the legal system. Also, mental health practitioners are called on to be consultants and experts for the legal system and need to understand the way courts make decisions in mental health and family cases (Saunders, 1993). This chapter provides a brief overview of the law in a number of substantive areas that are relevant to practice. Leading cases from each area of law are used to illustrate how the courts view the principal issues. Mental health professionals working with a particular population need to develop a deeper knowledge of population-specific legal issues in the jurisdiction in which they practice.

FAMILY LAW: MARRIAGE, DIVORCE, AND CUSTODY

> Marriage, as creating the most important relation in life, as having more to do with the morals and civilization of a people than any other institution, has always been subject to the control of the legislature.
>
> *Maynard v. Hill* (1888)

Marriage. There are certain legal prerequisites to being married. The rules vary slightly across jurisdictions but have three basic purposes: to protect public health, to assure that the parties have the legal capacity to consent to the marriage and to understand the obligations of that commitment, and to provide an official record of a marriage, which is required for various legal documents and proceedings (Saltzman & Proch, 1990). Most of the law governing marriage and divorce is found in state statutes and case law. The exception to this is where a particular state statute violates the constitutional rights of an individual. For example, in one municipality, a zoning ordinance limited occupancy of a single dwelling to members of a single family. The "acceptable" family members under this ordinance were narrowly defined. The Supreme Court ruled the ordinance unconstitutional, finding that it violated an individual's right to personal choice in matters of marriage and family life (*Moore v. City of East Cleveland,* 1977).

Laws regulating marriage are seen as supporting the institution of the family. By determining the conditions under which a person can marry and divorce, states encourage practices that are consistent with societal values and moral codes while denying sanction to those practices that are considered deviant. Because the law is inherently conservative, laws concerning marriage are slow to evolve. Justice Harlan of the Supreme

Court captured the essence of the role of the law in maintaining family structure:

> Perhaps no characteristic of an organized and cohesive society is more fundamental than its erection and enforcement of a system of rules defining the various rights and duties of its members, enabling them to govern their affairs and definitively settle their differences in an orderly, predictable manner. It is this injection of the rule of law that allows society to reap the benefits of rejecting what political theorists call the "state of nature." (*Boddie v. Connecticut,* 1971)

In addition, the rhetoric about family values always has been politicized, so that any effort to change the laws to reflect changes in family structure is subject to a difficult and slow legislative process. For this reason, the legislature has been an ineffective place to make changes in marriage laws; instead, the courts have supported the laws' evolution.

Clients of mental health practitioners are likely to experience issues in two areas of marriage law. First, because a marriage is a contract, it must be entered into freely (Schroeder, 1995). The question of whether a client is competent to consent to a marriage may be the subject of litigation. Sometimes the competency issue is related to the age of the individuals. Most states require parental or judicial permission for an underage person to marry. The policy is consistent with the legally presumed incompetency of a minor to enter into a contract. A second area of concern with competency involves individuals who are mentally ill or cognitively impaired. Clinicians may be called to testify as to the ability of a client to understand the marriage commitment and to testify as to whether the client is acting freely. Although many of the objectionable state marriage laws have been overruled or replaced with updated statutes, marriage laws continue to require the two parties to be of opposite sex. Courts and legislatures are currently dealing with the question of whether to sanction homosexual marriages. To understand how courts will handle these types of issues, clinicians must develop an awareness of the legal view of marriage as a fundamental aspect of American society (Guillerman, 1997).

Loving v. Commonwealth of Virginia (1967, opinion of the court). This case presents a constitutional question never addressed by this Court: Whether a statutory scheme adopted by the State of

Virginia to prevent marriages between persons solely on the basis of racial classifications violates the Equal Protection and Due Process Clauses of the Fourteenth Amendment. For reasons which seem to us to reflect the central meaning of those constitutional commands, we conclude that these statutes cannot stand.

In June 1958, two residents of Virginia, Mildred Jeter, a Negro woman, and Richard Loving, a white man, were married in the District of Columbia pursuant to its laws. Shortly after their marriage, the Lovings returned to Virginia and established their marital abode in Caroline County. A grand jury issued an indictment charging the Lovings with violating Virginia's ban on interracial marriages. The Lovings pleaded guilty to the charge and were sentenced to one year in jail; however, the trial judge suspended the sentence for a period of 25 years on the condition that the Lovings leave the state and not return to Virginia during that time.

Section 1 of the Fourteenth Amendment provides: All persons born or naturalized in the United States and subject to the jurisdiction thereof are citizens of the United States and of the State wherein they reside. No State shall make or enforce any law which shall abridge the privileges or immunities of citizens of the United States; nor shall any State deprive any person of life, liberty, or property, without due process of law; nor deny to any person within its jurisdiction the equal protection of the laws.

While the state court is no doubt correct in asserting that marriage is a social relation subject to the State's police power, the State does not contend in its argument before this Court that its powers to regulate marriage are unlimited, notwithstanding the commands of the Fourteenth Amendment. Instead, the State argues that the meaning of the Equal Protection Clause, as illuminated by the statements of the Framers, is only that state penal laws containing an interracial element as part of the definition of the offense must apply equally to whites and Negroes in the sense that members of each race are punished to the same degree. Thus, the State contends that, because its miscegenation statutes punish equally both the white and the Negro participants in an interracial marriage, these statutes, despite their reliance on racial classifications, do not constitute an invidious discrimination based upon race. There can be no doubt that restricting the freedom to marry solely because of racial classifications violates the central meaning of the Equal Protection Clause. These statutes also deprive the Lovings of liberty without due process of law in violation of the Constitution. The freedom to marry has long been recognized as one of the vital personal rights essential to the orderly pursuit of happiness by free men.

Marriage is one of the "basic civil rights of man," fundamental to our very existence and survival. To deny this fundamental freedom on so unsupportable a basis as the racial classification embodied in these statutes, classifications so directly subversive of the principle of equality at the heart of the Fourteenth Amendment, is surely to deprive all the state's citizens of liberty without due process of law. The Fourteenth Amendment requires that the freedom of choice to marry not be restricted by invidious racial discriminations. Under our Constitution, the freedom to marry, or not marry, a person of another race resides with the individual and cannot be infringed by the state.

These convictions must be reversed. It is so ordered. [Citations omitted; text edited for style and readability.]

Loving affirmed two important concepts in the law of marriage: First, because it is an institution that is so important to the social fabric, the courts are likely to be skeptical of any state laws that erect structural or procedural barriers to marriage. The key question is whether the statute or regulation is rationally related to permissible legislative purposes. Second, several areas of family life have been considered to be within the zone of personal privacy rights. As such, there is constitutional scrutiny of regulations that impinge on the right of individuals to make decisions about marriage and family life.

State legislatures occasionally have sought to implement a social policy by attaching conditions to the issuance of a marriage license. When the conditions have legitimate public health purposes (such as blood tests), or help to ensure that the decision to marry has been freely and conscientiously made (such as waiting periods and judicial approval of underage marriages), there is no constitutional problem with the conditions. However, legislatures cannot use the issuance of a marriage license to compel a certain behavior, even when it is a laudable goal, if the law unduly restricts the opportunity for marriage without serving a compelling state interest.

In *Zablocki v. Redhail* (1978), a Wisconsin statute provided that any resident of that state "having minor issue (child) not in his custody, and which he is under obligation to support by any court order or judgment" may not marry without an order of approval from the court, which cannot be granted absent a showing that the support obligation has been met and that children covered by the support order "are not then and are not likely thereafter to become public charges." The Supreme Court held this statute to violate the equal protection clause of the Fourteenth Amendment. The court relied on *Loving* to make the point that the right to marry is of fundamental importance, and the statutory classification involved here significantly interfered with the exercise of that right. More recently, a Missouri law restricting the right of prisoners to marry was invalidated by the Supreme Court for the same reason (*Turner v. Safley,* 1987).

Same-sex marriages. The question of same-sex marriages is relevant to this discussion. One could make a strong argument that the prohibition on same-sex marriages is based on a violation of equal protection, which is the primary rationale articulated in cases overturning marriage laws since *Loving.* In the same way that marriage is currently defined as between people of different sexes, it was previously defined as between people of the same race. As society has evolved, the latter restriction, once accepted, has become obsolete. Attempts have been made to gain legal recognition for a partnership through adult adoption (Green, 1996), but, as yet, no state has sanctioned same-sex marriages. Two recent high-profile cases, however, may foreshadow a trend toward acceptance of same-sex marriages.

In Hawaii, a series of state court rulings in the case *Baehr v. Lewin* (1993, subsequently known as *Baehr v. Miike*) support the equal protection rationale. A group of lesbian and gay individuals brought this suit. They argued that there are rights and benefits that accompany the state-conferred status of marriage (including such things as health and pension benefits for state employees, inheritance rights, and others). By refusing to recognize same-sex marriages, the state effectively was denying these benefits on the basis of an applicant's sex. The state supreme court found that the denial of benefits on the basis of the plaintiffs' classification was "suspect" with reference to the Hawaii Constitution. As a result, the state had the burden of showing that the ban furthered a "compelling" state interest and that the statute was narrowly drawn to avoid unnecessary abridgment of constitutional rights. At a trial in fall 1996, a circuit court judge found little credible evidence to support the ban on same-sex marriages and ordered the state to issue licenses to same-sex couples. The order will not take effect until after the decision is appealed. The case eventually will be reviewed by the state supreme court, but it appears that the court is ready to rule the ban unconstitutional.

As the Hawaii case worked its way through the courts, several state legislatures, including Hawaii, have attempted to pass legislation specifically banning same-sex marriages. On the federal level, Congress passed the Defense of Marriage Act (DOMA), which was signed by President Clinton in September 1996. DOMA defines *marriage* for all federal laws as being between one man and one woman. Further, the statute allows one state not to recognize a same-sex marriage from another state. The latter provision appears to violate the full faith and credit clause of the Constitution (Article IV, section 1), which requires each state to honor the court judgments of sister states (Guillerman, 1997). The prospect of large numbers of couples getting married in Hawaii and seeking to have the marriage recognized in their home state has many legislatures actively pursuing specific bans on same-sex marriages.

The second major case that militates for expansion of marital rights to same-sex couples was *Romer v. Evans* (1996). *Romer* represented the first time the U.S. Supreme Court had applied the equal protection clause to gays, lesbians, and bisexuals. The court struck down a voter-approved amendment to the Colorado Constitution that prohibited any governmental entity in the state from passing regulations to ban discrimination on the basis of sexual orientation. Given this result, a *Loving*-type case seems likely to be filed. Despite apparent public sentiment against expansion of marital rights to homosexual couples, the courts are providing a hospitable forum. If the purposes of marriage are to protect the parties and to legally recognize a life commitment, distinguishing same-sex couples from heterosexual couples is arguably unconstitutional.

There are a number of municipalities that have passed statutes recognizing domestic partnerships. The regulations provide legal recognition of these relationships and include various provisions such as granting rights in medical decision making, extending health insurance benefits to same-gender partners, granting hospital visitation rights, reforming tenant laws to allow domestic partners to assume leases of rent-controlled apartments, and making it illegal to discriminate against a person on the basis of sexual orientation (see, e.g., New York Domestic Partnership Acts, discussed in Green, 1996). The issue of formalizing and sanctioning the relationship becomes particularly important for same-gender partners to prove their "status" when seeking benefits.

---

390 West End Associates v. Wildfoerster (1997, opinion of the court). We agree with the majority at the Appellate Term and the trial court that there is essentially no evidence other than oral reflections of respondent and the deceased's friends that respondent's relationship with the deceased tenant of record was characterized by the "emotional and financial commitment, and interdependence" necessary for purposes of family member succession to the rent stabilized tenancy. Despite a 20-year relationship during which they lived together from 1976 to 1978 and again for more than two years prior to the tenant's death from AIDS in 1993, lacking are the normal indicia of a familial relationship. Although the tenant's close friends testified, and the trial court found, that the tenant and respondent had a very close, loving relationship, the trial evidence failed to sufficiently establish the respondent as a "family" member within the meaning of the applicable rent regulations.

The exact nature of respondent's living arrangements is unclear, given that he continued to receive his mail not at the deceased tenant's apartment but at 711 West End Avenue, listed that address on credit applications, and used it on his driver's license and tax returns. Moreover, although it is undisputed that respondent was totally dependent upon the tenant financially, there was no commingling of finances, no joint ownership of anything, not even an indication of sharing household or family expenses. Most significantly, there was no provision, financial or otherwise, made for the respondent at a time when the tenant knew or should have known that he was dying.

Thus the respondent seeks to have the petitioner landlord and this Court do what the deceased tenant never did in any fashion, which is acknowledge that their relationship could be described as having "family" attributes. What does emerge is a one-sided financial relationship. The respondent worked as the tenant's assistant in his business of producing cultural events but, while there was testimony that the respondent and the tenant occasionally entertained and traveled together, the tenant never acknowledged any family-type relationship with the respondent. There is no picture, letter, note, or other memento evincing a family-type relationship between the two and there were no other joint traditional "family-type" events or celebrations to evidence any interdependence in a familial sense.

Dissent. Under the test first articulated in *Braschi v. Stahl Associates Co.* (1989), and subsequently codified in various provisions of the rent stabilization regulations, the definition of a "family member" has been expanded beyond its traditional meaning to include any other person residing with the tenant in the housing accommodation as a primary residence, who can prove emotional and financial commitment, and interdependence between such person and the tenant. These regulations provide that evidence of whether such "commitment" and "interdependence" existed may include, but is not limited to, the following eight factors: (a) longevity of the relationship; (b) sharing of or relying upon each other for payment of household or family expenses, and/or other common necessities of life; (c) intermingling of finances as evidenced by, among other things, joint ownership of bank accounts, personal and real property, credit cards, loan obligations, sharing a household budget for purposes of receiving government benefits, etc.; (d) engaging in family-type activities by jointly attending family functions, holidays and celebrations, social and recreational activities, etc.; (e) formalizing of legal obligations, intentions, and responsibilities to each other by such means as executing wills naming each other as executor and/or beneficiary, granting each other a power of attorney, and/or conferring upon each other authority to make health care decisions each for the other, entering into a personal relationship contract, making a domestic partnership declaration, or serving as a representative payee for purposes of public benefits, etc.; (f) holding themselves out as family members to other family members, friends, members of the community or religious institutions, or society in general, through their words or actions; (g) regularly performing family functions, such as caring for each other or each other's extended family members, and/or relying upon each other for daily family services; and (h) engaging in any other pattern of behavior, agreement, or other action that evidences the intention of creating a long-term, emotionally committed relationship.

Notwithstanding this list, however, the regulations provide that "no single factor shall be solely determinative" in making such determination. This principle was also expressed in *Braschi*, which cautioned that although the enumerated factors are "most helpful," it should be emphasized that the presence or absence of one or more of them is not dispositive since it is the totality of the relationship as evidenced by the dedication, caring, and self-sacrifice of the parties that should, in the final analysis, control. [Citations omitted; text edited for style and readability.]

Mental health practitioners regularly interact with clients who face oppression because of their status. The lack of legal sanctions for same-sex relationships results in economic and psychic harm to gay, lesbian, and bisexual individuals. As experts in mental health, clinicians can be influential in advocating for passage of legislation that would provide legal recognition to same-sex relationships and protect individual rights. In the Hawaii case, the testimony of mental health professionals concerning the child-rearing capacities of homosexual couples rebutted the major argument supporting the ban on same-sex marriages (*Baehr v. Lewin*, 1993). The institution of marriage is a formal recognition of a committed relationship. As such, extending it to same-sex couples can only increase the stability of the family. If the legislatures are unwilling to take this political position, court decisions may become the primary impetus for social change.

> It is obvious that all sense has gone out of modern marriage; which
> is however, no objection to marriage but to modernity.
>   Nietzsche, *Twilight of the Idols* (1889)

Divorce. When a marriage ends, the state has an interest in protecting all parties (Saltzman & Proch, 1990). Decisions concerning child care and custody, distribution of property, and financial support for all parties need to be reached fairly. A divorce ends the legal relationship, freeing the spousal parties to remarry. Most states require couples to demonstrate that the marriage is irretrievably broken and to follow formal procedures for obtaining a divorce. The involvement of the courts enables decisions to be made that protect the rights and enforce the obligations of the parties.

Most states have liberalized their divorce laws and abandoned or minimized the use of fault systems. In the past, parties were forced to engage in the adversarial process of a trial to prove grounds for divorce such as adultery, physical cruelty, or abandonment. This process publicized private conflicts (Krause, 1986) and often increased the level of conflict. In some cases, the divorcing parties would agree to make up an acceptable story to obtain a divorce (Krause, 1986). As a result of these practices, most states have moved to a "no-fault" system or some combination of no-fault and fault grounds for divorce. In a no-fault system, one or both parties to the marriage can file an action for dissolution by claiming that the marriage has irretrievably broken down. Most states require a mandatory separation period, usually several months, prior to granting a divorce to guard against impulsive actions and to allow time for reconciliation efforts.

Because a divorce enables individuals to obtain legally enforceable agreements with respect to child custody, support payments, and property distribution, and because a divorce allows a person to be free to remarry, it is important that divorce be accessible to all citizens. The U.S. Supreme Court ruled that states must allow filing fees for a divorce to be waived for persons who are indigent to eliminate this barrier to the court system (*Boddie v. Connecticut,* 1971). Many states have developed divorce kits that allow people to represent themselves in divorce cases (called *pro se* representation). Mental health clinicians can be advocates for clients in this process to be certain their rights are being protected.

It is important to consider the alternatives to traditional lawyers for clients who are planning to divorce. From the perspective of many lawyers, divorce is a legal process in which legal rules and principles are applied to individual lives (Marlow, 1985). Lawyers are trained and socialized into the adversarial system, where the focus is on obtaining the best outcome for the client. Unfortunately, in divorce proceedings, some lawyers equate the winning of custody and property settlements as the best outcome. Often, the best outcome arises from the process that seeks agreement rather than animosity. Possibly the best thing mental health professionals can do for clients is to inform them of the option for divorce mediation services.

In divorce mediation, the focus is on "win-win" solutions (Severson & Bankston, 1995). Mediators may be attorneys or mental health practitioners with special training. The focus is on viewing the issues as personal problems that need creative and workable solutions. Clients are actively engaged in the process of problem solving and thus feel more empowered and in control than people who rely on their attorneys to work out the details. Mediation is not appropriate in all cases. For example, where a sufficient power differential exists between the parties or when there is a history of domestic violence, mediation is not the preferred option (Severson & Bankston, 1995). As the popularity of mediated settlements in divorce actions grows, more opportunities will be available for mental health practitioners to become trained and to specialize in this area. The traditional legal process doesn't fit well with the nature of family conflicts. It is time for mental health professionals to assume an increasingly active role in this area of law.

Custody. By and large, family courts do not work well to meet the needs of changing families or adequately resolve issues of child custody and support (Kenney & Vigil, 1996). The problems in family court are partly due to the clogged courts; the rotating of judges to various courts, which results in fewer "expert" family jurists; and the more basic issue of trying to use the adversarial legal system to resolve interpersonal conflicts. Procedures that allow child custody hearings to become a battlefield for the parents' anger are damaging to all parties. The past two decades have seen many improvements in the system, particularly where court service officers or other mental health professionals are part of the legal process. Clinicians must be active in efforts to continue the reform of family court.

Mental health professionals may assume a variety of roles within the custody determination. The most important factor in successful experiences for the clinician, the family, and the legal professionals is for there to be role clarity. A clinician who is working with a child or family should not be conducting an evaluation for the court. The custody evaluation should be performed by a detached professional who is charged with making a recommendation to a judge that is based solely on the child's best interests (Remley & Miranti, 1991). Custody evaluators should undertake advanced training in child development, family systems, cultural diversity, psychopathology, and the assessment of parental effectiveness. The evaluator must also have a clear understanding of the legal system as well as knowledge of the statutory language governing child custody decisions and the leading cases from the jurisdiction. Finally, the evaluator should be trained and experienced in serving as an expert witness.

There are other important roles the clinician can assume in child custody matters. Often the child and/or the family are being seen in treatment. Family members need information about the process and support in dealing with the system as well as with the emotional aspects of the custody determination. Other roles for the mental health clinician include serving as a consultant, mediator, or arbitrator to assist the decision-making process or being named as the guardian ad litem or advocate for the child. One role that could be developed as family courts continue to evolve is to have mental health workers employed by the court system. In this model, family courts would shift from solving disputes through litigation to solving disputes through therapeutic interventions (Kenney & Vigil, 1996). The needs of children could be emphasized rather than the rights of the parents. Under the legal model, the outcome is often phrased in terms of winning and losing: Which of the parents won? In a therapeutic resolution model, the resolution is focused on ways to ensure that the child emerges the winner.

Family courts decide issues of custody using the standard of the best interests of the child. It is vital that clinicians working in the system understand this concept and educate judges and attorneys concerning the child's interests. The best interests standard is amorphous and is sometimes used subjectively to justify a decision rather than as an objective basis for a decision. It is important for mental health clinicians to remind all parties that a court does not need to find one parent inadequate before awarding custody to the other (*Tucker v. Tucker,* 1996). Mental health clinicians can help to focus the court's consideration on the child's developmental needs, emotional attachments, parenting skills, and lifestyle issues as well as the expressed preferences of the child. The following well-known case illustrates the difficult, unique issues that must be dealt with in custody decisions.

In re Baby M (1988, opinion of the court). In this matter the Court is asked to determine the validity of a contract that purports to provide a new way of bringing children into a family. For a fee of $10,000, a woman agreed to be artificially inseminated with the semen of another woman's husband; she was to conceive a child, carry it to term, and after its birth surrender it to the natural father and his wife. The intent of the contract was that the child's natural mother, thereafter, would be forever separated from her child. The wife is to adopt the child, and she and the natural father are to be regarded as its parents for all purposes. The contract providing for this is called a "surrogacy contract," the natural mother inappropriately called the "surrogate mother."

We invalidate the surrogacy contract because it conflicts with the law and public policy of this State. While we recognize the depth of the yearning of infertile couples to have their own children, we find the payment of money to a "surrogate" mother illegal, perhaps criminal, and potentially degrading to women. Although in this case we grant custody to the natural father, the evidence having clearly proved such custody to be in the best interests of the infant, we void both the termination of the surrogate mother's parental rights and the adoption of the child by the wife/stepparent. We thus restore the "surrogate" as the mother of the child. We remand the issue of the natural mother's visitation rights to the trial court, since that issue was not reached below and the record before us is not sufficient to permit us to decide it de novo.

We find no offense to our present laws where a woman voluntarily and without payment agrees to act as a "surrogate" mother, provided that she is not subject to a binding agreement to surrender her child. Moreover, our holding today does not preclude the Legislature from altering the current statutory scheme, within constitutional limits, so as to permit surrogacy contracts. Under current law, however, the surrogacy agreement before us is illegal and invalid.

In February 1985, William Stern and Mary Beth Whitehead entered into a surrogacy contract. It recited that Stern's wife, Elizabeth, was infertile, that they wanted a child, and that Mrs. Whitehead was willing to provide that child as the mother with

Mr. Stern as the father. The contract provided that through artificial insemination using Mr. Stern's sperm, Mrs. Whitehead would become pregnant, carry the child to term, bear it, deliver it to the Sterns, and thereafter do whatever was necessary to terminate her maternal rights so that Mrs. Stern could thereafter adopt the child. Mrs. Whitehead's husband, Richard, was also a party to the contract; Mrs. Stern was not. Mr. Whitehead promised to do all acts necessary to rebut the presumption of paternity under the Parentage Act. Although Mrs. Stern was not a party to the surrogacy agreement, the contract gave her sole custody of the child in the event of Mr. Stern's death. Mrs. Stern's status as a nonparty to the surrogate parenting agreement presumably was to avoid the application of the baby-selling statute to this arrangement.

The history of the parties' involvement in this arrangement suggests their good faith. Due to financial considerations and Mrs. Stern's pursuit of a medical degree and residency, they decided to defer starting a family until 1981. Before then, however, Mrs. Stern learned that she might have multiple sclerosis and that the disease in some cases renders pregnancy a serious health risk. Her anxiety appears to have exceeded the actual risk, which current medical authorities assess as minimal. Nonetheless that anxiety was evidently quite real, Mrs. Stern fearing that pregnancy might precipitate blindness, paraplegia, or other forms of debilitation. The decision not to have a biological child had special significance for Mr. Stern. Most of his family had been destroyed in the Holocaust. As the family's only survivor, he very much wanted to continue his bloodline.

Mrs. Whitehead realized, almost from the moment of birth, that she could not part with this child. She had felt a bond with it even during pregnancy. Some indication of the attachment was conveyed to the Sterns at the hospital when they told Mrs. Whitehead what they were going to name the baby. She apparently broke into tears and indicated that she did not know if she could give up the child. She talked about how the baby looked like her other daughter, and made it clear that she was experiencing great difficulty with the decision. Nonetheless, Mrs. Whitehead was, for the moment, true to her word. Despite powerful inclinations to the contrary, she turned her child over to the Sterns on March 30 at the Whiteheads' home. The Sterns, concerned that Mrs. Whitehead might indeed commit suicide, not wanting under any circumstances to risk that, and in any event believing that Mrs. Whitehead would keep her word, turned the child over to her. It was not until four months later, after a series of attempts to regain possession of the child, that Melissa was returned to the Sterns.

The struggle over Baby M began when it became apparent that Mrs. Whitehead could not return the child to Mr. Stern. Due to Mrs. Whitehead's refusal to relinquish the baby, Mr. Stern filed a complaint seeking enforcement of the surrogacy contract. He alleged, accurately, that Mrs. Whitehead had not only refused to comply with the surrogacy contract but had threatened to flee from New Jersey with the child in order to avoid even the possibility of his obtaining custody. The court papers asserted that if Mrs. Whitehead were to be given notice of the application for an order requiring her to relinquish custody, she would, prior to the hearing, leave the state with the baby. And that is precisely what she did. After the order was entered, ex parte, the process server, aided by the police, in the presence of the Sterns, entered Mrs. Whitehead's home to execute the order. Mr. Whitehead fled with the child, who had been handed to him through a window, while those who came to enforce the order were thrown off balance by a dispute over the child's current name.

The Whiteheads immediately fled to Florida with Baby M. They stayed initially with Mrs. Whitehead's parents, where one of Mrs. Whitehead's children had been living. For the next three months, the Whiteheads and Melissa lived at roughly twenty different hotels, motels, and homes in order to avoid apprehension. From time to time Mrs. Whitehead would call Mr. Stern to discuss the matter; the conversations, recorded by Mr. Stern on advice of counsel, show an escalating dispute about rights, morality, and power, accompanied by threats of Mrs. Whitehead to kill herself, to kill the child, and falsely to accuse Mr. Stern of sexually molesting Mrs. Whitehead's other daughter.

Eventually the Sterns discovered where the Whiteheads were staying, commenced supplementary proceedings in Florida, and obtained an order requiring the Whiteheads to turn over the child. Police in Florida enforced the order, forcibly removing the child from her grandparents' home. She was soon thereafter brought to New Jersey and turned over to the Sterns. The prior order of the court awarding custody of the child to the Sterns was reaffirmed by the trial court. Pending final judgment, Mrs. Whitehead was awarded limited visitation with Baby M.

The Sterns' complaint, in addition to seeking possession and ultimately custody of the child, sought enforcement of the surrogacy contract. Pursuant to the contract, it asked that the child be permanently placed in their custody, that Mrs. Whitehead's parental rights be terminated, and that Mrs. Stern be allowed to adopt the child, that is, for all purposes, for Melissa to become the Sterns' child.

A trial was held to determine custody of the child. Soon after the conclusion of the trial, the trial court announced its opinion from the bench. It held that the surrogacy contract was valid; ordered that Mrs. Whitehead's parental rights be terminated and that sole custody of the child be granted to Mr. Stern; and, after hearing brief testimony from Mrs. Stern, immediately entered an order allowing the adoption of Melissa by Mrs. Stern, all in accordance with the surrogacy contract. Pending the outcome of the appeal, we granted a continuation of visitation to Mrs. Whitehead, although slightly more limited than the visitation allowed during the trial.

Mrs. Whitehead contends that the surrogacy contract, for a variety of reasons, is invalid. She contends that it conflicts with public policy since it guarantees that the child will not have the nurturing of both natural parents, presumably New Jersey's goal for families. She further argues that it deprives the mother of her constitutional right to the companionship of her child, and that it conflicts with statutes concerning termination of parental rights and adoption. With the contract thus void, Mrs. Whitehead claims primary custody (with visitation rights to Mr. Stern) both on a best interests basis (stressing the "tender years" doctrine) as well as on the policy basis of discouraging surrogacy contracts. She maintains that even if custody would ordinarily go to Mr. Stern, here it should be awarded to Mrs. Whitehead to deter future surrogacy arrangements.

In a brief filed after oral argument, counsel for Mrs. Whitehead suggests that the standard for determining best interests where the infant resulted from a surrogacy contract is that the child should be placed with the mother absent a showing of unfitness. All parties agree that no expert testified that Mary Beth Whitehead was unfit as a mother; the trial court expressly found that she was not "unfit," that, on the contrary, "she is a good mother for and to her older children," and no one now claims anything to the contrary.

The Sterns claim that the surrogacy contract is valid and should be enforced. They claim a constitutional right of privacy, which includes the right of procreation, and the right of consenting adults to deal with matters of reproduction as they see fit. As for the child's best interests, their position is factual: Given all of the circumstances, the child is better off in their custody with no residual parental rights reserved for Mrs. Whitehead.

Of considerable interest in this clash of views is the position of the child's guardian ad litem, wisely appointed by the court at the outset of the litigation. As the child's representative, her role in the litigation, as she viewed it, was solely to protect the child's best interests. She therefore took no position on the validity of the surrogacy contract, and instead devoted her energies to obtaining expert testimony uninfluenced by any interest other than the child's. We agree with the guardian's perception of her role in this litigation. She appropriately refrained from taking any position that might have appeared to compromise her role as the child's advocate. She first took the position, based on her experts' testimony, that the Sterns should have primary custody, and that while Mrs. Whitehead's parental rights should not be terminated, no visitation should be allowed for five years. As a result of subsequent developments, her view has changed. She now recommends that no visitation be allowed at least until Baby M reaches maturity.

One of the surrogacy contract's basic purposes, to achieve the adoption of a child through private placement, although permitted in New Jersey is very much disfavored. Its use of money for this purpose, and we have no doubt whatsoever that the money is being paid to obtain an adoption and not, as the Sterns argue, for the personal services of Mary Beth Whitehead, is illegal and perhaps criminal. In addition to the inducement of money, there is the coercion of contract: the natural mother's irrevocable agreement, prior to birth, even prior to conception, to surrender the child to the adoptive couple. Such an agreement is totally unenforceable in private placement adoption. Even where the adoption is through an approved agency, the formal agreement to surrender occurs only after birth, and then, by regulation, only after the birth mother has been offered counseling.

The surrogacy contract guarantees permanent separation of the child from one of its natural parents. Our policy, however, has long been that to the extent possible, children should remain with and be brought up by both of their natural parents. This is not simply some theoretical ideal that in practice has no meaning. The impact of failure to follow that policy is nowhere better shown than in the results of this surrogacy contract. A child, instead of starting off its life with as much peace and security as possible, finds itself immediately in a tug-of-war between contending mother and father.

Having decided that the surrogacy contract is illegal and unenforceable, we now must decide the custody question without regard to the provisions of the surrogacy contract that would give Mr. Stern sole and permanent custody. With the surrogacy contract disposed of, the legal framework becomes a dispute between two couples over the custody of a child produced by the artificial insemination of one couple's wife by the other's husband. Under the Parentage Act, the claims of the natural father and the natural mother are entitled to equal weight, that is, one is not preferred over the other solely because he or she is the father or the mother.

At common law the rights of women were so fragile that the husband generally had the paramount right to the custody of children upon separation or divorce. In 1860 a statute concerning separation provided that children "within the age of seven years" be placed with the mother "unless said mother shall be of such character and habits as to render her an improper guardian." The inequities of the common-law rule and the 1860 statute were redressed by an 1871 statute, providing that "the rights of both parents, in the absence of misconduct, shall be held to be equal." Under this statute the father's superior right to the children was abolished and the mother's right to custody of children of tender years was also eliminated. Despite this statute, however, the "tender years" doctrine persisted. This presumption persisted primarily because of the prevailing view that a young child's best interests necessitated a mother's care. Both the development of case law and the Parentage Act, however, provide for equality in custody claims.

There were eleven experts who testified concerning the child's best interests, either directly or in connection with matters related to that issue. Our reading of the record persuades us that the trial court's decision awarding custody to the Sterns (technically to Mr. Stern) should be affirmed. Our custody conclusion is based on strongly persuasive testimony contrasting both the family life of the Whiteheads and the Sterns and the personalities and characters of the individuals. The stability of the Whitehead family life was doubtful at the time of trial. Their finances were in serious trouble (foreclosure by Mrs. Whitehead's sister on a second mortgage was in process). Mr. Whitehead's employment, although relatively steady, was always at risk because of his alcoholism, a condition that he seems not to have been able to confront effectively. Mrs. Whitehead had not worked for quite some time, her last two employments having been part-time. Based on all of this we have concluded, independent of the trial court's identical conclusion, that the child's best interests call for custody in the Sterns.

The fact that the trial court did not address visitation is only one reason for remand. The ultimate question is whether, despite the absence of the trial court's guidance, the record before us is sufficient to allow an appellate court to make this essentially factual determination. We can think of no issue that is more dependent on a trial court's factual findings and evaluation than visitation. The trial court will determine what kind of visitation shall be granted to her, with or without conditions, and when and under what circumstances it should commence. It also should be noted that the guardian's recommendation of a five-year delay is most unusual, one might argue that it begins to border on termination. Nevertheless, if the circumstances as further developed by appropriate proofs or as reconsidered on remand clearly call for that suspension under applicable legal principles of visitation, it should be so ordered.

This case affords some insight into a new reproductive arrangement: the artificial insemination of a surrogate mother. The unfortunate events that have unfolded illustrate that its unregulated use can bring suffering to all involved. Potential victims include the surrogate mother and her family, the natural father and his wife, and, most important, the child. Although surrogacy has apparently provided positive results for some infertile couples, it can also, as this case demonstrates, cause suffering to participants, here essentially innocent and well intended. [Citations omitted; text edited for style and readability.]

States differ as to the treatment of surrogacy contracts with some approving them and others holding them to be invalid (Dickson, 1995). Regardless of the circumstances, the focus of the inquiry should remain on the child's interests. The issue of who is a "parent" and thus entitled to seek visitation and other custody-related rights has been litigated frequently. In the following case, a woman who helped to care for a child born to her same-sex partner attempted to get the court to grant her partial custody after the breakup of their relationship. Once again, the case provides interesting insight into the reasoning used by judges in making custody decisions. It is particularly difficult for a court to get to the actual issue of a child's needs and interests when there are many questions of law that must be addressed in a legal proceeding.

J. A. L. v. E. P. H. (1996, opinion of the court). We are asked to decide whether appellant Joan, the former lesbian life partner of appellee Elena [fictitious first names have been substituted for initials to improve readability] has standing to petition for partial custody of the child born to Elena during their relationship. We conclude that the trial court erred in denying standing to Joan. Therefore, we reverse and remand for consideration of appellant's petition for partial custody.

Joan and Elena entered into a lesbian relationship in 1980 and began living together as life partners in 1982, purchasing a home together in 1988. From quite early in the relationship, Elena wished to have a child. Following several years of discussion, the parties agreed that Elena would be artificially inseminated to attempt to conceive a child whom the parties would raise together. Together, Elena and Joan selected a sperm donor and made arrangements for a contract between Elena and the donor whereby the donor relinquished his parental rights in any child Elena might bear.

In August 1989, the insemination process began. The inseminations occurred in Joan's and Elena's home. For each insemination, the donor would produce the sperm in one room and Joan would receive the sperm and take them to Elena in another room, where Joan would perform the insemination. This procedure was repeated several times each month until Elena became pregnant. During the pregnancy, Joan accompanied Elena to doctor's visits and attended childbirth classes with her. Elena successfully carried the child to term, and Joan, as well as two friends of Elena, was present at the birth of the child in June 1991.

In registering the child's birth, Elena gave Joan's surname as the child's middle name; Elena subsequently had the child's middle name legally changed. During Elena's pregnancy, Elena and Joan consulted with an attorney regarding the status of the child. The attorney prepared drafts of several documents for the parties' consideration. The first document was a "Nomination of Guardian" in which Elena named Joan as the guardian of the child in the event of Elena's death or disability. The document included the following statement:

This nomination is based on the fact that [Joan] and I jointly made the decision that I should conceive and bear a child that we would then jointly raise. It is our intention that [Joan] will establish from birth a loving and parental relationship with the child. Further-more, my child will live with this adult from birth and will look to her for guidance, support and affection. It would be detrimental to my child to deprive my child of this established relationship at a time when I am unable to provide the security and care necessary to my child's healthy development.

The second document prepared for the parties was an "Authoriza-tion for Consent to Medical Treatment of Minor," permitting Joan to consent to medical or dental treatment of the child. The attorney also prepared a "Last Will and Testament" for each party, provid-ing for the other party and the child. Elena's will also included a clause appointing Joan as the guardian of the child.

The final document prepared by the attorney was a co-parenting agreement that set forth the parties' intention to raise the child together, to share the financial responsibility for the child, to make decisions about the child jointly, and for Joan to become a de facto parent to the child. The agreement also provided that in the event of the parties' separation, they would share custody, continuing to make major decisions about the child jointly and splitting the financial responsibility for the child's support. Shortly before the child's birth, the parties executed the nomination of guardian, the authorization for consent to medical treatment, and the wills. Joan refused to execute the co-parenting agreement, which the attorney advised the parties was not enforceable in Pennsylvania.

After the birth, Elena, Joan, and the child lived together in the house owned by Elena and Joan. Elena was the primary caregiver to the child, but Joan assisted with all aspects of the care of the baby, particularly during the first few weeks after the birth while Elena recovered from a cesarean section. Joan also cared for the baby alone from time to time when Elena went out. During Elena's maternity leave, Joan provided the primary financial support for the household, and throughout 1991, she continued to provide the majority of the household's income because Elena initially re-turned to work only part-time.

In late 1991, serious problems developed in the relationship be-tween Elena and Joan, and in the spring of 1992, Elena left the parties' home, taking the child with her and informing Joan that she intended to raise the child as a single parent. For the first year of the separation, by agreement of the parties, Joan took the child for visits twice a week, one on a weekday afternoon and the other for a full day on the weekend. During the second year of the separation, Elena reduced the visits. Both parties testified that the child enjoyed and looked forward to these visits and felt an attachment to Joan. Elena also testified that the child has similar visits and relationships with other adult "special friends."

In April 1994, Elena advised Joan that she no longer wished to have any contact whatsoever with Joan and that she also wished to end the visits between Joan and the child. Elena testified that she took this action because she felt that Joan was trying to establish a parental relationship with the child and to undermine Elena as parent, and that this could be harmful to the child. Although Joan sought to continue seeing the child, the parties were unable to come to any agreement to continue Joan's visits, and in February 1995, Joan initiated this action for partial custody.

In response to Joan's complaint for partial custody, Elena filed preliminary objections challenging Joan's standing. Following a hearing at which both parties and several other witnesses testified, the trial court granted the preliminary objections and dismissed the complaint for partial custody based upon Joan's lack of standing to bring such an action. This appeal followed.

The trial court in this case determined that because Joan was neither a biological nor an adoptive parent of the child, she must be viewed as a "third party" in her attempt to obtain partial custody and thus would have standing to seek custody only if she stood in loco parentis to the child. The court went on to conclude that Joan did not stand in loco parentis to the child because Elena never intended to grant her that status and Joan understood that she was considered only to be a friend, not a parent, of the child. Accordingly, the trial court held that Joan lacked standing to seek partial custody of the child. We hold that the trial court's application of the concept of standing in this custody matter was overly technical and mechanistic, and that it was an error to preclude Joan from seeking a judicial determination of her claim for partial custody of the child.

The concept of standing is a fundamental one in our jurisprudence. The purpose of this rule is to ensure that cases are presented to the court by one having a genuine, and not merely a theoretical, interest in the matter. Thus the traditional test for standing is that the proponent of the action must have a direct, substantial, and immediate interest in the matter at hand. In the area of child custody, principles of standing have been applied with particular scrupulousness because they serve a dual purpose: not only to protect the interest of the court system by assuring that actions are litigated by appropriate parties, but also to prevent intrusion into the protected domain of the family by those who are merely strangers, however well meaning.

Thus in custody cases, it has been held that an action may be brought only by a person having a "prima facie right to custody." Biological parents have a prima facie right to custody, but biological parenthood is not the only source of such a right. Cognizable rights to seek full or partial custody may also arise under statutes such as those permitting grandparents to seek visitation or partial custody of their grandchildren, or by virtue of the parties' conduct, as in cases where a third party who has stood in loco parentis has been recognized as possessing a right sufficient to grant standing to litigate questions of custody of the child for whom he or she has cared.

It is important to recognize that in this context, the term *prima facie right to custody* means only that the party has a "claim" to custody of the child. The existence of such a claim to custody only grants standing. In other words, it allows the party to maintain an action to seek vindication of his or her claimed rights. A finding of a prima facie right sufficient to establish standing does not affect that party's evidentiary burden: In order to be granted full or partial custody, he or she must still establish that such would be in the best interest of the child under the standards applicable to third parties. Thus, while it is presumed that a child's best interest is served by maintaining the family's privacy and autonomy, that presumption must give way where the child has established strong psychological bonds with a person who, although not a biological parent, has lived with the child and provided care, that of a parent. Where such a relationship is shown, our courts recognize that the child's best interest requires that the third party be granted standing so as to have the opportunity to litigate fully the issue of whether that relationship should be maintained even over a natural parent's objections.

In today's society, where increased mobility, changes in social mores, and increased individual freedom have created a wide spectrum of arrangements filling the role of the traditional nuclear family, flexibility in the application of standing principles is required in order to adapt those principles to the interests of each particular child. We do not suggest abandonment of the rule that a petitioner for custody who is not biologically related to the child in question must prove that a parent-like relationship has been forged through the parties' conduct. However, we hold that the fact that the petitioner lived with the child and the natural parent in a family setting, whether a traditional family or a nontraditional one, and developed a relationship with the child as a result of the participation and acquiescence of the natural parent must be an important factor in determining whether the petitioner has standing. Additionally, where only limited custody rights are sought, the limited nature of the intrusion into the biological family must be considered in deciding whether standing has been made out. Courts in several of our sister states that have addressed the issue of the standing of nonbiological parents have concluded that protection of the best interest of the child may require that traditional standing concepts be adapted to fit modern social patterns.

We have no difficulty in concluding that these facts sufficiently establish a parent-like relationship between Joan and the child to grant Joan standing to pursue the partial custody rights she seeks. We hold that the evidence of record in this matter, particularly the evidence that Joan and the child were co-members of a nontraditional family, is sufficient to establish that Joan stood in loco parentis to the child and therefore has standing to seek partial custody. Accordingly, we remand for a full custody hearing to determine whether partial custody by Joan is in the child's best interest. [Citations omitted; text edited for style and readability.]

It is important to note how the courts differ in their treatment of same-gender relationships when the focus of the hearing is on the child's interests. This case illustrates the primacy of the child's needs in custody cases. Clinicians must focus their evaluations and recommendations on this basis rather than on the relative strengths or weaknesses of a particular parent figure.

There are many roles for the mental health practitioner to assume in child custody cases. Maintaining a clear role and seeking to keep all parties focused on the needs of the child can result in improved outcomes. The legal system is poorly designed to address the question of what is best for the child. When the adversarial system is operating, it is in the interest of one parent to identify real, perceived, or even fabricated faults of the other parent. In this environment, the needs of the child cannot be the primary focus. The reform of the family court system is a worthy goal. Meanwhile, clinicians must be zealous advocates for the need to reach agreements rather than win "victories."

COMMITMENT AND THE RIGHT TO REFUSE TREATMENT

When dealing with issues of competency, commitment, and treatment refusals, mental health professionals must face the dilemma created by conflicting moral values. If an individual is in need of treatment, does society have a duty to provide services? The power of the state to compel treatment through commitment laws can be supported by the *parens patriae* doctrine. This orientation emphasizes that some individuals need services to avoid harming themselves or others but may not be able to ask for help (Reid & Popple, 1992). Those who support this position argue that it is not "freedom" when someone does not have the capacity to rationally decide on treatment.

On the other side of this debate are those who place a higher value on individual liberty. The power of the state to commit people who have a mental illness is seen as violating individual rights (Reid & Popple, 1992). The civil rights and consumer movements of the 1960s resulted in increased attention to protecting the rights of those who have a mental illness by requiring procedural protections and judicial scrutiny over commitment proceedings (Sales & Shuman, 1996). The concern over individual liberty reflected in these developments is firmly established in the historical values of the United States.

Persons in need of inpatient mental health treatment may agree to a voluntary admission or may be subject to an involuntary civil commitment. Mental health professionals are faced with difficult challenges in the process of evaluating individuals, protecting their civil rights, and attempting to provide treatment that will return the person to a more functional state. Within this system, professionals may assume the role of petitioner, asking the court to consider commitment, or the role of advocate, questioning the validity of committing a person (Saltzman & Proch, 1990). Most of the voluntary admissions involve significantly less formal procedures than needed for commitments.

There is valid concern that people could be detained in mental health treatment facilities because of their political beliefs; communication difficulties; the lack of family support, legal representation, or the services of an advocate; or simply due to a misdiagnosis. As a result, there are formal hearings, required reviews, and other procedural protections afforded to a person who is in an involuntary commitment proceeding. Most court reviews of commitment proceedings are focused on the civil rights of the patient. As such, they instruct mental health professionals to err on the side of protecting the individual's right to freedom over the need to provide treatment. The following case discusses the legal issues in commitment, both voluntary and involuntary.

Zinermon v. Burch (1990, opinion of the court). Burch, while allegedly medicated and disoriented, signed forms requesting admission to, and treatment at, a Florida state mental hospital, in apparent compliance with state statutory requirements for "voluntary" admission to such facilities. After his release, he brought suit under 42 U.S.C. section 1983 in the District Court against petitioners—physicians, administrators, and staff members at the hospital—on the grounds that they had deprived him of his liberty without due process of law. The complaint alleged that they violated state law by admitting him as a voluntary patient when they knew or should have known that he was incompetent to give informed consent to his admission, and that their failure to initiate Florida's involuntary placement procedure denied him constitutionally guaranteed procedural safeguards.

Burch apparently concedes that if Florida's statutes were strictly complied with, no deprivation of liberty without due process would occur. If only those patients who are competent to consent to admission are allowed to sign themselves in as "voluntary" patients, then they would not be deprived of any liberty interest at all. And if all other patients, those who are incompetent and those who are unwilling to consent to admission, are afforded the protections of Florida's involuntary placement procedures, they would be deprived of their liberty only after due process.

In their evaluation forms, hospital staff stated that, upon his arrival at the program (hereinafter ACMHS), Burch was hallucinating, confused, and psychotic and believed he was "in heaven." His face and chest were bruised and bloodied, suggesting that he had fallen or had been attacked. Burch was asked to sign forms giving his consent to admission and treatment. He did so. He remained at ACMHS for three days, during which time the facility's staff diagnosed his condition as paranoid schizophrenia and gave him psychotropic medication. On December 10, the staff found that Burch was "in need of longer-term stabilization" and referred him to a public hospital owned and operated by the State as a mental health treatment facility (hereinafter FSH). Later that day, Burch signed forms requesting admission and authorizing treatment at the public hospital.

On December 10, Doctor Zinermon wrote a "progress note" indicating that Burch was "refusing to cooperate," would not answer questions, "appears distressed and confused," and "related that medication has been helpful." A nursing assessment form dated December 11 stated that Burch was confused and unable to state the reason for his hospitalization and still believed that "this is heaven." On December 23, Burch signed a form entitled "Authorization for Treatment." This form stated that he authorized "the professional staff to administer treatment, except electroconvulsive treatment"; that he had been informed of "the purpose of treatment; common side effects thereof; alternative treatment modalities; approximate length of care"; and of his power to revoke consent to treatment; and that he had read and fully understood the Authorization. Dr. Zinermon, a staff physician at FSH, signed the form as the witness.

Dr. Zinermon, on December 29, made a further report on Burch's condition, stating that, on admission, Burch had been "disoriented, semi-mute, confused and bizarre in appearance and thought," "not cooperative to the initial interview," and "extremely psychotic, appeared to be paranoid and hallucinating." The doctor's report also stated that Burch remained disoriented, delusional, and psychotic. Burch remained at FSH until May 7, 1982, five months after his initial admission to ACMHS. During that time, no hearing was held regarding his hospitalization and treatment.

After his release, Burch complained that he had been admitted inappropriately to FHS and did not remember signing a voluntary admission form. His complaint reached the Florida Human Rights Advocacy Committee. The Committee investigated and replied to Burch by letter. The letter stated that Burch in fact had signed a voluntary admission form, but that there was "documentation that you were heavily medicated and disoriented on admission and . . . you were probably not competent to be signing legal documents." The letter also stated that, at a meeting of the Committee with FSH staff on August 4, 1983, "hospital administration was made aware that they were very likely asking medicated clients to make decisions at a time when they were not mentally competent."

Burch's complaint thus alleges that he was admitted to and detained at FSH for five months under Florida's statutory provisions for "voluntary" admission. These provisions are part of a comprehensive statutory scheme under which a person may be admitted to a mental hospital in several different ways. First, Florida provides for short-term emergency admission. If there is reason to believe that a person is mentally ill and likely "to injure himself or others" or is in "need of care or treatment and lacks sufficient capacity to make a responsible application on his own behalf," he may immediately be detained for up to 48 hours. A mental health professional, a law enforcement officer, or a judge may effect an emergency admission. After 48 hours, the patient is to be released unless he "voluntarily gives express and informed consent to evaluation or treatment," or a proceeding for court-ordered evaluation or involuntary placement is initiated

Second, under a court order, a person may be detained at a mental health facility for up to five days for evaluation, if he is likely "to injure himself or others" or if he is in "need of care or treatment which, if not provided, may result in neglect or refusal to care for himself and . . . such neglect or refusal poses a real and present threat of substantial harm to his well-being." Anyone may petition for a court-ordered evaluation of a person alleged to meet these criteria. After five days, the patient is to be released unless he gives "express and informed consent" to admission and treatment, or unless involuntary placement proceedings are initiated.

Third, a person may be detained as an involuntary patient if he meets the same criteria as for evaluation, and if the facility administrator and two mental health professionals recommend involuntary placement. Before involuntary placement, the patient has a right to notice, a judicial hearing, appointed counsel, access to medical records and personnel, and an independent expert examination. If the court determines that the patient meets the criteria for involuntary placement, it then decides whether the patient is competent to consent to treatment. If not, the court appoints a guardian advocate to make treatment decisions. After six months, the facility must either release the patient or seek a court order for continued placement by stating the reasons therefor, summarizing the patient's treatment to that point and submitting a plan for future treatment.

Finally, a person may be admitted as a voluntary patient. Mental hospitals may admit for treatment any adult "making application by express and informed consent" if he is "found to show evidence of mental illness and to be suitable for treatment." "Express and informed consent" is defined as "consent voluntarily given in writing after sufficient explanation and disclosure . . . to enable the person . . . to make a knowing and willful decision without any element of force, fraud, deceit, duress, or other form of constraint or coercion." A voluntary patient may request discharge at any time. If he does, the facility administrator must either release him within three days or initiate the involuntary placement process. At the time of his admission and each six months thereafter, a voluntary patient and his legal guardian or representatives must be notified in writing of the right to apply for a discharge.

Burch, in apparent compliance with the statute, was admitted by signing forms applying for voluntary admission. He alleges, however, that petitioners violated this statute in admitting him as a voluntary patient because they knew or should have known that he was incapable of making an informed decision as to his admission. He claims that he was entitled to receive the procedural safeguards provided by Florida's involuntary placement procedure, and that petitioners violated his due process rights by failing to initiate this procedure.

The Court usually has held that the Constitution requires some kind of a hearing before the State deprives a person of liberty or property. Burch alleges that he was deprived of his liberty interest in avoiding confinement in a mental hospital without either informed consent or the procedural safeguards of the involuntary placement process. Of course, if Burch had been competent to consent to his admission and treatment at FSH, there would have been no deprivation of his liberty at all. The State simply would have been providing Burch with the care and treatment he requested. Burch alleges, however, that he was not competent, so his apparent willingness to sign the admission forms was legally meaningless.

The risk is that some persons who come into Florida's mental health facilities will apparently be willing to sign forms authorizing admission and treatment but will be incompetent to give the "express and informed consent" required for voluntary placement. Indeed, the very nature of mental illness makes it foreseeable that a person needing mental health care will be unable to understand any proffered "explanation and disclosure of the subject matter" of the forms that person is asked to sign, and will be unable "to make a knowing and willful decision" whether to consent to admission. A person who is willing to sign forms but is incapable of making an informed decision is, by the same token, unlikely to benefit from the voluntary patient's statutory right to request discharge. Such a person thus is in danger of being confined indefinitely without benefit of the procedural safeguards of the involuntary placement process, a process specifically designed to protect persons incapable of looking after their own interests.

Persons who are mentally ill and incapable of giving informed consent to admission would not necessarily meet the statutory standard for involuntary placement, which requires either that they are likely to injure themselves or others, or that their neglect or refusal to care for themselves threatens their well-being. The involuntary placement process serves to guard against the confinement of a person who, although mentally ill, is harmless and can live safely outside an institution. Confinement of such a person not only violates Florida law but also is unconstitutional (there is no constitutional basis for confining mentally ill persons involuntarily "if they are dangerous to no one and can live safely in freedom"). Thus it is at least possible that if Burch had had an involuntary placement hearing, he would not have been found to meet the statutory standard for involuntary placement and would not have been confined at FSH. Moreover, even assuming that Burch would have met the statutory requirements for involuntary placement, he still could have been harmed by being deprived of other protections built into the involuntary placement procedure, such as the appointment of a guardian advocate to make treatment decisions and periodic judicial review of placement

The very risks created by the application of the informed-consent requirement to the special context of mental health care are borne out by the facts alleged in this case. It appears from the exhibits accompanying Burch's complaint that he was simply given admission forms to sign by clerical workers and, after he signed, was considered a voluntary patient. Burch alleges that petitioners knew or should have known that he was incapable of informed consent. This allegation is supported, at least as to Dr. Zinermon, by the psychiatrist's admission notes, described above, on Burch's mental state. Thus the way in which Burch allegedly was admitted to FSH certainly did not ensure compliance with the statutory standard for voluntary admission.

The Florida statutes, of course, do not allow incompetent persons to be admitted as "voluntary" patients. But the statutes do not direct any member of the facility staff to determine whether a person is competent to give consent, nor to initiate the involuntary placement procedure for every incompetent patient. A patient who is willing to sign forms but incapable of informed consent certainly cannot be relied on to protest his "voluntary" admission and demand that the involuntary placement procedure be followed.

The staff are the only persons in a position to take notice of any misuse of the voluntary admission process and to ensure that the proper procedure is followed. We express no view on the ultimate merits of Burch's claim; we hold only that his complaint was sufficient to state a claim under section 1983 for violation of his procedural due process rights. [Citations omitted; text edited for style and readability. (See Florida Statutes @ 394.463[1], 1981.)]

A voluntary admission presupposes that individuals, by recognizing the need for inpatient treatment, will be more receptive to and cooperative with the treatment program (Kopels, 1995). *Zinermon* has resulted in more careful screening of voluntary admissions to determine if there was actual consent to treatment. Although some have seen this result as antitherapeutic by making it more difficult for mental health facilities to provide treatment to those most in need, the principle of true informed consent is an important legal element of practice. The requirement of knowing consent, in fact, has been a part of the mental health system for many years. In a New York case, a court, reviewing a voluntary commitment, expressed its disapproval of a procedure allowing voluntary admissions of persons into hospitals who make "no positive objection" (*In re Certification of William R.*, 1958).

Mental health professionals need to understand that the inconvenience of the layers of procedural protection serve an important social function. Clients who are coerced into treatment in American society must be those who pose a real threat of danger to self or others or who are unable to care for themselves. Because most of the statutes and case law seem to prioritize the institutionalization of dangerous patients, there are those persons in need of treatment who will not meet the criteria for involuntary commitment and who refuse voluntary admission. However, it is not the presence of due process that blocks treatment, it is the lack of adequate community-based programs that is the primary impediment to providing services to all those in need. Decisions concerning the right to treatment and the right to be free from inappropriate, unwarranted confinement are not necessarily inconsistent. Perlin (1992) points out that the civil rights cases seeking to free those with mental illness and mental disabilities explicitly sought an expansion of a community-based network of services for the population (see, e.g., *Halderman v. Pennhurst State School and Hospital*, 1978). If more services were available in less restrictive environments than inpatient care, it would be possible to serve some of the clients who currently refuse hospitalization and other forms of treatment.

Right of refusal. Courts generally have been supportive of the rights of psychiatric patients to refuse to participate in treatment, to reject hospitalization or other inpatient therapy, and to refuse psychotropic medications. Although the debate in the literature generally assumes a for/against character, the courts have done less policy making and more individualized determinations. The issue of treatment refusal can have many faces. A person who is incompetent in some respects may have sufficient lucidity to make decisions on taking medication, particularly when side effects have been present. On the other hand, an individual who may present as "sane" may be dangerous to self or others to the extent that involuntary treatment is appropriate.

Mental health professionals, seeking a bright-line guide, have tried to understand court rulings, project trends, and set policy direction in response. Instead, clinicians must make the same individual determinations of treatment refusal cases as the courts. Supporting the right of a client to make treatment decisions supports the person's worth and dignity and sense of self-determination. In the long run, this intervention may be more successful than coerced treatment. The courts have been consistent in their view that the opinions of all patients, including incompetent ones, should be seriously considered with regard to treatment decisions (Stone, 1981). The following case demonstrates how the courts consider client rights in these matters. The most important issue is whether the institution followed a fair and consistent procedure for determining when to provide involuntary treatment. When the procedure is in place and is adhered to, courts are willing to support professional judgment.

Hightower, Ruff, Butts & Shepard v. Olmstead (1996, opinion of the court). This suit is a class action brought by a group of mental patients at a state mental hospital to stop the allegedly unlawful administration of psychotropic medication. Many medical authorities consider these drugs to be the primary treatment for acute and chronic mental disorders. On the other hand, psychotropic drugs also involve a risk of adverse side effects. Such side effects range from short-term discomforts, such as temporary sleepiness or dry mouth, to severe and possibly long-term impairments. One of the serious side effects is tardive dyskinesia, which involves involuntary movements of face, arm, and leg muscles. This condition does not generally respond to treatment and can persist after psychotropic drug use is discontinued. There is currently no way to predict who will develop dyskinesia or other severe side effects.

The Plaintiff class is made up of current and former patients at Central State Hospital in Georgia. Central State Hospital (CSH) is operated by the Georgia Department of Human Resources for the treatment of persons with mental illness, mental retardation, or substance abuse problems. Plaintiffs brought suit as a class to prevent doctors at CSH from medicating them with psychotropic drugs without their consent. Defendants include physicians at CSH and officials of the Georgia Department of Human Resources. Plaintiffs claim that state officials (a) did not properly inform them of the risks and benefits of medication before seeking consent to administer the drugs and (b) failed to provide standards or procedural safeguards for continuing forced medication when consent is not given. Plaintiffs argue that Georgia law provides insufficient substantive and procedural safeguards to protect their rights under federal law.

To challenge treatment decisions once they have been implemented, a patient or his representative may file a petition in the appropriate court alleging that the patient is being unjustly denied a right or privilege granted by statute, or that a procedure authorized by the statute is being abused. Upon the filing of such a petition, the court shall have the authority to conduct a judicial inquiry and to issue appropriate orders to correct any abuse.

The Georgia Division of Mental Health and Mental Retardation operates its facilities according to Policy Memorandum 1.200 (hereinafter "Policy Memo"). According to the Policy, all medication is to be used "solely for the purposes of providing effective treatment and protecting the safety of the patient and other persons and shall not be used as punishment or for the convenience of staff." For initial treatment with psychotropic drugs, consent is required. The attending physician is responsible for explaining the risks and benefits of psychotropic medication to the patient. In addition, it is the practice of CSH to place pamphlets describing the risks and benefits of these medications in areas accessible to the patients. If the patient is able to give legal consent and does so, then the physician must have the patient sign a consent form, which is placed in the Clinical Record.

The attending physician, in consultation with the Treatment Team, must also assess the patient's capacity to consent to the medication. "Assessment of capacity is a separate issue from whether or not the patient agrees to or refuses medication." The basis for the physician's decision must be documented in the Clinical Record. The 1993 and 1994 Policies note specific factors the doctor must consider in assessing capacity, such as a mental status exam, recent behavior, psychosocial data, the doctor's determination of whether the patient is physically and mentally able to understand the information, and the patient's ability to make and express a decision about medication.

If the patient is not legally competent to consent to medication, substituted consent must be sought. A parent, guardian, or other person temporarily in loco parentis may provide consent for a minor. A court-appointed guardian may provide substituted consent for an adult who has been judicially adjudged to be incompetent. If an adult, as a result of the doctor's assessment, is determined to be incapable of providing legally valid consent, then consent may be sought from one with a durable health care power of attorney, a spouse, parent, adult child, adult sibling, or grandparent. Substituted consent, and the reason therefor, must be made part of the Clinical Record by written form.

When consent to medication cannot be obtained from either the patient or one providing substituted consent, the doctor may medicate the patient only if he or she determines that failure to medicate the patient would render him "unsafe" to himself or others. Emergency medication may be continued under the attending physician's order finding the patient unsafe for a maximum of 72 hours. If the patient continues to refuse treatment and the physician determines that failure to medicate the patient is unsafe to him or others, then involuntary medication may be continued for up to 30 days, renewable once, with a concurring opinion from a second physician given prior to the expiration of the initial emergency period

The 1994 Policy requires the physician, with input from the treatment team, to conduct a status review every seven days during this stage of involuntary medication to determine if the patient continues to lack capacity to consent or whether he would be unsafe without medication. The results of this review must be documented in the Clinical Record. After the second thirty-day period, a Clinical Review is required to continue involuntary medication. The attending physician requests the Clinical Review and presents the case to the Review Panel. A Clinical Review Panel consists of three persons (two physicians and one person from an allied discipline) appointed by the Chief Medical Officer. None of these persons is permitted to be a member of the patient's treatment team.

The patient has certain procedural protections during the Review process. The patient or person providing substituted consent must be given written notification of the date, time, and location of the Review, the diagnosis, the rationale for the continued involuntary administration of psychotropic medication, the identity of those involved in presenting the case to the panel, and the fact that the patient may be interviewed. The patient also has the right to request assistance from a member of the Hospital's Human Rights Committee. The patient must be informed that he may ask for a review of the Panel decision by the Chief Medical Officer and may proceed with external process, including court action.

The effective treatment of mentally ill patients who have been committed to CSH is an important governmental interest. The state's power to act in parens patriae to ensure such treatment is appropriately invoked to accomplish the goal of returning patients to the community at large. In addition to the state's parens patriae interest, ensuring the safety of state-run institutions also represents an important state interest.

As discussed above, Plaintiffs clearly possess a liberty interest in remaining free from involuntary medication. On the other hand, the state of Georgia possesses a significant interest, indeed a significant duty, to provide a safe and effective environment within state-run institutions and to preserve the safety of Plaintiffs themselves. The means through which the state serves these interests unquestionably place limitations on Plaintiffs' important liberty interests. Therefore, the ultimate issue before this Court is whether the state's chosen means for serving its important interests strikes an appropriate balance between these interests and Plaintiffs' right to be free from unwanted medication.

Georgia's policy for the involuntary administration of psychotropic drugs appropriately balances the state's interests and Plaintiffs' right to be free from unwanted medication. First, the use of psychotropic drugs rationally serves the state's interests in running its institutions. Second, allowing patients to refuse the administration of these drugs under all circumstances would jeopardize the rights of other patients. Finally, Plaintiffs have not articulated another effective method of accommodating the competing interests at issue.

Consistent with due process, a state may not validly accept the consent of a mentally ill person without first determining his or her capacity to consent. As *Zinermon* (1990) instructs, dealing with mentally ill patients creates a foreseeable risk that some of the patients may not be competent to consent. Georgia's consent procedures comply with due process. Unlike the statutory scheme in *Zinermon,* Georgia provides for administrative procedures for determining a person's capacity to consent prior to the seeking of such consent.

Georgia's pre-deprivation and post-deprivation procedures depend on decisions made by medical professionals. Plaintiffs suggest that the decision to administer drugs against their will should not be made by a physician and should be made only by a court. However, due process does not require that the pre-deprivation fact finder be a judicial officer. The Supreme Court has further stated that "challenges to conditions in state institutions" must receive "limited judicial review" through deference to professional judgment. (*Youngberg*, 1982, p. 322). Thus, in medical decisions, deference is due the opinions of those skilled in the diagnosis and treatment of mental illness. Defendants' (physicians and DHR personnel) Motion for Summary Judgment is granted.

[Citations omitted; text edited for style and readability. (See Georgia Code Section @ 37-3-148.)]

One of the dilemmas of the debate concerning mental health treatment is that the civil rights and empowerment themes have sometimes been co-opted by those politicians who are seeking a reason not to pay for services. The debate is frequently murky and reflects political positions rather than a response to the needs of individuals. Along the continuum, there are people who are unjustly confined and who need advocacy to ensure that their rights are protected. On the other end of the continuum are those individuals who are currently unable to make a competent decision about treatment or medication. They need the protection of the state or even compelled treatment to return to a competent level of functioning where possible. For these individuals, the consequences of the legal decision are particularly significant. Is the individual's liberty enhanced by a return to functioning? Debating from the positions at the ends of the continuum leads to policy making governing the extremes. When this occurs, it has a negative effect on the majority of those whose cases requires individualized examination.

One other issue that is raised in the debate concerning commitment and compelled treatment is the concern that by allowing a client to refuse treatment, a mental health practitioner may be liable for the harm that occurs to the client or others. This risk is reduced by careful adherence to procedures. If a court or a review panel makes a determination, the clinician has acted reasonably and has limited exposure to being sued. Although clinicians have a duty to act professionally, recent decisions have recognized the need to protect mental health workers from the competing claims that can be made, regardless of whether the decision is to compel treatment or to allow an individual to refuse treatment. Some courts have found that there is no affirmative obligation on a mental health professional to initiate hospitalization or involuntary commitment proceedings (Bednar et al., 1991). A new California law provides that a hospital and its mental health staff are not civilly or criminally liable for detaining a person at the hospital for a period of up to eight hours if the client is evaluated as being dangerous to self or others. It also specifies that they are not liable for the postrelease actions of the client if attempts were made to find mental health treatment but they were unsuccessful (California Welfare & Institutions Code sec. 5150, 1996).

This type of legislative and judicial rule making helps clinicians to remain focused on the needs of the client rather than on a concern for potential liability.

CHILD WELFARE LAWS

Mental health professionals may be involved with a number of aspects of child welfare including the reporting of suspected child abuse; diagnosis, assessment, and treatment of children and families; and participation in the adjudication process determining whether a child should remain in the care and custody of parents or be cared for in an alternative setting. As with the other areas of practice discussed in this chapter, there are a variety of roles for the mental health practitioner. The key to effective performance is to understand the legal basis of each role and to let the role dictate professional actions.

Although child welfare has been a concern of mental health professionals dating back at least to the 1800s, the historic view of children as being the property of their parents has been slow to change (*Parham v. J. R.,* 1979). In 1873, Mary Ellen Wilson was removed from her foster home after suffering years of abuse at the hands of her foster parents. A friendly visitor sought to find help for Mary Ellen but discovered that there were no laws in the state of New York that specifically protected children from abuse or neglect by their caregivers. In an effort to publicize this problem and to find relief for Mary Ellen, a group of concerned persons attempted to file a court action under a statute that prevented cruelty to animals. Although the case was dismissed, the publicity generated the eventual passage of new laws specifically designed to protect children (Watson, 1990).

Mental health clinicians should understand the basic principles of child welfare laws to participate in the process. A case of child abuse may be brought in different types of court. When a complaint is made to the state child welfare agency, legal actions for temporary or permanent custody are brought by an attorney for the state in family or juvenile court, depending on the structure of the state courts. The focus of a family/juvenile court procedure is to determine whether there is sufficient evidence to justify the removal of a child. Because these cases are focused on the needs of the child rather than the "guilt" of the parents, the issues are framed as a question of whether the child is at risk of harm. For a child already in the system, the family/juvenile court judge is required to determine a set of expectations for parental behavior that would allow a child to be returned home, and to determine whether the temporary custody of a child should be extended or whether parental custody should be terminated. Mental health professionals and attorneys involved in these cases need extensive training, not only in their role but in the role of the other discipline. Where this understanding has occurred through training, there has been marked improvement in cooperation and effectiveness (Johnson & Cahn, 1995).

Separate from the civil child abuse proceeding, a criminal charge may be filed against the perpetrator of the abuse. State statutes specify criminal abuse definitions and punishments. In criminal court, the usual protections for the accused person are followed, whereas in family/juvenile court, the emphasis is on the safety of the child and the procedural rules are relaxed. A third type of legal action involving child abuse is a civil suit for the personal injuries suffered by the child. Often this type of suit is filed some time after the child reaches the age of majority, although there are statutory time lines for filing a suit of this type (see Chapter 5). Finally, child abuse and neglect charges are sometimes adjudicated in family court as part of a child custody hearing.

Many mental health practitioners find themselves faced with the dilemma of whether to report a case of possible child abuse. The typical scenario involves a therapist or counselor who is working with a family. In a treatment session, information emerges concerning an incident of abuse. The issue is worked on in the session and the therapist is satisfied that the child is in no danger. If a report is made to the child welfare agency, the treatment relationship—which has taken a long time to develop and now seems to be effective in helping the family to make changes—will be in jeopardy. Every state has a child abuse mandatory reporting law (Dickson, 1995). These laws identify the professionals who interact with children and require them to report reasonable suspicions of abuse. This is an important concept for mental health clinicians. There is no equivocation in the wording of most statutes. Clinicians *must* report reasonable suspicions. The clinician does not need to investigate to determine the actual truth; this is the role of the child protection agency. Nor does the clinician have the luxury under the law to decide which cases actually need protective services involvement and which cases should be left to the clinician to handle as part of the treatment of the family.

The best course of action in these cases is to let the family know that a report will need to be filed and to explain the statute's purpose of protecting all children. Some clinicians encourage the family to make the report with them to demonstrate the degree of openness to being helped. In any case, the failure of the local child protection agency to act in a therapeutic manner is not sufficient cause for a clinician to ignore the mandates of the child abuse reporting statutes. There could be severe sanctions, loss of license, or civil suits brought against clinicians who fail to report reasonable suspicions of abuse, regardless of the motivation. The mandatory reporting statutes generally grant immunity for a good faith report of suspected abuse so that a parent or other accused person cannot sue the professional unless the professional knowingly filed a false report.

Mental health clinicians who are employed by a child protection agency generally are required to act in good faith and within a standard of care. In a few cases, children or family members have filed suit against state agencies and their professionals. Even where a duty is identified, suits against the agency and the professionals may be barred by sovereign immunity statutes. The following case discusses the role of the state in providing protection to children who live in homes where they suffer abuse. It illustrates the general tendency of the courts to limit the legal duty to children in abuse cases.

DeShaney v. Winnebago County Department of Social Services (1989, opinion of the court). Joshua DeShaney, petitioner, is a child who was subjected to a series of beatings by his father, with whom he lived. The respondents, a county department of social services and several of its social workers, received complaints that the petitioner was being abused by his father and took various steps to protect him; they did not, however, act to remove the petitioner from his father's custody. Joshua's father finally beat him so severely that he suffered permanent brain damage and was rendered profoundly retarded. Joshua and his mother sued respondents under 42 U.S.C. section 1983 (a civil rights statute), alleging that respondents had deprived the petitioner of his liberty interest in bodily integrity, in violation of his rights under the substantive component of the Fourteenth Amendment's Due Process Clause, by failing to intervene to protect him against his father's violence.

The facts of this case are undeniably tragic. Joshua DeShaney was born in 1979. In 1980, a Wyoming court granted his parents a divorce and awarded custody of Joshua to his father, Randy DeShaney. The father shortly thereafter moved to Neenah, a city located in Winnebago County, Wisconsin, taking the infant Joshua with him. There he entered into a second marriage, which also ended in divorce.

The Winnebago County authorities first learned that Joshua might be a victim of child abuse in January 1982, when his father's second wife complained to the police, at the time of their divorce, that he had previously "hit the boy causing marks and was a prime case for child abuse." The Winnebago County Department of Social Services (DSS) interviewed the father, but he denied the accusations, and DSS did not pursue them further. In January 1983, Joshua was admitted to a local hospital with multiple bruises and abrasions. The examining physician suspected child abuse and notified DSS, which immediately obtained an order from a Wisconsin juvenile court placing Joshua in the temporary custody of the hospital.

Three days later, the county convened an ad hoc "Child Protection Team" (consisting of a pediatrician, a psychologist, a police detective, the county's lawyer, several DSS caseworkers, and various hospital personnel) to consider Joshua's situation. At this meeting, the Team decided that there was insufficient evidence of child abuse to retain Joshua in the custody of the court. The Team did, however, decide to recommend several measures to protect Joshua, including enrolling him in a preschool program, providing his father with certain counseling services, and encouraging his father's girlfriend to move out of the home. Randy DeShaney entered into a voluntary agreement with DSS in which he promised to cooperate with them in accomplishing these goals.

Based on the recommendation of the Child Protection Team, the juvenile court dismissed the child protection case and returned Joshua to the custody of his father. A month later, emergency room personnel called the DSS caseworker handling Joshua's case to report that he had once again been treated for suspicious injuries. The caseworker concluded that there was no basis for action. For the next six months, the caseworker made monthly visits to the DeShaney home, during which she observed a number of suspicious injuries on Joshua's head; she also noticed that he had not been enrolled in school, and that the girlfriend had not moved out. The caseworker dutifully recorded these incidents in her files, along with her continuing suspicions that someone in the DeShaney household was physically abusing Joshua, but she did nothing more. In November 1983, the emergency room notified DSS that Joshua had been treated once again for injuries that they believed to be caused by child abuse. On the caseworker's next two visits to the DeShaney home, she was told that Joshua was too ill to see her. Still DSS took no action.

In March 1984, Randy DeShaney beat 4-year-old Joshua so severely that he fell into a life-threatening coma. Emergency brain surgery revealed a series of hemorrhages caused by traumatic injuries to the head inflicted over a long period of time. Joshua did not die, but he suffered brain damage so severe that he is expected to spend the rest of his life confined to an institution for the profoundly retarded. Randy DeShaney was subsequently tried and convicted of child abuse.

Joshua and his mother brought this action against Winnebago County DSS and various individual employees of DSS. The complaint alleged that respondents had deprived Joshua of his liberty without due process of law, in violation of his rights under the Fourteenth Amendment, by failing to intervene to protect him against a risk of violence at his father's hands, of which they knew or should have known. The District Court granted summary judgment for the respondents, DSS, and the social workers.

Because of the inconsistent approaches taken by the lower courts in determining when, if ever, the failure of a state or local governmental entity or its agents to provide an individual with adequate protective services constitutes a violation of the individual's due process rights, and the importance of the issue to the administration of state and local governments, we granted certiorari. We now affirm.

The Due Process Clause of the Fourteenth Amendment provides that "no State shall . . . deprive any person of life, liberty, or property, without due process of law." Petitioners contend that the State deprived Joshua of his liberty interest in "freedom from . . . unjustified intrusions on personal security," by failing to provide him with adequate protection against his father's violence.

But nothing in the language of the Due Process Clause itself requires the State to protect the life, liberty, and property of its citizens against invasion by private actors. The Clause is phrased as a limitation on the State's power to act, not as a guarantee of certain minimal levels of safety and security. It forbids the State itself to deprive individuals of life, liberty, or property without "due process of law," but its language cannot fairly be extended to impose an affirmative obligation on the State to ensure that those interests do not come to harm through other means. If the Due Process Clause does not require the State to provide its citizens with particular protective services, it follows that the State cannot be held liable under the Clause for injuries that could have been averted had it chosen to provide them. As a general matter, then, we conclude that a State's failure to protect an individual against private violence simply does not constitute a violation of the Due Process Clause.

The petitioners contend, however, that even if the Due Process Clause imposes no affirmative obligation on the State to provide the general public with adequate protective services, such a duty may arise out of certain "special relationships" created or assumed by the State with respect to particular individuals. Petitioners argue that such a "special relationship" existed here because the State knew that Joshua faced a special danger of abuse at his father's hands, and specifically proclaimed, by word and by deed, its intention to protect him against that danger. Having actually undertaken to protect Joshua from this danger, which petitioners concede the State played no part in creating, the State acquired an affirmative "duty," enforceable through the Due Process Clause, to do so in a reasonably competent fashion. Its failure to discharge that duty, so the argument goes, was an abuse of governmental power that so "shocks the conscience" as to constitute a substantive due process violation.

We reject this argument. It is true that in certain limited circumstances the Constitution imposes upon the State affirmative duties of care and protection with respect to particular individuals. In *Youngberg v. Romeo* (1982), we extended this analysis, holding that the substantive component of the Due Process Clause requires the State to provide involuntarily committed mental patients with such services as are necessary to ensure their "reasonable safety" from themselves and others.

Had the State by the affirmative exercise of its power removed Joshua from free society and placed him in a foster home operated by its agents, we might have a situation sufficiently analogous to incarceration or institutionalization to give rise to an affirmative duty to protect. Indeed, several Courts of Appeals have held that the State may be held liable under the Due Process Clause for failing to protect children in foster homes from mistreatment at the hands of their foster parents.

Judges and lawyers, like other humans, are moved by natural sympathy in a case like this to find a way for Joshua and his mother to receive adequate compensation for the grievous harm inflicted upon them. But before yielding to that impulse, it is well to remember once again that the harm was inflicted not by the State of Wisconsin, but by Joshua's father. The most that can be said of the state functionaries in this case is that they stood by and did nothing when suspicious circumstances dictated a more active role for them. In defense of them it must also be said that had they moved too soon to take custody of the son away from the father, they would likely have been met with charges of improperly intruding into the parent-child relationship, charges based on the same Due Process Clause that forms the basis for the present charge of failure to provide adequate protection.

The people of Wisconsin may well prefer a system of liability which would place upon the State and its officials the responsibility for failure to act in situations such as the present one. They may create such a system, if they do not have it already, by changing the tort law of the State in accordance with the regular lawmaking process. But they should not have it thrust upon them by this Court's expansion of the Due Process Clause of the Fourteenth Amendment.

Dissent. The Court's baseline is the absence of positive rights in the Constitution and a concomitant suspicion of any claim that seems to depend on such rights. From this perspective, the DeShaneys' claim is first and foremost about inaction (the failure, here, of respondents to take steps to protect Joshua), and only tangentially about action (the establishment of a state program specifically designed to help children like Joshua). And from this perspective, holding these Wisconsin officials liable, where the only difference between this case and one involving a general claim to protective services is Wisconsin's establishment and operation of a program to protect children, would seem to punish an effort that we should seek to promote.

Wisconsin has established a child welfare system specifically designed to help children like Joshua. Wisconsin law places upon the local departments of social services a duty to investigate reported instances of child abuse. In this way, Wisconsin law invites, indeed, directs citizens and other governmental entities to depend on local departments of social services such as the respondent to protect children from abuse.

If DSS ignores or dismisses these suspicions, no one will step in to fill the gap. Wisconsin's child protection program thus effectively confined Joshua within the walls of Randy DeShaney's violent home until such time as DSS took action to remove him. Conceivably, then, children like Joshua are made worse off by the existence of this program when the persons and entities charged with carrying it out fail to do their jobs.

This court's past deference to a decision-maker's professional judgment (*Youngberg v. Romeo,* 1982) ensures that once a caseworker has decided, on the basis of her professional training and experience, that one course of protection is preferable for a given child, or even that no special protection is required, she will not be found liable for the harm that follows. Moreover, a social worker who simply makes a mistake of judgment under what are admittedly complex and difficult conditions will not find herself liable in damages under federal constitutional law.

My disagreement with the Court arises from its failure to see that inaction can be every bit as abusive of power as action, that oppression can result when a State undertakes a vital duty and then ignores it. Today's opinion construes the Due Process Clause to permit a State to displace private sources of protection and then, at the critical moment, to shrug its shoulders and turn away from the harm that it has promised to try to prevent. Because I cannot agree that our Constitution is indifferent to such indifference, I respectfully dissent. [Citations omitted; text edited for style and readability.]

In child abuse and neglect cases, there are limits to the ability of professionals to predict violence against children. As in malpractice cases discussed in Chapter 4, reasonable professional behavior must include ongoing training and professional development, regular supervision, consultation on difficult cases, and clear documentation of all decisions. Courts will be supportive of well-intentioned and professionally competent clinicians, even when the outcome, as in *DeShaney*, was tragic.

Mental health clinicians are often the primary witnesses in child abuse cases, regardless of the court. Those clinicians who had been treating the child or family are asked to testify as to their observations, their diagnoses, and the facts relevant to the abuse allegation. If a clinician is approved as an expert, the testimony can include information on the theories and dynamics of abuse in general (such as an explanation of the battered child syndrome and other similar information). The expert is also allowed to testify as to his or her opinion concerning whether the facts of the case are consistent with child abuse or neglect (Brooks, 1996).

CONCLUSIONS

This chapter has introduced some areas of the law with which mental health professionals interact. Obviously, there are many more legal issues. Most clinicians will have experience with the probate court system concerning guardianship, power of attorney and power of health care decisions, and wills and estates. Clients may have troubles that involve the criminal courts and correctional facilities, probation and parole standards, and victim restitution programs. Domestic violence and sexual assault laws tend to be highly specialized, and clinicians need to understand the details of the statutes and case law affecting clients. There are special protections for and applications of legal principles to persons with AIDS. It is vital to effective practice with this population that practitioners have a current knowledge of the law. Foster care and adoption laws guide the determination of who is eligible to provide care and what the procedures are for approval to be an eligible provider. Persons with disabilities are accorded certain rights by virtue of federal and state laws. Immigration laws specify the conditions under which a person can enter the country, obtain certain visas, and apply for permanent status and citizenship.

The scope of these legal issues for practice far exceeds the space available in this chapter. The issues that were selected represent examples of the way courts structure the legal rights, protections, and responsibilities of clients and professionals. It is clear from the limited review of family law, mental health law, and child protection law that mental health professionals must study the applicable law related to their areas of practice. Clinicians should be clear about the role they are playing when involved in a legal proceeding and should educate the lawyers concerning the appropriate clinical standards.

Finally, there are innumerable opportunities to exert influence over the development of the law through advocacy and legislative activism. Although the impact of a single clinician may seem negligible, it is not. Courts depend on the knowledge of mental health professionals to make proper decisions. Quality testimony, from both professional witnesses and experts, can be decisive in a case. The power of a professional organization can be even more significant than the interventions of a lone practitioner. By assuming a proactive role through introducing reforms and filing amicus briefs to educate a court about the effects of a particular ruling, organizations can exert enormous impact on the structure of the legal system as it affects clients and the practice environment. Professional organizations and advocacy groups, however, are effective only when their members participate. Clinicians should identify legal concerns that arise in practice and work within their professional associations to propose and/or support reform initiatives.

AFTERWORD

A living thing is distinguished from a dead thing by the multiplicity
of the changes at any moment taking place in it.

Herbert Spencer (*Principles of Biology,* 1865)

The premise explored at the start of this book was that the legal system
is an instrument of society used to regulate the conduct of its members.
Succeeding chapters demonstrated that the legal system is also a malleable system that requires information from a variety of sources to
establish rules and guidelines for behavior. Because of its perceived
authority and its obtuse terminology and procedures, the legal system
feels uncomfortable and is initially inaccessible for nonlawyers. But
there are many ways in which the mental health professions can influence the legal system so that the rules used to guide and judge the field
actually reflect the standards of the professions and the needs of clients.
The challenge for mental health professionals is to tolerate the discomfort of foreign terminology, procedures, purposes, and structures and
become a part of the system that exerts so much influence on practice.

The legal issues in social work, counseling, and psychotherapy often
have been viewed from the perspective of their "interference" with
professional practice. Clinicians are taught how to avoid legal problems
and reduce malpractice risks. Unfortunately, although useful in some
respects, this approach is insufficient. The main reason for legal system
involvement in mental health practice is to create and enforce standards
that protect the public. Most of the time, the legal complaints against

clinicians that reach the trial stage are substantive. There should be an available means to levy sanctions against offending practitioners and to award compensatory damages to injured clients. The mental health community should support this system. The standards of care for practice and the adherence to procedures to protect confidentiality and other rights of clients primarily exist to protect clients, not professionals. With this orientation, legal guidelines for practice can be viewed as consumer protection strategies, and adherence to their strictures is made more palatable.

The influence of the law on clinical practice. The influence of the legal system has been a reward, of sorts, for the growing legitimacy of counseling and psychotherapy in American society. As the field has developed, there has been an increasing need for standardization of practice methods and improved research to support common theoretical models. These standards should originate with the mental health professions. The professional associations must be active in refining guidelines for professional conduct as well as self-policing bad practice and dangerous practitioners. The legal system relies on such published standards, as well as expert witnesses, when there are lawsuits or other legal actions involving counselors, social workers, and psychotherapists.

Case law often makes bad law. When a court is considering a legal complaint charging malpractice, the focus is on the facts of the particular case. The testimony and evidence about the standard of care in the profession is solicited by the attorneys representing both parties. In the absence of clear, accepted standards, courts may substitute their judgment for that of the professional community. In a case where there is a well-defined standard of care for practice, plaintiff attorneys may seek "expert testimony" that contradicts the generally accepted view within the profession. In all such situations, clinicians must testify with integrity. Obviously, the information presented in court is that which is supportive of the case. The adversarial system requires the opposing side to present evidence to contradict or clarify the plaintiff's evidence. Then it is the job of the jury, or the judge in a bench trial, to listen to all of the evidence and determine whether there was an injury, whether the defendant was at fault, and whether damages should be awarded.

In this context, the evidence of the applicable standard of care may be overridden by sympathy for the injured party. If a jury returns a verdict in favor of a sympathetic plaintiff, it may be understandable, but no less dangerous. A decision in a high-profile lawsuit can result in other cases being filed using the same rationale and legal strategies. Before long, a trend of legal decisions has put the practice community on notice that the standard of care has changed. In response, professional associations publish articles about the new expectations, and individual practitioners who read about the results of the case adjust their practice accordingly to reduce their risk of liability.

The way social workers, counselors, and psychotherapists influence the law. The problem with the scenario outlined above is the degree to which it reflects a pattern of professional inaction followed by reaction. Professional standards must be developed in the context of research and theory as opposed to emotional court cases. Individual practitioners need to be involved in ongoing practice research to evaluate the effectiveness of current therapies. When these standards are published by professional organizations, it is difficult to argue that one expert should be believed over the collective voice of thousands of practitioners. Professional organizations must also be vigilant in monitoring legal cases that have the potential to affect practice. In this regard, the professional organizations deserve credit for having assumed a more active role in recent years. When amicus briefs are filed in important cases by the professional organizations, they generally are given considerable weight. Finally, when a case does result in a changed expectation from previously accepted practice standards, the professional organizations need to be active in the legislative arena to introduce bills to codify the proper standard, thereby eviscerating the precedential value of the court decision.

Many clients enter counseling or psychotherapy because their behaviors have caused problems in their lives. At times, it may be an inability to control anger or sadness, while at other times, it may be a difficulty controlling impulsive actions. One of the defining characteristics of an effective clinician is the ability to be nonjudgmental about these behaviors. Clinicians see behavior as functional in that it addresses some need of the client, even if the behavior seems self-destructive or otherwise difficult to accept. Mental health professionals must be able to use the same approach to working with attorneys. Generally attorneys are focused on zealous advocacy for their clients. At times, this causes the interactions between clinicians and lawyers to be strained but, most often, clinicians can improve the effectiveness of their interactions with lawyers by understanding the role each party is playing in a case. Lawyers must deal in facts in the courtroom and may have little patience for indecisiveness and soft information. On the other hand, attorneys generally are concerned about their clients and react well to efforts to support a client's emotional health.

Clinicians need to be mindful of the legal implications of their business practices and the policies that govern their interactions with clients. Carefully designed business and practice policies that ensure compliance with legal requirements are critical to protecting client rights and personal assets. If involvement with the legal system is accepted as a necessary and unavoidable reality in today's practice environment, clinicians will be prepared for handling questions about client confidentiality, issues about client records, and will understand how to respond to a subpoena.

The best strategy for asserting influence in the legal process begins with knowledge about the legal system. When mental health professionals understand the purpose of the proceeding, clarify the roles of the attorneys and other professionals, and prepare themselves for the roles they are being asked to play, they are granted opportunities to educate and thus influence the legal system.

REFERENCES

American Psychiatric Association, Board of Trustees. (1993). Statement on memories of sexual abuse. (Reprinted in *Journal of Clinical and Experimental Hypnosis, 42*[4], 261-264.)

American Psychiatric Association. (1994). *Diagnostic and statistical manual of mental disorders* (4th ed.). Washington, DC: Author.

American Psychological Association. (1992). *Ethical principles of psychologists and code of conduct.* Washington, DC: Author.

American Psychological Association, Committee on Legal Issues. (1996). Strategies for private practitioners coping with subpoenas or compelled testimony for client records or test data. *Professional Psychology Research and Practice, 27*(3), 245-251.

Americans With Disabilities Act (1990), 42 U.S.C. sec. 12101 et seq.

Anderson, B. S. (1996). *The counselor and the law* (4th ed.). Alexandria, VA: American Counseling Association.

Appelbaum, P. S. (1992). Practice guidelines in psychiatry and their implications for malpractice. *Hospital and Community Psychiatry, 43,* 341-342.

Appelbaum, P. S., Lidz, C. W., & Meisel, A. (1987). *Informed consent: Legal theory and clinical practice.* New York: Oxford University Press.

Appelbaum, P. S., & Zoltek-Jick, R. (1996). Psychotherapists' duties to third parties: Ramona and beyond. *American Journal of Psychiatry, 153*(4), 457-465.

Austin, K. M., Moline, M. E., & Williams, G. T. (1990). *Confronting malpractice: Legal and ethical dilemmas in psychotherapy.* Newbury Park, CA: Sage.

Bader, E. (1994). Dual relationships: Legal and ethical trends. *Transactional Analysis Journal, 24*(1), 64-66.

Barker, R. (1987). To record or not to record: That is the question. *Journal of Independent Social Work, 2*(2), 1-5.

Barker, R. L. (1995). *The social work dictionary* (3rd ed.). Washington, DC: NASW Press.

Barker, R. L., & Branson, D. M. (1993). *Forensic social work: Legal aspects of professional practice.* New York: Haworth.

Barnett, L. D. (1993). *Legal construct, social concept: A macrosociological perspective on law.* Hawthorne, NY: Aldine.

Baumoel, J. (1992). The beginning of the end for the psychotherapist-patient privilege. *University of Cincinnati Law Review, 60*(3), 797-826.

Bednar, R. L., Bednar, S. C., Lambert, M. J., & Waite, D. R. (1991). *Psychotherapy with high risk clients: Legal and professional standards.* Pacific Grove, CA: Brooks/Cole.

Bisbing, S. B. (1990). Recent legal developments and psychiatry. In R. I. Simon (Ed.), *Review of clinical psychiatry and the law* (Vol. 1, pp. 297-327). Washington, DC: American Psychiatric Press.

Black's law dictionary (abridged 5th ed.). (1983). St. Paul, MN: West.

Bollas, C., & Sundelson, D. (1995). *The new informants: The betrayal of confidentiality in psychoanalysis and psychotherapy.* Northvale, NJ: Jason Aronson.

Bowman, C. G., & Mertz, E. (1996). A dangerous direction: Legal intervention in sexual abuse survivor therapy. *Harvard Law Review, 109,* 549-602.

Bristol, M. C. (1936). *Handbook on social case recording.* Chicago: University of Chicago Press.

Brooks, C. M. (1996). The law's response to child abuse and neglect. In B. D. Sales & D. W. Shuman (Eds.), *Law, mental health and mental disorder* (pp. 464-486). Pacific Grove, CA: Brooks/Cole.

Brown, D. (1995). Pseudomemories: The standard of science and the standard of care in trauma treatment. *American Journal of Clinical Hypnosis, 37*(3), 1-23.

Butler, K. (1995). Caught in the crossfire. *Family Therapy Networker, 19*(2), 24-34, 68-79.

Charles, S. C. (1993). The doctor patient relationship and medical malpractice litigation. *Bulletin of the Menninger Clinic, 57*(2), 195-207.

Charles, S. C., Wilbert, J. R., & Franke, K. J. (1985). Sued and nonsued physicians' self-reported reactions to malpractice litigation. *American Journal of Psychiatry, 142*(4), 437-440.

Civil Rights Act, 42 U.S.C. sec. 1983.

Clarkson, P. (1994). In recognition of dual relationships. *Transactional Analysis Journal, 24*(1), 32-38.

Cohen, R. J., & Mariano, W. E. (1982). *Legal guidebook in mental health.* New York: Free Press.

Colorado State Statutes, sec. 13-90-107(1) (g), 6 C.R. S. (1985 Supp.)

Confidentiality in federal drug and alcohol programs. *Code of Federal Regulations 42,* Part 2.

Conroy, P. (1986). *The prince of tides.* New York: Bantam.

Conte, H. R., & Karasu, T. B. (1990). Malpractice in psychotherapy: An overview. *American Journal of Psychotherapy, 44*(1), 232-246.

Corcoran, K., & Vandiver, V. (1996). *Maneuvering the maze of managed care.* New York: Free Press.

Crowley, E. M. (1995). *In camera* inspections of privileged records in sexual assault trials: Balancing defendants' rights and state interests under Massachusetts's *Bishop* test. *American Journal of Law & Medicine, 21*(1), 131-164.

DeMott, D. A. (1988). Beyond metaphor: An analysis of fiduciary obligation. *Duke Law Journal, 1988,* 879-924.

Dershowitz, A. M. (1994). *The abuse excuse.* Boston: Little, Brown.

DeShaney v. Winnebago County Department of Social Services, 489 U.S. 189 (1989).

Dickson, D. T. (1995). *Law in the health and human services.* New York: Free Press.

District of Columbia: Washington, D.C. Law 6-2002(b) (1996).

Dombroff, M. A. (1987). *Expert witnesses in civil trials: Effective preparation and presentation.* Rochester, NY: Lawyers Cooperative.

Egley, L. C., & Ben-Ari, A. (1994). Making *Tarasoff* practical for various treatment populations. *Journal of Psychiatry and the Law, 21*(4), 473-501.

Employee Retirement Income Security Act (ERISA). (1974). 29 U.S.C. 1144 et seq.

Epstein, L. (1985). *Talking and listening: A guide to the helping interview.* St. Louis: Times Mirror/Mosby.

Faden, R. (1993, February 11-12). Keynote speech. In *Health records: Social needs and personal privacy: Conference proceedings* (Washington, DC: Omni Shoreham Hotel) (ISBN 0-16-043087-9, pp. 9-14). Washington, DC: Government Printing Office.

Farrand, M. (1923). *The framing of the Constitution.* New Haven, CT: Yale University Press.

Fernald, P. (1989). Puncturing the pretensions of a psychiatric witness. In A. H. Rutkin (Ed.), *Best of family advocate.* Chicago: American Bar Association.

Freedman, W. (1987). *Frivolous lawsuits and frivolous defenses: Unjustifiable litigation.* Westport, CT: Quorum.

Freedman, W. (1995). *Malpractice liability in the helping and healing professions.* Westport, CT: Quorum.

Gelman, S. R. (1992). Risk management through client access to case records. *Social Work, 37*(2), 73-79.

Givelber, D. J., Bowers, W. J., & Blitch, C. L. (1984). *Tarasoff,* myth and reality: An empirical study of private law in action. *Wisconsin Law Review, 1984*(2), 443-497.

Goldman, J. (1993, February 11-12). Consequences to the individual: Data collection, information use, and electronic health systems. In *Health records: Social needs and personal privacy: Conference proceedings* (Washington, DC: Omni Shoreham Hotel) (ISBN 0-16-043087-9, pp. 75-78). Washington, DC: Government Printing Office.

Greaney, T. L. (1996). Regulating the marketplace for competition among mental health providers: The roles of antitrust law and state mandates. In B. D. Sales & D. W. Shuman (Eds.), *Law, mental health, and mental disorder* (pp. 99-121). Pacific Grove, CA: Brooks/Cole.

Green, V. C. (1996). Same-sex adoption: An alternative approach to gay marriage in New York. *Brooklyn Law Review, 63,* 399-423.

Grisso, T., & Appelbaum, P. S. (1995). The MacArthur Treatment Competence Study: III. Abilities of patients to consent to psychiatric and medical treatments. *Law & Human Behavior, 19*(2), 149-174.

Guillerman, D. M. (1997). Comment: The defense of marriage act: The latest maneuver in the continuing battle to legalize same-sex marriages. *Houston Law Review, 34,* 425-452.

Gurry, F. (1984). *Breach of confidence.* Oxford: Clarendon.

Gutheil, T. (1980). In search of true freedom: Drug refusal, involuntary medication and "rotting with your rights on." *American Journal of Psychiatry, 137,* 327-328.

Handelsmen, M. M., Martinez, A., & Geisendorfer, S. (1995). Does legally mandated consent to psychotherapy ensure ethical appropriateness? The Colorado experience. *Ethics and Behavior, 5*(2), 119-129.

Herman, J. (1992). *Trauma and recovery.* New York: Basic Books.

Hirsh, H. L. (1995). Failed communications among health care providers about and with the patient. In F. Lane (Ed.), *Medical Trial Technique Quarterly, 1995 annual* (pp. 1-33). New York: Clark, Boardman, Callaghan.

Hirshman, A. O. (1991). *The rhetoric of reaction: Perversity, futility, jeopardy.* Cambridge, MA: Belknap.

Hogan, D. B. (1979). *The regulation of psychotherapists: Vol. 1. A study in the philosophy and practice of professional regulation.* Cambridge, MA: Ballinger.

Holmes, O. W. (1982). *The common law.* New York: Legal Classics Library/Gryphon Editions. (Original work published 1881)

Houston-Vega, M. K., Nuehring, E. M., & Daguio, E. R. (1997). *Prudent practice: A guide for managing malpractice risk.* Washington, DC: NASW Press.

Illinois Mental Health and Developmental Disabilities Confidentiality Act, 740 *ILCS* 110 (1996).

Jacobson, N. (1995). The overselling of therapy. *Family Therapy Networker, 19*(2), 41-47.

Jensen, P. S., Josephson, A. M., & Frey, J. (1989). Informed consent as a framework for treatment: Ethical and therapeutic considerations. *American Journal of Psychotherapy, 43*(3), 378-386.

Johnson, P., & Cahn, K. (1995). Improving child welfare practice through improvements in attorney-social worker relationships. *Child Welfare, 74*(2), 383-394.

Jones, A. J., & Alcabes, A. (1989). Clients don't sue: The invulnerable social worker. *Social Casework, 70*(7), 414-420.

Kagle, J. D. (1991). *Social work records* (2nd ed.). Belmont, CA: Wadsworth.

Kagle, J. D., & Kopels, S. (1994). Confidentiality after *Tarasoff. Health and Social Work, 19*(3), 217-222.

Kassin, S. M., Williams, L. M., & Saunders, C. L. (1994). Dirty tricks of cross-examination. In R. M. Krivoshey (Ed.), *Presentation of evidence to juries* (Vol. 3, pp. 513-524). New York: Garland.

Kendrick, M. M., Tsakonas, E. E., & Smith, P. M. (1993). The physician-patient, psychotherapist-patient, and related privileges. In S. N. Stone & R. K. Taylor (Eds.), *Testimonial privileges* (2nd ed., pp. 7-1–7-44). New York: Shepard's/McGraw-Hill.

Kenney, L. M., & Vigil, D. (1996). A lawyer's guide to therapeutic interventions in domestic relations court. *Arizona State Law Journal, 28,* 629-672.

Kneese, A. V., & Schultze, C. L. (1975). *Pollution, prices, and public policy.* Washington, DC: Brookings Institution.

Knuth, M. O. (1979). Civil liability for suicide. *Loyola of Los Angeles Law Review, 12,* 967-999.

Kopels, S. (1995). Heaven on earth creates a state of limbo: The Supreme Court and "voluntary" psychiatric hospitalization. *Journal of Law and Social Work, 5*(1), 83-90.

Kopels, S., & Kagle, J. D. (1994). Teaching confidentiality breaches as a form of discrimination. *Arete, 19*(1), 1-9.

Korner, S. (1995). Risk management and the resolution of treatment destructive resistances or consulting with patients to prevent malpractice. *Psychotherapy in Private Practice, 13*(4), 33-48.

Krause, H. D. (1986). *Family law* (2nd ed.). St. Paul, MN: West.

Leong, G. B., Spencer, E., & Silva, J. A. (1994). Silence or death: The limits of confidentiality when a psychotherapist is threatened by the patient. *Journal of Psychiatry & Law, 22*(2), 235-244.

Levin, R. B., & Hill, E. H. (1992). Recent trends in psychiatric liability. In R. I. Simon (Ed.), *Review of clinical psychiatry and the law* (Vol. 3, pp. 129-150). Washington, DC: American Psychiatric Press.

Loewen, J. W. (1982). *Social science in the courtroom.* Lexington, MA: Lexington Books.

Loftus, E., & Ketchum, K. (1994). *The myth of repressed memory: False memories and allegations of sexual abuse.* New York: St. Martin's.

LoPucki, L. M. (1996). The death of liability. *Yale Law Journal, 106*(1), 1-92.

Mackie, S. A. (1994). Proof of psychotherapist's negligence in diagnosing and treating a patient's mental condition. In *American Jurisprudence Proof of Facts 3d, 25* (pp. 117-187). Rochester, NY: Lawyers Cooperative.

Madden, R. G. (1995). Two eggs over medium: A narrative about *Billy. Reflections, 1*(3), 15-19.

Madden, R. G., & Parody, M. (1997). Between a legal rock and a practice hard place: Legal issues in recovered memory cases. *Clinical Social Work Journal, 25*(2), 241-265.

Malcolm, J. G. (1986). Treatment choices and informed consent in psychiatry: Implications of the *Osheroff* case for the profession. *Journal of Psychiatry & Law, 14*, 9-108.

Marks, M. A. (1981). *The suing of America.* New York: Seaview.

Marlow, L. (1985). Divorce mediation: Therapists in the legal world. *American Journal of Family Therapy, 13*(1), 3-10.

Mass. Gen. Laws Ann., ch. 112, sec. 135A(c)(2) (1991).

Mass. Gen. Laws Ann., ch. 233, sec. 20B (1992).

McIntyre, L. J. (1994). *Law in the sociological enterprise: A reconstruction.* Boulder, CO: Westview.

McLean, D. (1995). *Privacy and its invasion.* Westport, CT: Praeger.

Meisel, A. (1979). The exceptions to the informed consent doctrine: Striking a balance between competing values in medical decision making. *Wisconsin Law Review, 2*, 413-488.

Melton, G. B. (1994). Expert opinions: "Not for cosmic understanding." In B. D. Sales & G. R. VandenBos (Eds.), *Psychology in litigation and legislation* (pp. 55-100). Washington, DC: American Psychological Association.

Moore, W. J. (1989). When to let alone. *National Journal, 21*(41), 2518-2521.

National Association of Social Workers. (1996a). *Code of ethics.* Silver Spring, MD: Author.

National Association of Social Workers. (1996b, June). *Practice update: Evaluation and treatment of adults with the possibility of recovered memories of childhood sexual abuse.* Washington, DC: Author.

New Jersey Statutes Annotated, sec. 45:14B-28 (West 1978 & Supp. 1992).

Nurcombe, B., & Partlett, D. F. (1994). *Child mental health and the law.* New York: Free Press.

Packman, W. L., Cabot, M. G., & Bongar, B. (1994). Malpractice arising from negligent psychotherapy: Ethical, legal, and clinical implications of *Osheroff v. Chestnut Lodge. Ethics and Behavior, 4*(3), 175-197.

Perlin, M. L. (1992). The voluntary delivery of mental health services in the community. In B. D. Sales & D. W. Shuman (Eds.), *Law, mental health and mental disorder* (pp. 149-201). Pacific Grove, CA: Brooks/Cole.

Podgers, J. (1995). Compromising confidences. *American Bar Association Journal, 82*, 46-47.

Polinski, A. M., & Rubinfeld, D. L. (1993). *Sanctioning frivolous suits: An economic analysis* (Working paper series). Stanford, CA: Stanford University Law School.

Polowy, C. I., & Gorenberg, C. (1995). *Office of General Counsel law notes: Client confidentiality and privileged communications.* Washington, DC: National Association of Social Workers.

Pope, K. S. (1991). Dual relationships in psychotherapy. *Ethics and Behavior, 1*(1), 21-34.

Pope, K. S. (1996). Memory, abuse, and science: Questioning claims about the false memory syndrome epidemic. *American Psychologist, 31*(9), 957-974.

Pourtney, P. R. (1990). The evolution of federal regulation. In P. R. Pourtney (Ed.), *Public policies for environmental protection.* Washington, DC: Resources for the Future.

Reamer, F. G. (1990). *Ethical dilemmas in social service* (2nd ed.). New York: Columbia University Press.

Reamer, F. G. (1994). *Social work malpractice and liability: Strategies for prevention.* New York: Columbia University Press.

Regehr, C., & Antle, B. (1997). Coercive influences: Informed consent in court-mandated social work practice. *Social Work, 42,* 300-306.

Reid, P. N., & Popple, P. R. (1992). *The moral purposes of social work.* Chicago: Nelson-Hall.

Remley, T. P., & Miranti, J. G. (1991). Child custody evaluator: A new role for mental health counselors. *Journal of Mental Health Counseling, 13*(3), 334-342.

Rhode Island Supreme Court, Advisory Opinion to the House of Representatives, 469 A. 2d 1161 (R.I. 1983).

Richards, P. S., & Potts, R. W. (1995). Using spiritual interventions in psychotherapy: Practices, successes, failures, and ethical concerns of Mormon psychotherapists. *Professional Psychology Research and Practice, 26*(2), 163-170.

Rinella, V. J., & Gerstein, A. I. (1994). The development of dual relationships: Power and professional responsibility. *International Journal of the Law and Psychiatry, 17*(3), 225-237.

Roach, W. H., Chernoff, S. N., & Esley, C. L. (1985). *Medical records and the law.* Rockville, MD: Aspen.

Roback, H. B., Moore, R. F., Bloch, F. S., & Shelton, M. (1996). Confidentiality in group psychotherapy: Empirical findings and the law. *International Journal of Group Psychotherapy, 46*(1), 117-135.

Rozovsky, F. A. (1984; Supp., 1996). *Consent to treatment.* Boston: Little, Brown.

Saavedra, T. (1995, February 9). Nicole Simpson's therapist may lose license to practice. *Orange County Register,* p. A21.

Sadoff, R. L., & Gutheil, T. G. (1990). Expert opinion: Death in hindsight. In R. I. Simon (Ed.), *Review of clinical psychiatry and the law* (Vol. 1, pp. 329-340). Washington, DC: American Psychiatric Press.

Sales, B. D., & Shuman, D. W. (Eds.). (1996). *Law, mental health, and mental disorder.* Pacific Grove, CA: Brooks/Cole.

Saltzman, A., & Proch, K. (1990). *Law in social work practice.* Chicago: Nelson-Hall.

Saunders, T. R. (1993). Some ethical and legal features of child custody disputes: A case illustration and application. *Psychotherapy, 30*(1), 49-58.

Schneyer, T. (1996). Legal process scholarship and the regulation of lawyers. *Fordham Law Review, 65*(1), 33-70.

Schoeman, F. D. (1984). Privacy: Philosophical dimensions of the literature. In F. D. Schoeman (Ed.), *Philosophical dimensions of privacy* (pp. 1-33). New Rochelle, NY: Cambridge University Press.

Schopp, R. F., & Wexler, D. B. (1989). Shooting yourself in the foot with due care: Psychotherapists and crystallized standards of tort liability. *Journal of Psychiatry & Law, 17*(2), 163-203.

Schroeder, L. O. (1995). *The legal environment of social work* (rev. ed.). Washington, DC: NASW Press.

Severson, M. M., & Bankston, T. V. (1995). Social work and the pursuit of justice through mediation. *Social Work, 40*(5), 683-691.

Shapiro, D. L. (1990). Standard of care in the prediction of violent behavior. *Psychotherapy in Private Practice, 8*(2), 43-53.

Shuman, D. W. (1993a). The psychology of deterrence in tort law. *University of Kansas Law Review, 42*(1), 115-168.

Shuman, D. W. (1993b). Making the world a better place through tort law? Through the therapeutic looking glass. *New York Law School Journal of Human Rights, 10*(3), 739-758.

Simon, R. I. (1991). The practice of psychotherapy: Legal liabilities of an "impossible" profession. In R. I. Simon (Ed.), *Review of clinical psychiatry and the law* (Vol. 2, pp. 3-91). Washington, DC: American Psychiatric Press.

Simon, R. I. (1992). *Clinical psychiatry and the law* (2nd ed.). Washington, DC: American Psychiatric Press.

Slaughter, M. E. (1996). Note: South Dakota Supreme Court: Misuse of the psychotherapist-patient privilege in *Weisbeck v. Hess*: A step backward in the prohibition of sexual exploitation of a patient by a psychotherapist. *South Dakota Law Review, 41*(3), 574-623.

Slind-Flor, V. (1994). He says "recovered" memories ruined him. *National Law Journal, 16*(33), 10.

Slovenko, R. (1966). *Psychotherapy, confidentiality, and privileged communication.* Springfield, IL: Charles C Thomas.

Slovenko, R. (1989). Commentary: Misadventures of psychiatry with the law. *Journal of Psychiatry & Law, 17*(1), 115-156.

Slovenko, R. (1993). Commentary: Liability insurance coverage in cases of psychotherapy sexual abuse. *Journal of Psychiatry & Law, 21*(2), 277-288.

Slovenko, R. (1996). Surveying the attacks on psychiatry in the legal process. *International Journal of Evidence & Proof, 1*(1), 48-75.

Sobel, S. B. (1992). Small town practice of psychotherapy: Ethical and personal dilemmas. *Psychotherapy in Private Practice, 10*(3), 61-69.

South Dakota Statutes, 36-26-30(2) exception (2) (1996).

Steadman's medical dictionary (5th lawyer's ed.). (1982). Cincinnati, OH: Anderson.

Stone, A. (1981). The right to refuse treatment: Why psychiatrists should and can make it work. *Archives of General Psychiatry, 36,* 351-354.

Stone, J., & Mathews, J. (1996). *Complementary medicine and the law.* New York: Oxford University Press.

Stromberg, C., Haggarty, D. J., Leibenluft, R. F., McMillan, M. H., Mishkin, B., Rubin, B. L., & Trillings, H. R. (1988). *The psychologist's legal handbook.* Washington, DC: Council for National Register of Health Service Providers in Psychology.

VandeCreek, L., Knapp, S., & Herzog, C. (1988). Privileged communications for social workers. *Social Casework: The Journal of Contemporary Social Work, 69*(1), 28-32.

Vandenberg, G. H. (1993). *Court testimony in mental health: A guide for mental health professionals and attorneys.* Springfield, IL: Charles C Thomas.

Warren, S. D., & Brandeis, L. D. (1890). The right to privacy (the implicit made explicit). (Reprinted in F. D. Schoeman, Ed., 1984, *Philosophical dimensions of privacy,* pp. 75-103, New Rochelle, NY: Cambridge University Press.)

Watkins, S. (1989). Confidentiality and privileged communications: Legal dilemmas for family therapists. *Social Work, 34*(2), 133-136.

Watson, S. (1990). The Mary Ellen myth. *Social Work, 35,* 500-503.

Weiner, J. G. (1995). Comment: "And the wisdom to know the difference": Confidentiality vs. privilege in the self-help settings. *University of Pennsylvania Law Review, 144,* 243-306.

Wexler, D. B. (1990). *Therapeutic jurisprudence: The law as a therapeutic agent.* Durham, NC: Carolina Academic Press.

Wexler, D. B. (1996). Therapeutic jurisprudence in clinical practice. *American Journal of Psychiatry, 153*(4), 453-455.

Wexler, D. B., & Winick, B. J. (1992). The potential of therapeutic jurisprudence: A new approach to psychology and the law. In J. R. P. Ogloff (Ed.), *Law and psychology: The broadening of the discipline* (pp. 211-240). Durham, NC: Carolina Academic Press.

Wiener, R. L. (1992). A psycholegal and empirical approach to the medical standard of care. In J. R. P. Ogloff (Ed.), *Law and psychology: The broadening of the discipline* (pp. 381-424). Durham, NC: Carolina Academic Press.

Whitaker, C. (1996). *Architecture and the American dream.* New York: Clarkson N. Potter.

Whitfield, C. (1995). *Memory and abuse: Remembering and healing the effects of trauma.* Deerfield Beach, FL: Health Communications.

Wigmore, J. H. (1961). *Evidence in trials at common law* (Vol. 8, McNaughton Revision). Boston: Little, Brown.

Williams, L. M. (1994). Recall of childhood trauma: A prospective study of women's memories of childhood sexual abuse. *Journal of Clinical and Consulting Psychology, 62,* 1167-1176.

Winick, B. J. (1986). The right to refuse psychotropic medication: Current state of the law and beyond. In D. Rapoport & J. Parry (Eds.), *The right to refuse antipsychotic medication* (pp. 7-31). Washington, DC: American Bar Association.

Winnicott, D. W. (1965). *The maturational processes and the facilitating environment.* New York: International Universities Press.

Wisconsin Statutes Annotated, 940.22(2) (West Supp. 1984).

Woman testifies against holistic approach of her therapist. (1994, July 12). *Providence Journal-Bulletin,* p. C5.

Wrightsman, L. S., Nietzel, M. T., & Fortune, W. H. (1994). *Psychology and the legal system* (3rd ed.). Pacific Grove, CA: Brooks/Cole.

Yang, J. E. (1997, January 11). Ethics panel tries to settle dispute. *Washington Post,* pp. A1, A9.

Youngren, J. N., & Skorka, D. (1992). The non-therapeutic psychotherapy relationship. *Law and Psychology Review, 16,* 13-28.

Ziskin, J. (1981). *Coping with psychiatric and psychological testimony.* Venice, CA: Law and Psychology Press.

Zoltek-Jick, R. R. (in press). For whom does the bell toll? Repressed memory and challenges for the law: Going beyond the statute of limitations. In P. S. Appelbaum, L. Vyehara, & M. Elin (Eds.), *Trauma and memory: Clinical and legal controversies* (pp. 89-101). Oxford: Oxford University Press.

LEGAL REFERENCES

A. B. v. C. D., 14 Dunlop 177 (1851). (p. 45)

Adams v. Elgart, 623 N.Y.S.2d 637 (1995). (p. 75)

Addington v. Texas, 441 U.S. 418 (1979). (p. 6)

Alberts v. Devine, 479 N.E.2d 113 (Mass. 1985). (p. 65)

American Home Assurance Company v. Stephens, 943 F. Supp. 703 (So. D. Tex., Hou. Div. 1996). (p. 138)

American Home Assurance Company v. Stone, 864 F. Supp. 767 (1994); 61 F.3d 1321, 1330 (7th Cir. 1995). (pp. 138, 139, 141)

Arnett v. Baskous, 856 P.2d 790 (Alaska Sup. Ct. 1993). (p. 93)

Baehr v. Lewin, 852 P.2d 44 (1993). (pp. 212-213, 216)

Bala v. Powers Ferry Psychological Association, 1997 Ga. App. LEXIS 367 (1997). (p. 115)

Bellah v. Greenson, 146 Cal. Rptr. 535 (App. 1978). (p. 78)

Bird v. W. C. W., 868 S.W.2d 767 (Sup. Ct. Tex. 1994). (pp. 172, 180)

Boddie v. Connecticut, 401 U.S. 371 (1971). (pp. 209, 217)

Brady v. Hopper, 570 F. Supp. 1333 (D. Colo. 1983). (p. 74)

Brandt v. Grubin, 329 A.2d 82 (Sup. Ct. N. J. 1974). (pp. 140, 143)

Braschi v. Stahl Associates Co., 74 N.Y.2d 201 (Ct. App. 1989). (pp. 215-216)

Canterbury v. Spence, 464 F.2d 772 (D.C. Cir. 1972). (p. 129)

Chizmar v. Mackie, 896 P.2d 196 (Alaska Sup. Ct. 1995). (p. 68)

Clausen v. New York State Department of Health, 648 N.Y.S.2d 842 (N.Y. App. Div. 1996). (p. 139)

Cobbs v. Grant, 502 P.2d 1 (Cal. 1972). (p. 131)

Cobo v. Raba, 481 S.E.2d 101 (N.C. Ct. App. 1997). (pp. 148-149)

Commonwealth v. Bishop, 617 N.E.2d 990 (Mass. 1993). (pp. 95-96)

Commonwealth v. Kobrin, 395 Mass. 284 (1985). (p. 101)

Commonwealth v. Wilson, 602 A.2d 1290 (Pa. 1992). (p. 97)

Editor's Note: Page numbers at the end of the legal references refer to pages in this book.

Lacock v. United States (No. 95-35778, U.S. Ct. of App. 9th Cir. 1997) (1997 U.S. App. LEXIS 783). (p. 69)

Landeros v. Flood, 551 P.2d 389 (Cal. 1976). (p. 43)

Lee v. Corregedore, 925 P.2d 324 (Haw. Sup. Ct. 1996). (p. 174)

Lindgren v. Moore, 907 F. Supp. 1183 (N. D. Ill. 1995). (pp. 168-169, 181)

Lipari v. Sears Roebuck & Co., 497 F. Supp. 185 (D. Neb. 1980). (pp. 68, 69, 75)

Lorenzo v. Fuerst, 1997 Ohio App. LEXIS 12 (1997). (p. 79)

Lovett v. Superior Court, 203 Cal. App. 3d 521 (5th App. Dis. 1988). (p. 85)

Loving v. Commonwealth of Virginia, 388 U.S. 1 (1967). (pp. 209-211, 212)

Lujan v. Mansmann, Neuhausel & Genesis Associates, 1997 U.S. Dist. LEXIS 2960 (E.D. Pa. 1997). (pp. 111, 125, 166-167)

MacDonald v. Clinger, 84 A.D.2d 482; 446 N.Y.S.2d 801 (Sup. Ct. 1982). (pp. 46, 47, 48)

Magwood v. Giddings, 672 A.2d 1083 (D.C. Ct. App. 1996). (p. 178)

Manning v. Crockett, 1996 U.S. Dist. LEXIS 16118 (N.D. Ill. E.D.1996). (p. 121)

Marlene F. v. Affiliated Psychiatric Clinic, 770 P.2d 278 (Cal. 1989). (p. 171)

Masterson v. Board of Examiners, 1995 Del. Super. LEXIS 589 (1995). (pp. 136-137, 141)

Maynard v. Hill, 125 U.S. 190 (1888). (p. 208)

McMartin v. Children's Institute International, 212 Cal. App. 3d 1393 (1989). (p. 172)

Meier v. Ross General Hospital, 445 P.2d 519 (Cal. 1968). (pp. 43, 176-177)

Menendez v. Superior Court, 3 Cal. 4th 435 (1992). (pp. 83-84)

Michigan v. Regts, 555 N.W.2d 896 (Mich App. 1996). (p. 135)

Michigan v. Stanaway & Michigan v. Caruso, 521 N.W.2d 557 (1994). (pp. 96, 97)

Molien v. Kaiser Foundation Hospital, 616 P.2d 813 (Cal. App. 1980). (p. 167)

Moore v. City of East Cleveland, 431 U.S. 494 (1977). (p. 208)

Moore v. Regents of University of California, 793 P.2d 479 (Cal. 1990). (p. 129)

Ms. B. v. Montgomery County Emergency Services, 799 F. Supp. 534 (E.D. Penn. 1992). (pp. 70-73)

Noto v. St. Vincent's Hospital and Medical Center of New York, 537 N.Y.S.2d 446 (N.Y. Sup. Ct. 1988). (p. 139)

O'coin v. Woonsocket Institution Trust Co., 535 A.2d 1263 (Rhode Island 1988). (p. 93)

Paddock v. Chacko, 522 So.2d 410 (Fla. Dist. Ct. App. 1989). (p. 74)

Parham v. J. R., 442 U.S. 584 (1979). (p. 247)

Peck v. Counseling Service of Addison County, 499 A.2d 422 (Vermont 1985). (pp. 35, 68)

Pennsylvania v. Ritchie, 480 U.S. 39 (1987). (p. 95)

People v. Clark, 789 P.2d 127 (Cal. 1990). (pp. 82, 83)

People v. Foggy, 521 N.E.2d 86 (Ill. 1988). (p. 97)

People v. Wharton, 53 Cal.3d 522 (1991). (p. 84)

Perry v. Fiumano, 61 A.D.2d 512 (1978). (p. 82)

Pettus v. Cole, 49 Cal. App. 4th 402 (1996). (pp. 57-61)

Petyan v. Ellis, 200 Conn. 243 (1986). (pp. 93, 181)

Pisel v. Stamford Hospital, 180 Conn. 314 (1980). (p. 110)

Psychiatric Institute of Washington v. Allen, 509 A.2d 619 (Dist. Col. App. 1986). (p. 177)

Ramona v. Isabella (C61989, Napa, Calif., Sup. Ct.) [*National Law Journal*, 4-18-94]) (1991). (pp. 164, 168)

Renzi v. Morrison, 618 N.E.2d (Ill. App. 1st Dis. 1993). (pp. 63-64, 92)

Romer v. Evans, 116 S. Ct. 1620 (1996). (p. 213)

Rost v. State Board of Psychology, 659 A.2d 626 (Com. Ct. Pa. 1995). (pp. 190-192)

Rousey v. United States, 921 F. Supp. 1550 (D. Kentucky 1996). (pp. 68, 69)

Russell v. Adams, 482 S.E.2d 30 (Ct. App. N.C. 1997). (p. 179)

St. Paul Fire & Marine Ins. Co. v. Love, 459 N.W.2d 698 (Minn. 1990). (pp. 138, 146)

Salgo v. Stanford University Board of Trustees, 317 P.2d 170 (Cal. 1957). (p. 129)

Sarchie v. Roe, 618 So.2d 905 (La. Ct. App. 1993). (p. 48)

Schloendorff v. Society of New York Hospital, 105 N.E. 92 (N.Y. 1914). (p. 125)

Schwarz v. Regents of the University of California, 226 Cal. App. 3d 149 (1990). (p. 171)

Shahzade v. Gregory, 923 F. Supp. 286 (D. Mass. 1996). (pp. 158, 164)

Shelnitz v. Greenberg, 509 A.2d 1023 (Conn. Sup. Ct. 1986). (p. 176)

Simmons v. United States, 805 F.2d 1363 (9th Cir. 1986). (p. 136)

Smith v. Driscoll, 94 Wash. 441 (1917). (p. 46)

Smith v. Pust, 23 Cal. Rptr. 2d 364 (Cal. App. 4th Dis. 1993). (p. 169)

Snow v. Koeppel, 159 Wis.2d 77 (1990). (pp. 63, 64)

State v. Andring, 342 N.W.2d 128 (Minn. 1984). (p. 85)

State v. Boucher, 652 A.2d 76 (Sup. Jud. Ct. Maine 1994). (p. 86)

Sullivan v. Cheshier, 846 F. Supp. 654 (N.D. Ill. 1994). (p. 168)

Tarasoff v. Regents of University of California, 17 Cal.3d 425, 551 P.2d 334 (1976). (pp. 12, 18, 43, 52, 65, 72, 74, 116, 214, 216)

390 West End Associates v. Wildfoerster, 1997 N.Y. App. Div. LEXIS 7826 (1997). (pp. 214-216)

Turner v. Safley, 482 U.S. 78 (1987). (p. 212)

Tucker v. Tucker, 910 P.2d 1209 (Sup. Ct. Utah 1996). (p. 219)

Tuman v. Genesis Associates, 935 F. Supp. 1375 (E.D. Pa. 1996). (pp. 166-167, 179, 181)

United States v. Butt, 955 F.2d 77 (1st Cir. 1992). (p. 94)

United States v. Gambino, 741 F. Supp. 412 (S.D. N.Y. 1990). (p. 94)

United States v. Layton, 90 F.D.R. 520 (N.D. Cal. 1981). (p. 106)

United States v. Nixon, 418 U.S. 683 (1974). (p. 49)

United States v. Willis, 737 F. Supp. 269 (1990). (pp. 41, 102-103)

Weisbeck v. Hess, 524 N.W.2d 363 (S. D. Sup. Ct. 1994). (pp. 98-101)

Whalen v. Roe, 429 U.S. 589 (1976). (p. 39)

Youngberg v. Romeo, 457 U.S. 307 (1982). (pp. 245, 253, 254)

YWCA-ARCH v. Commonwealth, No. 94-J-442 (Mass. App. Ct., June 1, 1994). (p. 96)

Zablocki v. Redhail, 434 U.S. 374 (1978). (p. 212)

Zamstein v. Marvasti, 240 Conn. 549 (Sup. Ct. 1997). (pp. 170, 171)

Zinermon v. Burch, 494 U.S. 113 (1990). (pp. 234-240, 245)

INDEX

Stare decisis, 200
Statutory law. *See* Lawmaking
Statute of limitations, 35-36, 162-163,
    181
Subpoena, 186-194
    elements of, 188-189
    in camera review process, 193
    responding to, 188-192
    contesting, 192-194
Substance abuse. *See* Addiction
Substantive due process.
    See Constitutional rights
Substitute judgment, 67
Suicide, 174-178
    See also Duty to protect
Supervision, 8
    and liability, 143-145
    and handling transference, 136-137
Surrogacy, 220-227

Technology forcing, 6-7, 115
Tender years doctrine, 223, 226
Termination, clinical:
    abandonment, 140-143
    and managed care decisions, 142
    duty to effectuate a referral, 143
    for self interest, 141
    through death or incapacity, 140
Termination of parental rights.
    See Child welfare
Testimony, 194-203
    preparation for, 196
    guidelines, 197-198
    See also, expert witness
Testimonial privilege, 172
Therapeutic relationship, 10, 121-122
Therapist as defendant, 98-102
Third party liability, 164-173
    and alienation of affection actions,
        169-170
    and child abuse evaluations, 170-173

direct victim standard, 165-170
Slap suits, 166
Standing to initiate, 165-167
Third party payers. *See* Managed care
Tort law, 11, 47, 109-111
    and deterrence, 12
    as distinguished from criminal, 109
    breach of duty, 110
    damages, 110
    duty of care, 109-110
    elements of, 109
    intentional infliction of emotional
        distress, 181-182
Transference, 122, 135-136

United States Constitution.
    See Constitutional rights

Vicarious liability:
    of supervisor, 143-145
    of agency, 144
    and impaired colleagues, 145
Video Privacy Protection Act, 40
Violence. *See* Dangerousness;
    Duty to warn
Voluntary commitment, 234-240
    and competency, 236
    and informed consent, 240

Waiver of privilege, 81-92
Wexler, D. B., 117-118
Whitfield, C. 153-155
Wiener, R. L., 115, 120
Witness, *See* Testimony
    See also Expert witnesses

Ziskin, J., 201

ABOUT THE AUTHOR

Robert G. Madden is Associate Professor at Saint Joseph College (1678 Asylum Avenue, West Hartford, Connecticut 06117). He teaches social policy and field practice in the Baccalaureate Social Work Program. He holds a master's degree in social work from Columbia University and a law degree from the University of Connecticut. He has extensive clinical social work experience and currently maintains a private law practice, which provides representation, consultation, and training to the social work community. He serves on the board of directors of the Children's Law Center, a nonprofit group that represents children in Connecticut. He has published articles on issues at the intersection of law and social work including child welfare, disability law, HIV disease, recovered memory, and psychotherapy practice. He is also active with the Education and Legislative Action Network of the Connecticut Chapter, National Association of Social Workers.